ENOC
MAGIC
IN PRACTICE

ALSO BY FRATER YECHIDAH

Enochian Magic in Theory

As a Contributor:

Commentaries on the Golden Dawn Flying Rolls

Mishkan ha-Echad
http://mishkan-ha-echad.blogspot.com

PRAISE FOR THIS BOOK

"This book is one of the most concise and detailed books on the practical application of Dr. John Dee's magical system. Frater Yechidah skillfully combines many of Dee's original practices with the techniques from the original manuscripts of the Order of the Golden Dawn to produce a truly practical manual. Any Adept studying Enochian Magic should have this book as a guide through which this complex world of Enochian Magic is fully explained."

— Darcy Küntz,
editor of *The Enochian Experiments of the Golden Dawn*

"In recent years it has become fashionable for those who follow the 'Dee Purist' Tradition to dismiss the Golden Dawn's contribution to the Enochian System of Magic. However, as Frater Yechidah reminds us, 'the changes or innovations the Golden Dawn made were clearly made with intent, and were largely based on precedences within the Dee diaries themselves.' *Enochian Magic in Practice* clearly explodes the myth that Golden Dawn Enochian Magic begins and ends with the Elemental Watchtowers. In this sequel to *Enochian Magic in Theory*, the author examines portions of Dee's diaries with the eyes of an experienced practitioner and decodes their sometimes cryptic meanings. This book builds upon the previous work and provides readers with an effective system for practical Enochian ritual magic that yields results. Highly recommended for anyone who seeks an in-depth, working knowledge of the Angelic System."

— Charles "Chic" Cicero and Sandra "Tabatha" Cicero,
Chief Adepts of the Hermetic Order of the Golden Dawn,
authors of *The Golden Dawn Enochian Skrying Tarot*

"Picking up where *Enochian Magic in Theory* left off, this new volume explores the practical aspects of the Enochian tradition, such as prayer and devotion, skrying and astral vision, communicating with angels, interpretation of visions and symbols, the importance of the Enochian ritual tools, the making of Enochian talismans, angelic evocation, and more. Frater Yechidah also provides us with some example rituals—such as openings for both the Sigillum Dei Aemeth and the Great Table, the invocation of Heptarchic and Watchtower angels, skrying the Aethyrs/Parts of the Earth, and several sample records of astral visionary experiences. The author even explores the rarely-mentioned Gebofal operation—the opening of the 48 Gates of Heaven.

"As he did in the first volume, Frater Yechidah has overcome the decades of contention between Dee-purist and post-Golden Dawn Enochian tradition, choosing instead to draw from both sides of the fence. He covers material found only in Dee's original journals, but freely references the writings and techniques developed by the likes of Samuel Mathers, William Westcott, Aleister Crowley, and Benjamin Rowe. This book continues the revelation of a greater emerging Enochian tradition."

— Aaron Leitch,
author of *The Essential Enochian Grimoire*

ENOCHIAN MAGIC IN PRACTICE

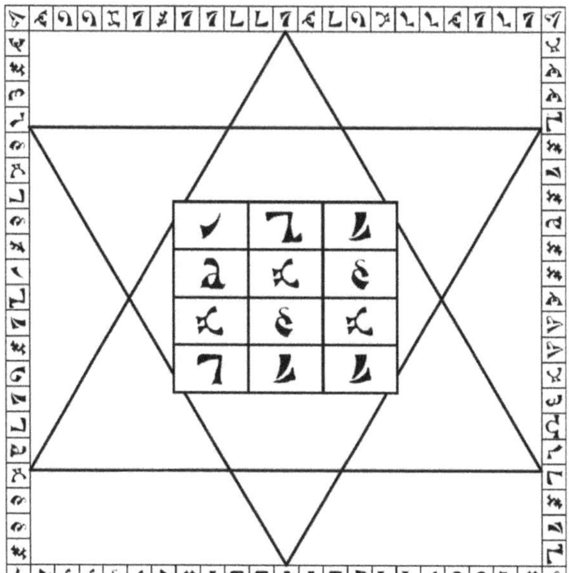

FRATER YECHIDAH

KERUBIM PRESS
DUBLIN 2016

Cover design and interior graphics by Frater Yechidah

First Paperback Edition 2016

ISBN 978-1-908705-14-3

Published by Kerubim Press
Dublin, Ireland

www.kerubimpress.com
enquiries@kerubimpress.com

CONTENTS

I

INTRODUCTION

Enochian magic is widely considered to be one of the most powerful occult systems out there, attracting a lot of attention, and yet there has been relatively little written about its practical use.

To answer this riddle, it is important to understand that there is far less in the way of practical instruction in the material Dee received, making it somewhat difficult to produce an authentic practical guide without reading between the lines or incorporating material or mechanics from elsewhere.

In many ways, the approach Dee would have taken with this would be similar to other grimoire-style magic, such as the Key of Solomon, which makes the tools (found mostly in the Heptarchic system) of paramount importance. Prayer—or invocation—then becomes the primary means through which contact with the angels is obtained. To some, this will be a less exciting approach, but I cannot overemphasise the importance of prayer to Dee, and so I have dedicated an entire chapter to this. Indeed, I could have almost dedicated an entire book.

The Golden Dawn took a different approach, applying its own

unique take on the system, which has become perhaps the most influential conception of Enochian magic since. The reason for its popularity can be attributed to two things: 1) it works; and 2) it provides detailed practical instructions.

It has become popular in recent years to deride the Golden Dawn's approach to this system, especially now that many magicians have gained easy access to some or all of the original diaries (a point, it must be noted, was not quite so easy back in Victorian times). On discovering the sometimes stark differences between the original instructions and the Golden Dawn variations, it is easy to see why some would dismiss the latter, or see them as being inherently wrong. In some cases, it has been argued that Mathers and Westcott simply made mistakes, or did not understand the material they were reading. Having studied and practised both approaches, I strongly disagree with this viewpoint, because the changes or innovations the Golden Dawn made were clearly made with intent, and were largely based on precedences within the Dee diaries themselves. They were not, as some have suggested, merely plucked out of thin air.

It has also been posited that the Golden Dawn ignored some parts of the system in favour of others, but the reality is that what has been published to date is not the totality of the Golden Dawn corpus, nor is what was written the entirety of what was planned for the various higher grades in that Order's curriculum. Individual members of the historical Order, and its offshoots, also explored other parts of the Enochian material beyond the Watchtower system. There are surviving papers that give a full breakdown of the Heptarchic system, and at least one member of a Golden Dawn offshoot actively worked with Liber Loagaeth.

I point out the above because there are many misconceptions about the Golden Dawn and its teachings, partly due to incomplete or inaccurate material in the public domain. The same is true of Enochian in general, and I encourage any efforts to address the widespread misinformation in the occult world.

Indeed, even those following the "Dee purist" approach face choices and challenges. For the former, there is, of course, the Original Great Table or the Reformed Great Table. Some see this as a simple choice, but I am not so sure. Many of the arguments levelled against the Reformed version can easily be applied to other corrected material delivered throughout the entire Enochian workings, and yet these largely go unquestioned. For the latter, there are many gaps in instruction, which require assumptions to be made. Context helps, but at the end of the day even the purest approach will tend to incorporate elements from elsewhere.

Of course, it is entirely up to the individual magician as to which approach, if any, he or she wishes to take to this beautiful and powerful system of magic. There are pros and cons to both. It also does not end with Dee and the Golden Dawn, as there have been many others who have discovered new ways to look at old material, and this is perhaps something of a legacy that will be passed on to others.

This book includes some of those different approaches to Enochian magic, from "Dee purist" to Golden Dawn, along with some more unique instructions that come from more modern magicians, myself included. In an effort to be as comprehensive as possible, I wanted to showcase a variety of methods, so that the reader may select those most suitable for themselves.

Some of the approaches included here come from the Order of the Sons and Daughters of Light (OSDL), a now-defunct group I once belonged to that focused primarily on Enochian magic. Its teachings and techniques evolved (sometimes rather quickly) over time, but at its core it was an experimental, experiential collective, focusing on the practical use of magic.

Where possible, I will point out if something is from Dee's diaries or a later source, as I believe it is important to know this, so that the magician can make an informed choice as to which approach he or she wishes to take. I have also included quotations and citations, so that the reader may see the original instruction, from which they may glean a different interpretation than my own.

Like the first book, *Enochian Magic in Theory*, I have updated the English spelling, and sometimes the grammar, in quotations from Dee's diaries. This is to make the passages more readable, as the English Dee used can be quite difficult for modern readers to understand. For those truly dedicated to working this system, I encourage reading the original source material.

For references, I have primarily cited the more accessible volumes *John Dee's Five Books of Mystery* and *A True and Faithful Relation*. The latter has been somewhat vilified lately, but the reality is that the majority of it is accurate, if perhaps not very appealing in its layout. A more readable version, with corrections, can be found in *Dr. John Dee's Spiritual Diaries*, edited by Stephen Skinner. I have also consulted, where possible, the original Sloane manuscripts.

I have attempted to cover as wide a range of practical topics in this book as possible, including skrying, evocation, talismans, and larger scale operations. There are many things covered here which I have not seen mentioned in other books on the subject, and yet there are even more gems in Dee's diaries to mine.

It has been almost half a millenium since this system was first delivered, and Dee's accounts continue to fascinate both scholars and magicians alike. Though there have been many documented communications with spirits, nothing quite rivals the scope and intensity of that experienced by the Queen's astrologer.

With such interest continuing, and perhaps even growing, I offer this book as, hopefully, a helpful hand to those looking to begin their journey with Enochian magic. Perhaps it may also provide some additional insights and approaches for more seasoned magicians. Indeed, many of the procedures and principles found here can be applied to other forms of magic.

In closing, I hope this book will offer something of value in the legacy of Dee and Kelley, and their myriad angelic cohorts, some of which, perhaps, with the help of these instructions, may become the cohorts of the reader too.

— Frater Yechidah
Dublin, Ireland
21 December 2015

י

II

THE POWER OF PRAYER

When it comes to actually engaging with the Enochian angels like Dee and Kelley did, there is no more ubiquitous practice than prayer. While most modern magicians have a different idea of what magic is all about, with banishing and invoking, it was through prayer that the system was delivered. This, therefore, must be our first tool in practising Enochian magic.

Prayer is often seen as petitionary in nature—i.e. we ask God for what we want. It can also be used to forge a closer connection to the divine, to give thanks for what we have (or, perhaps, what we have petitioned for previously), and as a form of worship. In the right hands, prayer is a powerful magical method, which can work just as effectively as more elaborate approaches.

To understand the importance of prayer within the Enochian system, we have to look at how the system was delivered, and to whom it was delivered. Dee and Kelley were both devout Christians, though they were more than a little unorthodox. While Dee had access to many magical texts, and potentially used them to great effect, his primary method of communing with the divine, and achieving what many today would consider magical effects, was prayer. Likewise for

Kelley.

When we look at the surviving records of their communication with the angels, we see that they are flooded with prayer. Prayer begins and ends operations, and prayer sustains workings while they are going on. Prayer is used to combat the interference of demons, to call forth angelic entities, to periodically praise the divine, and even to apologise when Dee or Kelley made errors or offensive remarks to the angels. Indeed, in the words of the angel Ilemese to Dee, "Prayer is the key of all good things."[1]

Dee wrote that he gave prayers in Latin, English, or "another unique and particular manner,"[2] which is perhaps a reference to prayers in the Enochian language. He said it was "most gratifying to [him] to pour forth [his] prayers to God."

In fact, Dee theorised that the name of the "angel or intelligence presiding over the whole world," given in *Liber Primus* as Annael, came from the Hebrew word Anna (אנא), meaning to beseech or pray. Dee wrote: "It may not be unreasonable that it indicates praying and confessing God."

It could be argued, therefore, that if Dee believed Annael to be the angel set over the entire world, and that this name indicated prayer, Dee saw prayer as the ultimate practice. Whether or not one agrees with that assessment, it is clearly evident that prayer is a pivotal element of Enochian practice, especially for those seeking to mimic Dee.

The potency of prayer is captured in the following quotation from Eliphas Levi:

> "A word is a requisite formula of a thought, an act is an exhibition of will. This is why prayer is a necessity, and may obtain all that it asks. A prayer is a perfected act of the will, it is a link connecting the human words with the divine will. All ceremonies, consecrations, ablutions, and sacrifices are prayers in action, and are symbolic formulas; and they are the most potent prayers because they are translations of word into action, showing will power and persistence, seeing that they require more

1 Joseph H. Peterson, ed. *John Dee's Five Books of Mystery*, p. 375.

2 Ibid., p. 55.

> constrained attention than silent prayer, or prayer expressed in words; and so they constitute real work, and such work demands a man's whole energy."[3]

The question is: what is it that makes prayer truly effective? At its most basic level, there are two necessary ingredients: a form in which the prayer takes (the vessel), and a force which propels the prayer to its desired end (the energy). This is described in the Golden Dawn as Imagination and Will. Essentially, we are talking about the words used and the emotion behind it.

The wording is of clear importance, as it is in invocations in general. We are perhaps all familiar with the adage "be careful what you wish for," or tales of poorly-worded spells and workings that resulted in unintended effects. A prayer or invocation should be clear in its intent. It is often a good idea to define the manner in which the intended result should be made manifest, and even to include a time frame for this. I also find it useful to repeat, in the same or different words, the goal in question, as this reinforces the intent. Repetition has long been part and parcel of the activity of prayer.

Of course, it is important not to fall into the trap of saying prayers just for the sake of it, like in many modern orthodox religions. As someone who grew up as a Roman Catholic, I distinctly remember the rapid mumbling through prayers as if it were a race, and the clear boredom and disinterest people had in their prayers. If it is seen and treated as a chore, it might as well be dispensed with entirely.

Just saying the words is not enough. There needs to be meaning. Infusing prayer with emotion creates a much stronger effect, and, indeed, is the pivotal second part of the equation, where the energy is raised and directed towards the intended goal.

Aleister Crowley summarised the importance of this infusion of emotion in the chapter on invocation in his *Magick in Theory and Practice*:

> "... the secret of success in invocation has not hitherto been disclosed. It is an exceedingly simple one. It is practically of no importance whatever that the invocation should be 'right.' There are a thousand different ways of

3 Eliphas Levi, *The Magical Ritual of the Sanctum Regnum*, pp. 2-3.

> compassing the end proposed, so far as external things are concerned. The whole secret may be summarised in these four words: 'Enflame thyself in praying.'"[4]

Here then we see that the vessel may take many forms, but regardless of what form it takes, it must be filled if it is to be effective. Whether we call it invocation or prayer is largely irrelevant, for, when practised correctly, it is essentially practised the same way.

This concept of putting one's all into a prayer, instead of just saying it by rote, can be found referenced throughout occult literature, including here in Abramelin:

> "Know ye that although in the beginning your prayer be but feeble, it will suffice, provided that ye understand how to demand the Grace of the Lord with love and a true heart, whence it must be that such a prayer cometh forth. Also it serveth nothing to speak without devotion, without attention, and without intelligence; nor yet to pronounce it with the mouth alone, without a true intent; nor yet to read it as do the ignorant and impious. But it is absolutely necessary that your prayer should issue from the midst of your heart, because simply setting down prayers in writing, the hearing of them will in no way explain unto you how really to pray."[5]

It was also stressed by the angel Ave, when he told Dee the following:

> "Invocation proceedeth of the good will of man, and of the heat and fervency of the spirit: And therefore is prayer of such effect with God."[6]

Like most magic, prayer can be enhanced through additional tools. In Judaism, for example, there is the *talith* or *tallit*, a kind of prayer shawl designed to essentially give a miniature temple space better

4 Aleister Crowley, *Magick in Theory and Practice*, Chapter XV.

5 S.L. MacGregor Mathers, trans. *The Book of the Sacred Magic of Abramelin the Mage*, p. 65.

6 *A True and Faithful Relation*, p. 188.

suited to prayer. The word means "little tent," and it can be placed over the head to block out any distractions from the everyday world. Its potential parallel with the Tabernacle gives it an extra dimension of meaning and resonance.

In Christianity, like in many other religions, prayer or rosary beads are common. Interestingly, the common word "bead" actually derives from an Old English word (*bede*) that means prayer, showing the strong place of these physical objects in religious worship. They act as a counting device, which helps keep the user's focus on the prayer itself, rather than worrying where he or she is in the prayer cycle. They can also help occupy the mind, and so prevent it from wandering to more mundane matters.

In the later days of the OSDL, we experimented with the use of prayer beads. I incorporated a set of 21 beads with one of the Enochian letters painted on each of them, and the Hieroglyphic Monad employed as a kind of "cross." Specific prayers can be assigned to each bead, though it is a good idea to first skry the letters to find their meanings, so that you can assign prayers most appropriate to those meanings. Alternatively, one may even use the beads during skrying sessions, holding the bead of the appropriate letter for the duration of the working. This gives an additional link to the forces of that letter, and may even help ground the experience. As for the Hieroglyphic Monad symbol, Dee's most common prayer (given later in this chapter) can be assigned to it.

Prayer, therefore, can be enhanced with these kinds of tools, just as we would employ various wands and regalia in ceremonial magic. The donning of special clothes, and the tactile sensation of special implements, helps trigger the magical mindset, making it easier to make the most of a particular ritual or prayer session.

It is interesting to note that despite the fairly obvious magical nature of Dee's work, he did not see, or at least did not readily admit, that he actually practised magic, but rather wanted help "in [his] philosophical studies."

> "And I truly excused myself therein as not in the, vulgarly accounted Magic, neither studied, or exercised."[7]

---

7 Joseph H. Peterson, ed. *John Dee's Five Books of Mystery*, p. 66.

While this is likely Dee's attempt to defend himself against his many critics, who accused him of sorcery, he may have genuinely believed his work was different to the "vulgar" magic of the Medieval period, especially since his primary methodology was, in fact, prayer.

Dee commonly made prayers of the self-effacing kind. I am personally of the opinion that such prayers, if used, should be used frugally, because I do not think that regular and repeated use of this kind of wording does any good for the psychological health of an individual. It is one thing to remind oneself of how small one is in the grand scheme of things (something easily done if, for example, one looks at some of the amazing images of the vastness of space), or how much greater the divine is, but it is quite another to belittle and degrade oneself. There is a very big difference between humility and humiliation, and my view is that, while we should not inflate our egos, we should not entirely deflate them either. They serve a very necessary purpose *when in their appropriate place.*

For the specific forms a prayer should take, the magician may write his or her own, or use established ones. The benefit of the former is customisation and personal connection, but the benefit of the latter is that those words have already been regularly infused with emotion over many generations, giving them some added strength. There is a lot to be said for tapping into the wellspring of tradition.

The Book of Psalms (or *Tehillim* in Hebrew, meaning "Praises") is a common go-to resource for established prayers, offering a wide range of beautifully-worded passages for a number of different purposes. In fact, Dee is told that the best way to call upon the archangel Michael is with the Shepard Psalms. He also frequently used a Psalter book, "with short prayers annexed to every Psalm."[8]

Yet Dee was not shy of writing his own prayers, many of which are quite long. At the beginning of *Liber Primus*, Dee provides a Latin prayer which he called his "most frequently used."[9] He referred to it as: "My morning and evening prayer for wisdom."[10] I give below the English translation of this prayer made by scholar Joseph H. Peterson.

---

8 *A True and Faithful Relation*, p. 183.

9 Ibid.

10 Ibid.

Morning and Evening Prayer for Wisdom

In the name of God the Father, God the Son, God the Holy Spirit.

Amen.

O almighty, eternal, true and living God, be pleased to deliver me! O Lord of Lords, King of Kings, Jehovah Zebaoth, make haste to help me!

Glory be to God the Father, and to the Son, and to the Holy Spirit: as it was in the beginning, is now, and ever shall be, world without end. Amen.

Teach me to perceive and understand properly (O Creator of all things), for your wisdom is all I desire. Fix your word in my ear (O Creator of all things), and fix your wisdom in my heart.

O Lord Jesus Christ (you who are the true wisdom of your eternal and omnipotent Father) I most humbly beg your Divine Majesty that you consider it proper to send me the speedy help of some pious wise man and experienced philosopher for realizing and perfecting above all fully those things which will be of greatest value for increasing your praise and glory. And if no such mortal man now lives upon the earth who is fitting for this work, or who may have been assigned by your eternal providence to the performing of that service for me, then truly I most humbly, most ardently, and most faithfully ask from your divine majesty that you grant to send me down from heaven your good spiritual ministers and angels, namely Michael, Gabriel, Raphael, and also Uriel: and (from your divine favor) any other true and faithful angels of yours, who may completely and perfectly train and teach me in the true and accurate knowledge and understanding of your secrets and wonders (concerning all your creatures, and their nature, properties, and best use) and necessary knowledge for us mortals, to the praise, honour, and glory of your name, to my firm solace and otherwise (through me) the solace of the greatest number of your faithful, and to the confusion and ruin of the wicked. Amen. Let it be O Jehovah Zebaoth; let it be O Adonay; let it be O Elohim. O blessed and omnipotent Trinity, praised above all things, grant me (John Dee) this petition, in such a manner that will be most pleasing to you.

Amen.

III

TOOLS OF THE TRADE

The next most prominent aspect of the Enochian system, particularly the Heptarchic element, is the prevalence of numerous tools and furnishings. This is pretty standard stuff for grimoire-style magic, and in many ways the creation of these items acts as an initiation into the system itself.

Many modern magicians, particularly those inspired by the Golden Dawn, use very few tools, often limiting themselves to the Watchtowers, and maybe the Sigillum Dei Aemeth. For those looking for a Dee purist approach, every single tool must be used, and must be built to exact specifications (or as close to exact as possible). There is a middle ground, of course, and we will explore in this chapter just how much we need to do if we are to get the most out of the numerous tools.

The big question, of course, is: do we really need to make these tools to the standard initially asked for by the angels? To answer this, I will explore the concept of tools, and the materials and approaches taken to them, by both the Golden Dawn and Dee (or, rather, the angels' instructions to him).

In the Golden Dawn system it is the symbolism rather than the material that is stressed, and while many modern magicians have created quite ornate and beautiful tools, the original Order members often created theirs out of cardboard and coloured paper.

For example, W.B. Yeats' surviving Rose Cross Lamen, on display in the National Library of Ireland, is thin cardboard, and there are also many talismans present, where coloured paper was used to form the various geometric shapes.

Instructions for this approach are explicitly given in numerous Golden Dawn documents, such as the paper on the Lotus Wand, which states:

> "The Lotus flower may be made of sheet metal or cardboard."[11]

A Theoricus Adeptus Minor paper on the Ring and Disc (not to be confused with a ring worn on the figure) is even more clear that the material is not of great concern:

> "The Ring and the Disc may be made of any material—cardboard will do—not too light, or the elasticity of the thread may vitiate its action."[12]

For those practising Enochian magic within the Golden Dawn system, therefore, this precept of the importance of symbolism over material can be followed. It is easy to see, therefore, why Lon Milo DuQuette suggests using a paper Ring.[13] In fact, he often provides cardboard Rings and Lamens during his practical workshops.

However, the Golden Dawn's approach is largely at odds with many grimoires, which call for very specific, and often very hard to find, items. While some magicians stress the symbolic nature of these instructions, others attempt to follow them as given, going to great lengths to find lion skins, etc.

Enochian magic, if we are to follow the instructions as given, follows this grimoiric tradition. Dee is told not just what he must acquire, but the *material form* it must come in. The best examples of

11 *Ritual D – The Lotus Wand*, Private Collection.

12 *Ritual Beta – The Ring and Disc*, Private Collection.

13 Lon Milo DuQuette, *Enochian Vision Magick*, p. 37.

this are the Sigillum Dei Aemeth, which was "to be made of perfect wax"[14] (or beeswax), and the PELE Ring and Lamen, which were to be made of "perfect gold."[15]

Another question is if the tools need to be made by the magician alone or if they can be acquired by others. For many (though not all) Golden Dawn tools, at least those personal to the Adept, the instructions require that no one else touch the item, having no part in its construction or consecration. In some cases, adaptation is fine.

Yet Dee found that he lacked certain skills, such as engraving metal, and he wondered if he could have someone else do this for him, as shown here:

> "Δ How shall I do for the graving of the ring; May not another man do it, though, E.T. grave it not?
>
> Mi: Cause them to be made up, (according to Instruction) by any honest man."[16]

This allows for the Ring to be crafted and engraved by any "honest" metalworker. Dee was clearly put off by the idea of doing this himself, likely due to him lacking the necessary skills, and this might likewise be the case for many modern magicians. This, again, is in stark contrast to many Golden Dawn instructions, where the magician is generally required to make the tool his or herself (within reason). It is easy, therefore, to see why Mathers and Westcott did not require more elaborate materials for such tools.

Of course, this only makes the manner of crafting the Ring easier. It does not help with the fact that it should be gold, which may be too expensive for many people. Unfortunately, most of us have not found the alchemical secret of turning lead into gold, and many of us do not enjoy quite the same patronage as some of our predecessors (where, for example, Queen Elizabeth I provided funds for Dee, and Annie Horniman provided funds for Mathers).

In light of this, I have found that a governing principle in

---

14 *John Dee's Five Books of Mystery*, ed. Joseph H. Peterson, p. 79.

15 Ibid., p. 214.

16 Ibid., p. 179. (Δ is the symbol Dee used for himself. "Mi" is Michael. "E.T." is Edward Talbot, the initial name that Kelley went by.)

approaching magic is the following passage from *The Sacred Magic of Abramelin the Mage* (translated by Mathers):

> "Thus in this point as in all the others, we should rule and govern ourselves according unto the means at our disposal."[17]

Indeed, the passage preceding this called for the use of a censer of bronze, "or of silver if one hath the means." What one man or woman has at his or her disposal should not dictate the same requirements for someone else with less. Do not let a lack of means be an obstacle to practice.

While obviously we cannot take the rules of one system and apply them to another, it does show that there can be some flexibility in grimoire magic, and that even a purist approach to Enochian magic can allow for whatever financial circumstances we find ourselves in.

It is interesting to see that at times even Dee himself was attempting to adopt some compromises with the angels on their instructions. For example, during the same session where he asked if someone else could make the Ring for him, he asked about the chamber for practice:

> "May my farthermost little chamber, serve, if the bed be taken down?"[18]

Interestingly, Michael evaded this question, stating he would answer it in the next working. It was much later before Dee got an answer, and he had to ask again if his "chamber of practice" would do the trick, this time to Uriel, who responded:

> "The place can not Sanctify the Action, but the Action the place. But I answer thee, after the manner of men. It is sufficient."[19]

---

17 S.L. MacGregor Mathers, trans. *The Sacred Magic of Abramelin the Mage*, p. 76.

18 Joseph H. Peterson, ed. *John Dee's Five Books of Mystery*, p. 179.

19 Ibid., p. 404.

Thus we see that a specific chamber set aside for this work is not necessarily needed (though it is obviously ideal, for many reasons), and though Dee worried extensively about this, the angels deemed his efforts in this regard "sufficient." For the place is not sacred—the work makes it so.

Let me, however, stress the old adage of "you get out what you put in." If it is in any way feasible for one to follow the instructions to the letter, no matter the expense or time commitment, then one should do so, for lazy practice will produce lazy results, if it produces results at all.

Indeed, I was told in no uncertain terms by the angels in instructions for one elaborate ritual designed for a major outcome that if what I wanted was to come "fully adorned," then my method of practice should be "fully adorned" as well. In other words, it must have the full assortment of tools, including a wax Sigillum and gold Ring. This is not to say that a lesser outcome would not manifest without these, but it would, I was assured, most definitely be lesser.

In the end, however, any material is better than none at all, and it is better to practise with what one has at his or her disposal than to never practise at all. We must all strike a balance between the search for perfection and the realisation that true perfection cannot, in purely human terms, be achieved.

Materials aside, what of the specific measurements given for the tools? Must they be followed exactly, or is there any leeway for being slightly off? In many cases, the angels gave very specific instructions on the height, width, and thickness of things, so it wise to follow these as closely as possible. Indeed, in the case of the Sigillum Dei Aemeth, Uriel said it "*must* be 9 inches in diameter"[20] (my italics for emphasis). Yet, Dee's surviving Seal (assuming it is actually his) is slightly larger than 9 inches (roughly 22.9cm) in diameter, measuring 23.2cm instead. Likewise, the thickness, which was to be an inch and an eight (roughly 2.9cm), is different to Dee's finished product, which is 3.4cm in thickness. Interestingly, beeswax tends to shrink slightly when it cools (a point worth noting when constructing the Sigillum Dei Aemeth), but this would not explain why Dee's seal is actually larger. He may have simply found it easier to construct this way. So, while every effort should be made to get the measurements

20 Ibid., p. 71.

right, clearly there is some room to be slightly off.

Another thing to consider is the order in which names and symbols are inscribed upon the tools. These should ideally be done in the order in which they were delivered. For example, the Sigillum Dei Aemeth should be inscribed first with the outer wheel, then moving inwards steadily until it is completed. Full breakdowns of the delivery and derivation of the key tools can be found in *Enochian Magic in Theory*.

Consecration of tools is typical in grimoire tradition, but Dee did not receive instructions of this nature. For those who wish to adopt something, the Key of Solomon includes exorcisms (essentially consecrations) for many different types of item, including anything made of beeswax, which could therefore potentially be employed for the material of the Sigillum before the design is carved therein. Some may find this particularly beneficial if the beeswax has been handled by others, as will likely be the case, before coming to the magician.

STORING MATERIALS

Storage is another important consideration. The Golden Dawn recommends that tools be stored in (typically) white silk or linen. A cloth in a similar colour to the one used to cover the Table of Practice could be used instead. This was initially described as red, but later was to be of "diverse colours, the most changeable that can be gotten."[21] If nothing else, this will keep the shewstone from getting scratched, etc., for any imperfections may affect the workings.

Likewise, the Watchtower Tablets, if divided up, may be stored in coloured cloths related to the Elements, if employing the Golden Dawn correspondences, or in alchemical colours, as shown in the vision Kelley had, where cloths of black, red, white and green were employed.

Regarding the shewstone that Dee mysteriously acquired during one of his workings, he was told, "Let no mortal hand touch it, but thine own."[22] This injunction is similar to instructions given by the Golden Dawn for the Adept's personal tools.

21 Ibid., p. 398.

22 Ibid., p. 254.

The reason for keeping magical objects clean of the energies of other people is that they can, intentionally or unwittingly, influence the subsequent workings that employ those tools. When skrying it can be hard enough to keep one's own subconscious at bay, let alone the subconscious of another.

THE PROVENANCE OF THE OBSIDIAN MIRROR AND OTHER ITEMS ATTRIBUTED TO DEE

Before I end this chapter, I would like to take this space to cover a "pet peeve" of mine when it comes to some individuals, typically those unfamiliar with Dee's work, theorising about the process he employed in his spirit workings.

It is widely believed today that the Obsidian Mirror on display in the British Museum was used by Dee and Kelley, a matter that is largely taken for granted, thanks to it being in the same display cabinet as other items linked with Dee, and its attribution to the Elizabethan magician by museum staff.

This Mirror is purportedly of Aztec origin, leading some to suggest a possible Aztec link to the Enochian workings. Yet this is all based on the assumption that this device was, in fact, Dee's, whereas there is no real evidence that this is actually the case.

This assumption is primarily based on a claim by Horace Walpole, who received this item in 1771. The note pasted to the accompanying case, believed to be written in Walpole's handwriting and initialled by him, reads: "The Black Stone into which Dr Dee used to call his Spirits." It was not acquired by the British Museum until 1966, where it continues to be labelled as Dee's "Magical Mirror" or "Magical Speculum," based solely on Walpole's unverified claim.

Some even believe this was the object that mysteriously appeared by the window during one of Dee and Kelley's workings, but this has no basis. The stone that Dee found was described by Kelley as being "as big as an egg: most bright, clear and glorious," while Dee said it was "roundish, and less than the palm of my hand."[23] Given that the Mirror in the British Museum has a height of 22cm (including the small handle) and a diameter of 18.4cm, this clearly cannot be

23 Ibid., p. 253.

the same object that fit in Dee's hand. Indeed, it is almost as large as the Sigillum Dei Aemeth itself. While Dee later described the stone as being half an inch in thickness, which the Mirror roughly is, the other dimensions simply do not match. I would also argue that Dee's description of the object he found being "roundish," and the numerous references to it being a "stone" (and not a "glass") suggest it was spherical, not to mention Kelley's description of it being "bright" and "clear"—in other words, a classic crystal ball, not a black mirror. Alternatively, the small thickness may suggest it was a crystal lens, as posited by Aaron Leitch.[24]

Of course, Dee had several objects in his possession for skrying, so it could be argued that the Obsidian Mirror was one of these. However, I have yet to find a single reference to this object in any of Dee's diaries, whereas there are numerous mentions of his various shewstones. One would think that if this Mirror was "used to call his Spirits," there would be mention of it somewhere, particularly given Dee's meticulous record-keeping, not to mention its alleged origin in the New World, in which Dee had a vested interest.

The authenticity of this object has also been challenged by several scholars, including Christopher Whitby, who wrote about it at length, stating finally "the evidence connecting the mirror with Dee is very circumstantial."[25]

Further, in an article on the provenance of the items associated with Dee in the British Museum, written by Silke Ackermann, a former curator of the British Museum, and Louise Devoy, curator of the Royal Observatory, they noted that "at the present time, and without further evidence, any suggestion of a direct link between the obsidian mirror and John Dee remains conjectural."[26]

They also categorically denied a link between the Golden Talisman and Dee, stating, "we have established that the engraving of the Vision of the Four Castles is based upon Casaubon's erroneous diagram of 1659, and can therefore state that the disc certainly did

24 Aaron Leitch, *The Essential Enochian Grimoire*, p. 131.

25 Christopher Whitby, *John Dee's Actions With Spirits*, p. 141.

26 Silke Ackermann, Louise Devoy, *'The Lord of the smoking mirror': Objects associated with John Dee in the British Museum*; Studies in History and Philosophy of Science Part A, Volume 43, Issue 3, September 2012, p. 543.

not belong to Dee, nor was it made during his lifetime."[27] While they noted a lack of definitive evidence linking the wax seals with Dee, they recognised that the internal evidence (of how closely they match the instructions and diagram in Dee's diaries) offers "the strongest potential link to Dee."[28]

Indeed, even the provenance of the crystal ball on display in the British Museum is highly questionable, and it was not originally associated with Dee by museum staff. Ackermann and Devoy noted that it "has virtually no documentary evidence to support its description as Dee's 'shew stone.'"[29] Indeed, it is only one of several devices that have been attributed to Dee over the years.

For example, there is another crystal ball in the Science Museum in South Kensington, which Nicholas Culpeper claimed was given to him by Dee's son Arthur. Culpeper apparently used this stone, which is of a purplish hue and is contained within a metal frame upon a small chain, until 1651, when he said he encountered within it a lewd and depraved entity. It is difficult to say if this object was genuinely possessed by Dee.

There is also a convex Claude glass in a circular case in the Science Museum that is attributed to Dee and his spirit workings, but this is more likely to be the one that Dee used to display optical illusions to people,[30] including Queen Elizabeth I, if indeed it is Dee's at all.

We see, therefore, that many people have claimed to have received one of Dee's magical devices over the years. Indeed, Francis Barrett noted in 1801 that there were as many as seven people purporting to have one of these illustrious heirlooms:

> "Although *Dee's* manuscripts, and his Magic Chrystal, are to be seen at the Museum, there are six or seven individuals in *London* who assert they have the stone in their possession; thereby wishing to deceive the credulous, and to tempt them to a purchase at an

27 Ibid., p. 548.
28 Ibid., p. 547.
29 Ibid., p. 548.
30 See Dee's *The Mathematical Preface to Elements of Geometry of Euclid of Megara*, where he describes this object.

enormous price."[31]

Given Dee's popularity (or notoriety), it is not surprising why people would make such claims, but it does considerably muddy the water in terms of scholarship, not to mention leading to unsupported (though evidently very popular) beliefs like that of Dee's alleged Obsidian Mirror.

This is important in a practical sense, because there are many people attempting to recreate the process used by Dee and Kelley, employing a similar black mirror instead of the more traditional shewstone (which we know Dee did use, even if the one on display is not his). While there is nothing stopping anyone from using any object they desire in their own personal spirit workings, it seems very unlikely that they would actually be emulating Dee in this regard.

31 Francis Barrett, *The Magus*, Book II, p. 196 (footnote).

IV

ANGELIC RULERS OF THE TOOLS

An important consideration when it comes to the tools is the specific angelic rulers set over them, the names of whom can be used in invocations, while the angels themselves can be beseeched for additional insight into those devices.

There are several places where such angelic rulers are mentioned or alluded to in Dee's diaries. For example, in one of his earliest workings, on 22 December 1581 (when Saul acted as skryer, as Dee had not yet met Kelley), Dee set his shewstone in the metal frame before the angel Annael (sometimes written by Dee as Anael) and asked if there was any "good angel" assigned to it.[32]

Annael showed the Hebrew letters for the name Michael (מיכאל). To verify, Dee asked if this was the same good angel "mentioned in scripture" (i.e. the Bible), which Annael confirmed. Thus, not only is Michael set over the shewstone Dee possessed, but he is the same archangel who is described in the Book of Daniel as a "great prince" who protects the people of Israel, and who defeats Satan in the Book

32 *John Dee's Five Books of Mystery*, ed. Joseph H. Peterson, p. 63.

of Revelation.

In the next working documented in Dee's *Mysteriorum Liber Primus*, Kelley enters the scene. It is three months later, 10 March 1582, and Kelley is eager to prove his skills to Dee, who brings forth his shewstone in the ornate frame. Kelley connects with the angel Uriel, who confirms he is one of those answerable to the stone. When Dee asked if there were others, Uriel responded:

> "Michael and Raphael. But, Michael is the foremost in our works."[33]

From this one might be inclined to believe that Michael is therefore set over all shewstones adopted for skrying in the Enochian system, or in magic in general, but my experience suggests otherwise. In one ceremony I was told by an Enochian angel that Gabriel was set over a shewstone I acquired through a friend, which came to him, and then to me, in unusual circumstances (which I shall briefly describe later).

Subsequent workings suggested to me that shewstones are primarily ruled by one of the four archangels, Michael, Raphael, Gabriel, or Uriel, and that the respective ruler should be called upon for magical workings with that shewstone.

Interestingly, a similar "stone in a frame" to that which Dee possessed was mentioned by the astrologer William Lilly. It was owned by one Gilbert Wakering, and then "Gladwell of Suffolk," and Lilly described it as follows:

> "It was the largeness of a good big orange, set in silver, with a cross on the top, and another on the handle; and round about engraved the names of these angels, Raphael, Gabriel, Uriel."[34]

It is intriguing to note the omission of Michael, who might have had no relation to that particular shewstone. Alternatively, Wakering or Gladwell might have seen Michael as being set over the stone, and employed the other three names upon the frame itself as a form of balance. Further still, the names may have been carved as an aid in

33 Ibid., p. 67.

34 *John Dee's Actions with Sprits*, Christopher Whitby, p. 92.

calling those particular angels forth (Lilly noted that Gladwell once had the conference of Uriel and Raphael, but subsequently lost this communication). It seems that the latter is the most likely scenario.

The use of the names of the four archangels in relation to the shewstone is confirmed in the instructions of Trithemius on how to conjure an angel into a crystal, where part of the preparatory work requires that a small metal plate of pure gold is used to encompass half of the crystal, while on the reverse of the plate Trithemius tells us: "let there be engraven '*Michael, Gabriel, Uriel, Raphael*;' which are the four principal angels ruling over the *Sun*, *Moon*, *Venus* and *Mercury*."[35]

Of course, Dee's diaries do not prescribe such a practice, though they do suggest etching the names of five angels from the Sigillum Dei Aemeth upon the back of the Lamen, in the midst of which would be placed the stone.[36] This may have been designed to form a link between the two, especially considering the more traditional shewstone was to placed within the centre of the Seal, which would be roughly within the circumference of those same names.

As an aside, it is worth considering the manner in which Dee received his shewstones. The "stone in the frame" was given to him by a friend, and he later came upon another shewstone in unusual circumstances, finding it beside the window in one of his workings. Such apparent "materialisation" of a physical object is one of the stranger episodes in the diaries, but similarly odd occurrences have been reported by more modern magicians.

For example, I will share the story of how my own primary shewstone came to me, which was also given to me by a friend. The friend in question (who requested to remain anonymous, so I will simply refer to him as X) was at the time receiving numerous messages from the Enochian angels for me, as at that period my own psychic abilities were significantly less developed, whereas he was very naturally receptive.

After extensive ritual work, which initially appeared fruitless, X felt compelled to follow what seemed like a series of signs, which led him around Ireland, eventually bringing him to Ennis in County

35 Francis Barret, *The Magus*, Book II, p. 135.

36 See Aaron Leitch, *The Essential Enochian Grimoire*, p. 134 for a depiction of this.

Clare. While wandering through the hills, attempting to understand the message he was receiving, it started to rain. Caught in the torrent, he was invited in by an old lady who lived in the solitary cottage in the area. She inquired why in Heaven's name he was out in the rain, and he told her truthfully that he was following signs. She asked to hear more, then wandered off, before producing a dark purple cylindrical container, in which was a crystal ball wrapped in purple and white cloth. She felt it was for him, and though he knew that this was the answer he was looking for, the key to his amazing journey, he felt the shewstone was for me. This occurred very early in my Enochian work (2005), and this magical device has been with me ever since.

I have heard of similarly strange means of acquiring shewstones from other Enochian magicians, suggesting that there might be more to this than at first appears. Just as Dee was told that he needed a "meet receptacle,"[37] (suggesting that the one he was already using was not sufficient for future work), the same may be required for those working extensively with the Enochian system. Unfortunately, situations like what I described above cannot exactly be actively created, but tend to manifest mysteriously while the magician is conducting other magical work. I posit that such strange means of shewstone procurement is not a requisite for successful work with the Enochian angels, but is still curious all the same.

To find out the name of the archangel who rules over one's shewstone, one could replicate my simple method: ask the angels. They might give a direct answer or might beat around the bush a little, forcing you to decipher their response. For me, the Enochian angel in question said he answered to *Fortitudo Dei*, the Latin title for Gabriel (meaning "Strength of God"), and that the latter is set over the shewstone in my possession. Interestingly, this Latin title was also attributed to Michael in Dee's diaries, but it was clear in my workings that Gabriel was intended.

The shewstone is not the only tool which has a governing angel. The PELE Ring was delivered to Dee by the archangel Michael, who is the same angel who delivers the Ring to Solomon. It can therefore safely be said that Michael also rules this Ring. This angel does *not* differ for each magician, however, as Michael is employed to help control and subdue any demons that would disrupt the work.

37 *John Dee's Five Books of Mystery*, ed. Joseph H. Peterson, p. 253.

Since this is the same angel that rules over Dee's shewstone, it is clear, therefore, that Michael had a special place in the work of Dee. Indeed, Uriel told him that "Michael is the angel who illuminates your path."[38] This, and my own personal experience (where Gabriel has become quite prominent), suggests that a different angel may illuminate the paths of others.

For those wondering just how to contact Michael, Dee had the same question in mind:

> "Δ: What may I, or must I do, to have the sight, and presence, of Michael, that blessed Angel?
>
> UR: Request and invoke our appearance with sincerity and humility."[39]

Admittedly, this is not particularly helpful by way of instruction, and clearly Dee felt the same, for he asked again:

> "Δ: I know no means or order to use in the invocating of Michael.
>
> UR: He is to be invocated by certain of the psalms of David, and prayers. The which psalms are nothing else, but a means unto the seat and Majesty of God, whereby you gather with your selves due power, to apply your natures to the holy Angels. I mean the psalms, commonly called the Seven psalms. You must use pleasant savours, with hand and heart, whereby you shall allure him and win him (through God's favour) to attain unto the thing you have long sought for. There must be conjunction of minds in prayer, betwixt you two, to God continually."[40]

This is much more useful, as it gives us the specific Psalms to use as part of an invocation. These are the Seven Penitential Psalms, commonly attributed to King David, and they number as follows:

38 Ibid., p. 68.

39 Ibid.

40 Ibid., p. 70.

6, 32, 38, 51, 102, 130, and 143. It is likely that Dee used the Latin versions of these, but the English will be sufficient for most modern magicians.

I provide below an example invocation of Michael for use with either the shewstone or the Ring, based on material from these Psalms. I employ the King James Version for its poetry, but feel free to adopt a different translation. Feel free also to write your own invocation based on those Psalms, or perhaps even read out the full text of all seven one after the other.

> Hear my prayer, O Lord, and let my cry come unto thee, for I beseech thee: send forth your good angel Michael, that I might better understand thy mysteries through him.
>
> Create in me a clean heart, O God; and renew a right spirit within me. Purge me with hyssop, and I shall be clean: wash me, and I shall be whiter than snow.
>
> Behold, thou desirest truth in the inward parts: and in the hidden part thou shalt make me to know wisdom. Thou art my hiding place; thou shalt preserve me from trouble; thou shalt compass me about with songs of deliverance.
>
> Lord, hear my voice: let thine ears be attentive to the voice of my supplications. Hear me, O God, thou God of my salvation, and my tongue shall sing aloud of thy righteousness.
>
> O Lord, open thou my lips; and my mouth shall show forth thy praise. I meditate on all thy works; I muse on the work of thy hands. Of old hast thou laid the foundation of the earth, and the heavens were crafted by thee.
>
> Let your good angel Michael say unto me: 'I will instruct thee and teach thee in the way which thou shalt go: I will guide thee with mine eye.'
>
> Let him utter unto my ears: 'Be ye not as the horse, or as the mule, which have no understanding: whose mouth must be held in with bit and bridle, lest they

> come near unto thee.'
>
> And let him speak further: 'Be glad in the Lord, and rejoice, ye righteous, and shout for joy, all ye that are upright in heart.'
>
> For in thee, O Lord, do I hope: thou wilt hear, O Lord my God.
>
> And when all is done, depart from me, all ye workers of iniquity; for the Lord hath heard my supplication; the Lord will receive my prayer.

One will note that the above form naturally includes a kind of purification at the beginning and a kind of License to Depart at the end, two elements of standard magical practice. We can see, therefore, how a prayer can be turned into an invocation, a magical act, with some careful thought and planning.

For the Sigillum Dei Aemeth, the Seven Angels before the throne of God bear an obvious prominence, though there are also planetary angels, and a variety of other names, many of which I use to "open" the Seal before most workings (see Chapter VIII). It could even be argued that Levanael, whose name enjoys the central position of the Seal, has a special governance over this tool.

It is possible, and highly probable, that there are angelic rulers set over other items within the Enochian system, but I have not yet conducted workings to see who those might be. I leave this as a possible expansion upon the system by other magicians.

V

COMMUNICATING WITH ANGELS

Enochian magic is largely focused on communication. Dee desired the communication of the angels, which he received in abundance. The manner of working is largely focused on dialogue between the angels and the Operator, the Skryer being the conduit for that discourse. And, of course, the system comes with the Angelic tongue itself. Effective communication, therefore, is of vital importance to successful magical practice.

SEER AND SCRIBE

The traditional mode of operation for this style of magical work, and the one that Dee and Kelley adopted, requires two roles to be filled: 1) one to act as a vessel for the communication; 2) the other to, typically, perform the invocations, ask the questions, and to record the answers.

These roles have historically gone by a number of names: Seer and Scribe, Skryer and Magician, Medium and Operator, but the roles can essentially be summed up in the terms "passive" and "active."

In many cases this style of working largely rested on the natural talents of both parties. Instead of training one's intuitive faculties, the magician would employ someone who is already gifted (or, depending on the perspective, cursed) with psychic ability.

Interestingly, Dee did try looking into the shewstone himself in his earliest workings, reporting in 1581 that he "had sight in Χρυσταλλω [*Crystallo*, or Crystal] offered me, and I saw."[41] He did not describe what he saw, but presumably his vision was not good enough, or he had trouble replicating it, because within months he was employing Barnabas Saul as Seer.

I imagine that Dee's lack of natural talent in this area caused him immense frustration, and this frustration further inhibited his ability, for such "lusting for results" is not conducive to good skrying.

Dee employed several skryers over the years, but none of them were remotely of the calibre of Kelley. It is important to recognise that Kelley's abilities are somewhat rare, and his volatile nature and sometimes difficult personality were likely tied up with that ability.

Dee also used his son Arthur for some skrying sessions, though this proved unproductive, with Arthur seeing very little, particularly in comparison to Kelley's vivid visions. The use of child skryers was very common at the time, and instructions on this can be found in many grimoires. Nowadays, such practice would tend to be frowned upon. On this topic, Mathers wrote:

> "If the Operator himself has developed the clairvoyant faculty; which the training he has subjected himself to for six months ought to have greatly aided, and be pure in mind, I can see no necessity for the employment of a Child as Seer."[42]

Let us consider for a moment why children were even considered for this role. It largely has to do with the idea that they are untainted by the world, that their innocence makes them a better vehicle through

41 James Orchard Halliwell, ed. *The Private Diary of Dr. John Dee*, p. 11

42 S.L. MacGregor Mathers, trans. *The Sacred Magic of Abramelin the Mage*, p. 82 (footnote).

which the communion with angelic forces can occur. Whether or not adults can faithfully replicate this purity I leave for the reader to decide, but surely the piety shown by Dee and Kelley in prayer was enough for the angels to appear, and so it can be also with magicians today.

Yet there is another factor, and that is the imaginative faculty, and the natural psychic ability that lies dormant in us all. These tend to be stronger in children, where, for example, the idea of "invisible friends" is common, but societal conditioning largely forces us to grow out of that, to shut away those natural talents. Yet we were all children once, and though we may have forgotten those days, and locked away those ways of looking upon the world, they still remain.

Thus, that clairvoyant ability is latent within us all, and can be accessed, and can be trained, so that we may be either the magician or seer, or both. Of course, taking on both roles is more difficult, and success will require more effort, but it can and *has* been done. Yet those wishing to employ the strictest definition of Dee purism may wish to employ a separate Seer for the work.

RECORD-KEEPING

An important consideration in magical work of this nature is keeping a diary. Skrying records, conversations with spirits, and impressions and experiences before and after a working are all valuable pieces of information that may make more sense later on, and may need to be referred to to better understand some instruction, or to compare with other magicians to see if there are common experiences. Indeed, if it were not for Dee's meticulous records throughout numerous diaries, we would not have the Enochian system today.

During a working, the magician may be forced to hastily scribble down what he or she sees or hears, and this may result in a rather messy scrawl of text, like many of Dee's records of the spirit workings, that will need to be deciphered later. It is wise to go over this text soon after the working has ended and transcribe it into a more legible format, perhaps with additional explanatory notes. If too much time passes between the former and the latter, the text may be difficult to read and elements of the working will likely be forgotten.

Some magicians, especially those working alone, prefer to use a tape recorder, which is less distracting in the magical working. Indeed, some people find they keep better records of things in a particular format, be it shorthand, drawings, audio/video recordings, digital files, or good old-fashioned hand-written diaries. The format does not matter, and no one should feel obligated to work in a format that they find unproductive. The important thing is that the information is documented.

A VOICE OR NO

Perhaps the most common question when dealing with angels and other beings is: how do they communicate with us? If they do not have a mouth, how do they speak? Is the form we see their real form, or a creation of our own minds?

Understanding this is important for practical work, because many people have misconceptions about how these communications occur, and thus become disheartened if they cannot replicate what they believe is supposed to happen.

In the majority of cases, dialogue with the angels, or any spiritual entity, occurs in the imagination. Now, by this I do not mean to say that they are "made up," in the sense that they are therefore not real, but rather "forming mental images or concepts of what is not actually present to the senses."[43] The communication thus happens internally, to the inner senses, not with the five common external senses. This does not make them any less real; it simply makes them of a different, more subtle nature.

When a magician states that an entity has *said* something to him or her, it is rare that this is heard as an audible voice externally. In many cases, it is not even an internal voice, but more of a thought, or strong feeling that seems to be implanted in the mind. Likewise for visual appearances of entities. It is uncommon for spirits to manifest to visible (outer, external) appearance, and typically a medium of some kind is needed, such as the commonly touted incense smoke.

43 Definition of *imagination* from dictionary.com.

Advanced *clairvoyance* and *clairaudiance* can seem just as "real" as our everyday senses, and it is possible for spirits to affect the physical world, but one should not feel that such physical manifestations are in any way necessary to consider a working successful.

One might wonder, then, if this really is all just the magician deluding him or herself, but there is a very noticeable difference to one's own inner voice, intuition, inspiration, and general mental faculties compared to the act of spiritual communication. It will not only *feel* incredibly different, to the point of being unmistakeable when it happens, but there are tried and tested means of validating such experiences, which will be explored in the next chapter.

Before we move on, let us look at how the angels described their process of communication to Dee himself. The angel Uriel told Dee the following:

> "Think not, that you could speak or talk with me, unless I did greatly abase myself, in taking upon me so unlikely a thing in form as to myself."[44]

Dee further clarified this in a footnote:

> "Angels abase themselves, to pleasure man by their instructions, when they take upon them, or use any sensible evidence of themselves or voices, etc."[45]

Uriel then asked Dee: "Have we any voice or no?" Dee answered:

> "I do think you have no organs or instruments apt for voice, but are mere spiritual and nothing corporeal, but that you have the power and property from God to insinuate your message or meaning to ear or eye, in such sort as man's imagination shall be, that both they hear and see you sensibly."[46]

Uriel further stated: "We have no voice, but a full noise that filleth

44 Jeffrey H. Peterson, ed., *John Dee's Five Books of Mystery*, pp. 351-352.
45 Ibid., p. 351.
46 Ibid.

every place."

The nature in which they appear to us was further clarified when Galvah told Dee that the angels "neither are man nor woman,"[47] but take on a form at the will of the angel and the office it is in charge of.

TIMING

Some may wonder when is the most appropriate time to contact the angels. Dee received sometimes conflicting advice on this, being told at one time not to conduct workings on the Sabbath (which makes sense within the Christian context), and yet when he wondered if there was a special time or hour to contact Michael, Uriel responded with, "Every hour is our hour."[48]

There is, however, a long-standing occult tradition where certain hours are most conducive to certain types of energies, and any spirits relating to those energies are more easily called forth during those hours. Tables of these can be found in multiple sources, including Agrippa. It is worth noting that, despite these tables, Uriel's statement remains correct. Angels can be called at any time. It is just *easier* to call them at certain times. When attempting to contact a specific force, it is wise to put oneself into as much sympathy and harmony with the force in question as possible, and this includes adopting specific names and symbols, and operating within specific times. The more pieces that line up, the easier the line of communication will be, and the clearer the message.

Therefore, in an Enochian context, the angels of the Bonorum, which relate to planets, may best be approached in their respective planetary hours, while the angels of the Watchtowers, which relate to the elements (at least in the Golden Dawn variant), can best be approached during their Tatvic tide.

ACQUIRING ANSWERS

One great difficulty many magicians face when working with spirits

47 *A True and Faithful Relation*, p. 13.

48 Jeffrey H. Peterson, ed., *John Dee's Five Books of Mystery*, p 68.

of any kind is getting clear and direct answers to questions. It is often the case that an answer is given in a roundabout way, or the question is evaded entirely.

Dee faced this on a regular basis, and it is something I, and many other Enochian magicians, have also encountered. Evasiveness tends to be a basic quality of spiritual entities, and there may be many reasons for this:

1. An inability to answer, due to it not being of their office.
2. A deliberate attempt to keep the magician engaged, and so string them along for more workings (this appears to have been common with Dee and Kelley).
3. A kind of jealous guarding of the secrets of Nature, Man, and God.
4. A lack of clarity in the question.
5. They may think the question is answered, and consider it a limitation of human understanding.
6. The magician is simply not ready for the answer.

How then do we deal with this common issue?

The first thing to consider is that questions should ideally be prepared beforehand, not on the spur of the moment. Of course, it is impossible to predict every eventuality, and one may have to go with the flow of a particular working or conversation, but the magician should know what he or she is intending to find the answer to before beginning the operation.

The second point is that the questions should be unambiguous if the answers are to be unambiguous too. Be as specific as possible. In the classic sense of *be careful what you wish for*, the magician should be careful what he or she asks the answers of too.

The third matter is: do not ask questions one can find the answer to easily elsewhere. As much as someone on an internet forum might be irked by another person asking a basic question instead of "googling" it, the Enochian entities tend not to respond well to being asked questions that are answered through a bit of study, especially if they can be found quite readily in a book.

The fourth consideration is perseverance. If one does not get an answer to a question, or if the answer is unclear, even after due reflection, then one should simply ask again. The magician may find that the angel approached is not permitted to answer, and another may be more suitable. Indeed, they can even be asked for the name of whomever the magician should speak with on this. In many cases, they will give it. In some, they will evade that question too. Persistence is key here.

THE DIFFERENCE BETWEEN THE HEBREW AND ENOCHIAN ANGELS

A common question regarding the nature of the Enochian entities, and why we should even bother working with them, is how they differ from the common Hebrew angels we are familiar with from Judaeo-Christian tradition.

It is important to consider that the Hebrew angels actually feature heavily in the Enochian system, and largely facilitated the transmission of it. Many of their names are found on the Heptarchic tools, and their names are even used to uncover other names and spirits. We cannot, therefore, totally separate the two, and it is not in any way improper to beseech the Hebrew angels for aid in understanding the finer details of Enochian magic.

Yet, it begs the question why we need the Enochian system at all. Why not just go straight to Michael and company if they were the ones who delivered this complicated array of material in the first place?

A very succinct answer to this is given by S.L. MacGregor Mathers, one of the founders of the Golden Dawn, in a section of Ritual X:

> Those Hebrew Angel Names which have been taught unto the First Order are rather general than particular, alluding especially to an office or rule whereunto such an Angel is allotted, as it is written, "One Angel doth not undertake two messages."
>
> For these mighty Angels [the Hebrew ones] do

> rather show forth their power in the governance of the Four Great Sephirotic Columns of Severity and Mercy when projected in a Sphere, and this also is under the Presidency of the Sephiroth.
>
> But the Names of the Angels of the Tablets [the Enochian ones] do rather express particular adaptations of Forces, shewing forth all variations and diverse combinations of which are in the other case manifested in a more general manner."[49]

So, in summary, if one's issue or question is of a general nature, the Hebrew angels are most appropriate; if it is of a more specific or particular nature, the Enochian angels are a better fit. Of course, some particular entities are better for different things, as shown in Chapter VII.

49 Ritual X (Private Collection).

VI

TESTING SPIRITS AND VISIONS

If the angels largely appear to us through our imagination, it begs the question if we are simply inventing the experience, deluding ourselves, or, if the experience is indeed real, how do we know that the angels are who they say they are?

This is where testing experiences comes in. Dee sometimes tested the spirits he worked with, and the Golden Dawn introduced a slew of methods to test spirits, and also to test visions in general, some of which I will outline later in this chapter.

The first thing to consider here is the nature of evil spirits, which are frequently deceitful, as evidenced by most experiences with the Goetia. Illuding spirits may take on the vestures of angels, or wear like a shell the forms of the dead, and may claim to be any other spirit, and may outwardly appear to be true. They may do this to gain an audience with the magician, to gain power, to feed off the energy of the magician or working, to interfere with the spiritual or magical aims of the magician, to impart false information, sigils, seals or devices (by which they may further gain power, authority, experience, or connections to others), or simply to cause general confusion, disenchantment, and mischief.

Dee faced such illuding spirits on a regular basis, and we see one such entity appear in the very first working Dee and Kelley did together, when the spirit Lundrumguffa appeared as the angel Uriel, delivering a false lamen (and only being discovered as a fake some time after), before Uriel told Dee to discharge the demon with brimstone.

To give an example of how Dee would test a spirit, he issued the following challenge to the spirit called Il:

> "Who art thou? Art thou one that loveth and honoureth our Creator?"[50]

There are two parts to this basic challenge: 1) asking the name of the spirit; and 2) asking it to confirm that it is a holy creature by acknowledging God or Christ.

The first part is pretty self-explanatory, but the second part warrants some attention. It has long been tradition, both in exoteric and esoteric society, that evil spirits cannot abide the names of God or Christ, or honour the same.

The power of divine names, and the Tetragrammaton in particular, is exemplified in this passage by Agrippa (or pseudo-Agrippa, as the case may be):

> "As the final and highest authority, the magician utters the ineffable name (*nomen ineffabile*) of God, which appears in the prayer in three forms: the Greek (written in Latin characters), the Hebrew, and the Latin—'Tetragrammaton, יהוה, Jehovah.' This is the ultimate authority in magic, above which there is no higher power, 'by the sound of which the elements are overthrown, the air is shaken, the sea runs back, the fire is extinguished, the earth quakes, and all the terrestrial, celestial, and infernal hosts tremble, are troubled and confounded.'"[51]

50 Jeffrey H. Peterson, ed., *John Dee's Five Books of Mystery*, p. 353.

51 Donald Tyson, ed. *The Fourth Book of Occult Philosophy*, pp. 236-237.

Indeed, King Bnaspen of the Heptarchic system, who revealed his office as being that of evil spirits, and who could be employed to cast out the same, told Dee:

> "Blessed be his name, whose Glory is everlasting food to the Just, and sempiternal [terror] to the Wicked."[52]

In order to deal with such spirits, Agrippa (or pseudo-Agrippa) writes:

> "Castor tells [Pollux] that the most certain method [of driving evil spirits away] is by speaking the name 'Jesus.' Origen, he says, had often seen the use of this name drive away innumerable spirits from both the souls and bodies of men. ... Cyprian advised that devils be 'conjured away' by invoking the name of the 'true God.'"[53]

It follows that if such divine names have the power to expel and banish evil spirits, they also have the power to compel such spirits to reveal their true identity. Indeed, merely speaking them in the presence of illuding spirits can be enough to set them in flight, which in and of itself reveals that they were not true.

Those who are not Christian, or do not themselves acknowledge an Abrahamic deity, may have difficulty with this use of holy names, but it is important to consider that the context of the Enochian material is overtly Christian, and both Dee and Kelley professed to be pious Protestants. It is difficult to extricate the system from the religious milieu in which it was delivered.

There are, however, other means of testing an entity, and as many as possible should be employed. The first example given by Dee, of simply asking the spirit its name, can be expanded by challenging the spirit to show that it is who it claims to be. The spirit may then show its name in English, Enochian, or some other language, upon its girdle, chest, forehead, heart, or so forth. Generally speaking, illuding spirits will be unable to show a false name in this manner.

52 Jeffrey H. Peterson, ed., *John Dee's Five Books of Mystery*, p. 242. (Dee thought he misheard or forgot a word here, suggesting it was "perhaps terror.")
53 Donald Tyson, ed. *The Fourth Book of Occult Philosophy*, p. 318.

They may speak falsely, but they cannot have the name etched upon them.

We see an example of the latter in the same exchange with Il, when the angel answered Dee's test by showing his heart, whereon was the name El. Dee recorded elsewhere that his name was "Il or El," and typically a spirit showing a name on its body like this can be taken as proof that it is genuine. Yet it may also be that the angel was trying to show that it did indeed love and honour God, as Dee asked, by displaying the Hebrew divine name El ("God") upon its heart.

This did not satisfy Dee and Kelley, however, nor did the angel's general behaviour, for he "skipped here and there," and showed himself to be "a very merry Creature." His lack of seriousness and solemnity meant that Dee and Kelley "took him to be an Illuder," and so Dee challenged him again, to which he replied:

> "My answer is Threefold: I answer by gesture, by my apparel, and will answer thee by my words."[54]

This appears to have satisfied Dee, and it is worth noting these three elements by which we may judge a spirit. Yet these are also elements which may be faked by a spirit, so the magician should not rely on appearances alone. To me, the spirit bearing its heart is a greater sign of proof than the above.

Another example of a common initial challenge by Dee to a spirit is the following (translated from the Latin):

> "In the name of Jesus Christ, who art thou?"[55]

Again, this assumes an innate power in divine names, a matter which Dee took as fact. Indeed, in an exchange with the angel Ave on how to deal with the evil spirits, or Cacodaemons, of the system, Dee made the use of Christ's name very clear:

> "We call upon the name of Jesus in the expulsing of devils, saying in the name of Jesus, etc."[56]

54 Jeffrey H. Peterson, ed., *John Dee's Five Books of Mystery*, p. 353.

55 Ibid., p. 62.

56 *A True and Faithful Relation*, p. 188.

Ave responded that the name of God is used "against the wicked," not "to allure the devil."

At one time Kelley challenged the angel Galvah, asking her "how can you persuade me that ye be no deluders?" to which she replied:

> "I will prove it by contrary.
>
> The servants of darkness have their Garments stained; their mouths stink of blasphemy, and lies, but our Garments are no such, neither do our lips speak any untruth; and therefore we are of God, for whosoever is of truth, is of God."[57]

Judging by appearances can be useful as a first test, particularly with lower-ranking spirits, who are less capable of deception than their superiors. In a working with a spirit of Fire, if the entity shows up in blue vestures, carrying a cup of water, or other such contradictory imagery, it can likely be taken to be untrustworthy (either being a product of one's own imagination or an illuding spirit, or maybe even a sign that the magician has wandered off into the wrong territory). Yet relying on appearance alone is unwise, as highlighted previously.

However, Galvah provided another measure of proof:

> "In one thing thou mayest know us differing from Devils. The wicked spirits always abhor this word *Mercy*."[58]

The magician may add this word to his or her arsenal.

Dr. Rudd, who appears to have had some experience of the Enochian system before the Golden Dawn popularised it, provided this advice in a treatise copied by Peter Smart (who was likely the original author) in 1712:

> "... mark and observe well the manner, shape, form, corporature, gesture, vestments and foregoing sign thereof, and if in all symbolical likelihood and probable symptoms the Apparition seemeth to be no less, or otherwise conjectured than what is from hence to be

57 Ibid., p. 20.

58 Ibid.

expected."[59]

An example of a challenge (and, indeed, the entire exchange with a spirit) when in doubt of its veracity is given by Dr. Rudd as follows:

> "'In the name of JESUS who art thou?' Then perhaps it will say, 'I am the Servant of God.' Then you may say – "Art thou come from God? Art thou sent from him with good tidings or message?' Then perhaps it will say to you, or some such like words – 'What I am he knoweth of whom I bear witness.' Then you may ask its name, saying then – 'What is your name? Either as it is notified among the blessed Angels or called by of mortal man, if you be of verity and so of charity you cannot mistake my speeches.' Then it will tell you its name, or say nothing at all. But if it doth tell you his name, then you may say to it – 'If you be in the name of Jesus, say that all wicked Angels are justly condemned, and that by the mercies of God in the merits of Christ, Mankind elect is to be saved.' Then it will give you a sufficient answer to satisfy you or else it will be gone from you. And then if it be of good and hath answered your request, then perhaps it will say, 'This much thou hast required.' Then you may say – 'I did so for so is his Judgement and Justice against the Impertinent and his mercy to his Elect. Test is Truth.'"[60]

This exchange is important, as it highlights the lengths the magician may need to go to verify that the spirit in question is true. The magician should not be concerned about testing genuine spirits, which they will generally recognise as being important. Some illuding spirits, on the other hand, may feign offence and indignation, and may challenge the magician in turn, asking who the magician thinks he or she is to ask anything of that spirit, and perhaps even suggesting that they are lucky the spirit showed up at all. It is important not to be fooled by such responses.

How far one wishes to go with this line of testing is up to the

59 Adam McLean, ed. *A Treatise on Angel Magic*, p. 183.
60 Ibid. p. 185.

individual. By forcing a spirit to confess to something against its nature (i.e. an evil spirit confessing the truth of certain accepted religious dogma), the nature of the spirit can be revealed. Several clauses can be employed, which should help weed out and root out particularly evasive and illusive spirits. Indeed, the spirit can be held to a full obligation, including a clause of punishment if it violates any aspect of the oath. Here we see, therefore, how the very initiation ceremonies many occult societies adopt contain important magical formulae that can adapted for formal ritual work.

One basic form of testing involves drawing the spirit's name before the spirit, in any relevant language, and seeing if the image weakens, blurs, or dissipates, or, in some cases, if the spirit recoils or immediately leaves. Any of the above demonstrates that the spirit was not whom it claimed to be. We might wonder why drawing a name can have such an effect, but in the case of spirits, the name is more than just an allusion to the entity—it is the very essence of the entity itself. When it is spoken or drawn before the correct being, that being should be enhanced and strengthened by it. Otherwise, it will weaken the form of any other being not consonant with the nature of those letters.

The Golden Dawn introduced many new forms of testing. The first involves giving a grade sign, which must then be answered in kind (or with the complementary sign). Grade signs related to the Elemental Grades would then be employed to test Elemental entities. These various signs mean less for those not heavily involved in the Golden Dawn tradition, but they can still be very effective.

The second is by drawing pentagrams, hexagrams, or other sacred symbols relevant to the nature of the entity or vision. For example, a Fire spirit should strengthen, not weaken, if an invoking Fire Pentagram is drawn. Likewise, a spirit of Mars should not baulk in the face of an invoking Mars Hexagram. Banishing figures should obviously not be drawn at spirits to test them, as this will simply banish them, whether they are good or evil.

Some spirits may actually pre-empt the magician's tests, by giving all the necessary names and signs when they appear, or may even request an exchange of signs themselves. They do this not for their own benefit (they know who we are), but for ours. In some cases they do this to hurry the proceedings, being somewhat "matter of fact" and taking little heed of pleasantries. While true spirits tend not to object to being tested, they may find the process tedious, or may desire to be tested in a different manner more appropriate to their nature, rank or office.

Other spirits may challenge the magician to prove their worth. For example, in one of Dee's early workings (with Saul instead of Kelley), the angel Annael asked, "By whom is your power?"[61] Dee was confused by this, wondering why he was challenged thus. Annael replied with, "It means you haven't satisfied me." In these cases, it should be more than sufficient to say: "My power comes from God." Remember that the magician is authorised by God alone, and it is this divine authority that allows him or her to command the angelic hosts. Within a Golden Dawn context, the magician may also employ their motto, grade, title/s, and so forth. Merely wearing one's regalia, including one's sash, may be enough on these occasions.

Such tests are also important for "skrying" work in general, because there is a definite risk of self-delusion, which is an even bigger threat than external deceit, for it can be very subtle, and can play on the magician's desires, not to mention his or her inexperience.

Mathers warned of this in relation to clairvoyance within the Golden Dawn system, pointing to a common error of the beginner:

> "... he believes himself to have gone away and to see elsewhere, and may be but among the confused images of his own aura."[62]

Seeing something, therefore, is not the goal. Seeing something *accurate* and truly representative of the plane or force the magician is working with is what is important. It is relatively easy to get a vision, but it may be made up of memories, mental worries, and external influences, not to mention the potential for the intrusion of illuding entities.

This is likely one of the reasons why Mathers advocated that such vision work was to be conducted alone, not with a group, as the

---

61 Jeffrey H. Peterson, ed., *John Dee's Five Books of Mystery*, p. 63.

62 Flying Roll XI, *Clairvoyance*, by G.H. Frater D.D.C.F. (Mathers), in the words of G.H. Frater N.O.M. (Westcott).

potential for the energies and experiences of others to influence one's own experience is very real. This is why I am not particularly keen on, for example, group skrying of the Aethyrs. It can be done, but it requires significant shielding, and a high degree of trust and faith in those with whom one is working.

Indeed, Mathers viewed a "Skryer" as being more than just a "Seer," in that he or she does not just passively receive visions, but "descries" them, which means that he or she sees clearly, employing discernment and skill. This is largely where the modern magical path diverges from the standard that was employed in the time of Dee, where the Operator was the active, guiding, critical force, and the Seer was almost entirely passive and receptive. It is possible to take on both roles, carefully receiving, without letting the floodgates open, but it does require some training.

The Golden Dawn provided a means to test if an experience is coming from various internal influences, such as memory or emotion, by formulating in the imagination one of the Hebrew letters associated with the planets:

Planet	**Letter**	**Cause of Illusion**
Saturn	Tav ת	Memory
Jupiter	Kaph כ	Imagination
Mars	Resh ר	Anger
Sol	Peh פ	Vanity
Mercury	Beth ב	Lies/Intellectual Untruth
Luna	Gimel ג	Wavering Mind
Venus	Daleth ד	Pleasure

If the vision alters or dissipates after testing with one of these letters, it can be considered false. The letter should be imagined in white. The magician can either test with all of the above, one by one, or by whichever letter relates to the cause he or she feels may be misleading them. If there are doubts, then testing should always be employed.

One might wonder why these letters work. On a basic level, the planets exert an influence over us, and each has a special nature or power over a particular force. The magician, over time, aims to free him or herself from these influences, and so gain control over the full direction of his or her life. In a ritual setting, these holy letters, each having an affinity with their particular planet, offer a direct means of control over the vision in question, and so help avoid illusion.

It is also wise not to conduct magical work, especially of a visionary or divinatory manner, when angry, sick, fearful, highly distracted, tired, or disinterested. Any of these states of mind are liable to induce false visions or experiences, or cause the magician to forget an important step, or neglect some vital process.

There are more methods of testing, some of which will come naturally to the magician with experience, and some which are more suited to certain practices than others. Indeed, some spirits may even teach new forms, such as giving a sigil or seal by which they, and they alone, may be called. It goes without saying, of course, that these spirits should be tested too, in order to determine if those teachings or sigils are false.

I cannot stress enough how important testing and the employment of discernment is. One may argue that one of the keywords of the Enochian system is Aemeth (or Emeth אמת), Hebrew for Truth. If we are seeking truth, and not just comfort, then we cannot accept everything we are told, or all that we experience, until it has shown itself to be true.

VII

THE USES OF ENOCHIAN

One of the most common questions regarding the Enochian system, and perhaps all magical systems in general, is: what can it be used for? There are a myriad of potential applications, and perhaps the limit really is only the imagination of the magician in question, but I have provided some examples below based on my experience, study, and discussion with fellow magicians.

- **Healing:** Dispositors/Cacodaemons
- **World Issues/Politics/Influence:** Governors/Parts of the Earth/Kerubic Angels
- **Money and Worldly Gain:** Bonorum/Dispositors
- **Weather:** Bonorum
- **Initiation:** Governors of the Aethyrs/Letters
- **Knowledge:** Kings, Seniors, Bonorum

- **Understanding of Nature:** Kerubic Angels
- **Travel:** Kerubic Angels
- **Crafts and Mechanics:** Kerubic Angels
- **Secrets of Men:** Kerubic Angels
- **Metals:** Dispositors
- **Transformation:** Dispositors
- **Elements:** Dispositors
- **Understanding of the Cosmos:** Seniors
- **Work with Primal Forces:** Overseers
- **Vengeance:** Kings (Severe)
- **Forgiveness:** Kings (Mercy)

Healing: Dispositors/Cacodaemons

The Dispositors or Servient Angels of the upper left-hand sub-angle (Air of [Element] in the Golden Dawn system) are, according to the instructions Dee received, in charge of medicine.

Indeed, these Angels gain additional healing potency when their names are prefixed, for Ave told Dee:

> "If it be an incurable disease (in the judgement of man) then add the letter that standeth against the name, and make him up five; then he cureth miraculously."[63]

63 *A True and Faithful Relation*, p. 180.

Those using the Golden Dawn approach may wish to narrow this down further by considering which element the particular ailment belongs to. For example, issues with blood or other fluids being Water, injury of muscles being Earth, difficulties with the lungs or speech being Air, and problems like fever being Fire. Then the relevant Servient Angels of that particular Tablet can be worked with.

Further, the Cacodaemons can be bound in order to address physical, mental, emotional or spiritual wounds. This is covered in some detail in Chapter XIII.

World Issues/Politics/Influence: Governors/Parts of the Earth/Kerubic Angels

The most obvious entities or forces to use for changing the world on a political level are the Governors or Parts of the Earth. There is some debate over whether these are the names of places or rulers (see Chapter XII of *Enochian Magic in Theory*), but my experience shows that they are both, and thus we can use their names in either context.

Because we have sigils for these, drawn from the Great Table, it is very easy to create talismans. The sigils can also be used while evoking the entities or entering the astral equivalent of the Part of the Earth, and for testing the Governors to ensure they are who they say they are.

The Kerubic Angels of the lower right-hand sub-angle (Earth of [Element] in the Golden Dawn system) are, according to the instructions Dee received, in charge of "secrets of kings." This was at a period when royalty equated with political rule, but the word "kings" can be taken for anyone in political office today, particularly those of senior office, such as presidents and prime ministers.

Again, for those using the Golden Dawn approach, it is possible to further pinpoint the most useful Kerubic Angels for this by considering the politician in question and the intended result, and which element best fits this. For example, a ritual designed to instil passion and fervour into lacklustre and immoveable political bodies may best employ the Fire Tablet.

Money and Worldly Gain: Bonorum/Dispositors

One of the most, if not *the* most, common desires when it comes to magic is the acquisition of riches, preferably vast riches, so much so that the search for buried treasure features frequently in grimoires. The Enochian system is no different, and this was a particular focus of Edward Kelley, who did indeed find some buried treasure that led on to his alleged acquisition of the power to transmute lead into gold.

Some of the best angels for this purpose are the Bonorum, or the Good Angels of the Heptarchic system, who are largely tasked with earthly things.

Another set of angels that may be applicable are the Dispositors of the upper right-hand sub-angle (Water of [Element] in the Golden Dawn system), which are, according to the instructions Dee received, in charge of metals, particularly the knowledge, finding and use of them, as well as stones. Since coins are obviously made of metal, and gold is worth so much, this is one potential area to explore if the magician is interested in acquiring wealth. Of course, these angels may prove unhelpful when it comes to paper money, but since paper money is valued on the basis of gold, and is effectively an "IOU" note for that gold, it could be argued that this is all interlinked. Whether or not these angels accept that argument remains to be seen.

Weather: Bonorum

The Bonorum are also useful for other earthly affairs, including altering the weather.

I have only ever performed this form of magic once, and it proved highly successful. It was a particularly bad Winter, much more than normal, and we had heavy snow in Dublin (which is somewhat of a rarity), which threatened to impede an important event that would include several initiations, and prevent people from flying in. We employed King Bobogel and Prince Bornogo (who are linked with the Sun), and within a day or two (well within the 49 hours deadline we gave), the snow had largely disappeared, allowing the event to go ahead unimpeded.

Generally speaking, I see very little reason to use magic to alter the weather, given that the time, energy, and will can perhaps be better spent elsewhere. However, in certain cases, where a greater purpose demands a particular form of weather, this line of magic may be explored.

Initiation: Governors of the Aethyrs/Letters

While Dee was not given much detail on the nature or use of the Aethyrs, subsequent work by Aleister Crowley and others, myself included, has shown that Aethyrs are depositories of experience and knowledge, and entering them amounts to a form of initiation.

Another area worth exploring is the Enochian letters themselves, skryed in three groups of seven, each group acting as a form of initiation. This is covered in much more detail in Chapter IX.

Knowledge: Kings, Seniors, Bonorum

For the acquisition of knowledge, particularly knowledge of arcane matters, the secrets of nature, the meaning of life, and so forth, the highest-ranking entities of the system are the best bet. This includes the Kings, the Seniors, and the Bonorum.

It has been my experience, and that of others I worked with, that the Kings are more approachable if the Seniors are worked with first. Essentially, we are gaining entry into the royal court, and gaining favour with the King by already having the favour and recommendation of his key advisors. In a purely structural way, we can see this exemplified in the fact that the names of the Seniors surround and lead out from the central squares that mark the nature of the King.

Understanding of Nature: Kerubic Angels

The Kerubic Angels of the upper left-hand sub-angle (Air of [Element] in the Golden Dawn system) are, according to the instructions Dee received, in charge of nature, particularly "the conjoining and knitting together of Natures," and "the destruction of Nature, and of things that may perish."

Thus, the idea of life and death, of growth and decay, falls under these angels, and they may be of use for those attempting to come to terms with the decease of loved ones and the magician's own mortality.

Travel: Kerubic Angels

The Kerubic Angels of the upper right-hand sub-angle (Water of [Element] in the Golden Dawn system) are, according to the instructions Dee received, in charge of travel, particularly "moving from place to place, as into this Country, or that Country at pleasure."

Dee and Kelley travelled frequently throughout Europe, and Dee was highly invested in the imperial exploits of the British Empire (a term he is credited with having invented, though it was actually used earlier than him), so magical aids to travel were no doubt of particular import.

While travel between countries in those days was much more limited, all forms of travel, including by plane and even the burgeoning space tourism business, would fall under the care of these angels.

Crafts and Mechanics: Kerubic Angels

The Kerubic Angels of the lower left-hand sub-angle (Earth of [Element] in the Golden Dawn system) are, according to the instructions Dee received, in charge of hand-crafts, particularly the "knowledge of all crafts Mechanical."

These angels are therefore good for any form of creativity involving the use of the hands (even robotic hands), from sculpture to mechanical engineering. While production lines and businesses focused on making computer parts were not envisaged by Dee, they would also be applicable here.

Secrets of Men: Kerubic Angels

The Kerubic Angels of the lower right-hand sub-angle (Fire of

[Element] in the Golden Dawn system) are, according to the instructions Dee received, in charge of the "secrets of kings," a quality Dee extended to "discovering the secrets of all men" in his invocations, showing that this skill is not limited to those of high office. Further, the angels appointed "all human knowledge" to these Kerubic Angels, and while that may seem very broad, I think it is more likely meant as "all knowledge in human minds," as in their deepest, darkest secrets.

Metals: Dispositors

The Dispositors of the upper right-hand sub-angle (Water of [Element] in the Golden Dawn system) are, according to the instructions Dee received, in charge of "the knowledge, finding and use of Metals," "the virtues of themselves," and "the congelations and virtues of Stones."

This area could arguably be extended to sources of fuel, or rare earth elements (or metals), which are in short supply. Finding new caches of these resources would obviously be very beneficial, both to the magician and humanity as a whole.

Transformation: Dispositors

The Dispositors of the lower left-hand sub-angle (Earth of [Element] in the Golden Dawn system) are, according to the instructions Dee received, in charge of transformation. Of this, Dee was told "formal transformation, but not essential." Alchemy may be considered to come under this heading.

Elements: Dispositors

The Dispositors of the lower left-hand sub-angle (Fire of [Element] in the Golden Dawn system) are, according to the instructions Dee received, in charge of the elements, including "the knowldge of all elemental Creatures." These may be taken to be both the animal forms among us (the fish of the waters, the birds of the air, etc.) and the spirits called Elementals.

Understanding of the Cosmos: Seniors

The Seniors offer, according to the instructions Dee received, "knowledge and judgement of human affairs, according to the nature of their parts" (which is to say that the Seniors of the East, or Air, offer a different take on the above than those of the other directions or elements).

My experience has shown that the Seniors, linked with the 24 Elders of the Apocalypse, and attributed to the planets in the Golden Dawn system, are perhaps the best "go-to" figures for gaining understanding of the universe, especially that part which is most immediate to us (our solar system and galaxy). This was also largely the experience of Benjamin Rowe in his explorations with the Seniors of the Tablet of Earth,[64] though much of those visions are personal to him.

It is a good idea not to go to the Seniors with "small matters," in much the same way we would not waste the time of elders in our society with similarly trivial requests. They are concerned solely with the greater truths and the grander questions, and will look with scorn on any who beseech their aid in unimportant affairs.

Work with Primal Forces: Overseers

These beings, which are essentially the combined root essence of an entire Watchtower, are the rulers of the primal element, and any experience with them will deal with the raw, pure, unaltered and unfiltered essence of that element. As such, these are volatile, difficult and dangerous forces to work with, and I caution extreme care be taken.

My experience is that the Overseers (referred to elsewhere as Great or Supreme Elemental Kings) are the Watchtowers themselves as an animated force. They are, in essence, the collective energy of all that is contained within them, and therefore they represent a kind of raw and primal power. Within a Golden Dawn context this would be elemental.

These entities, or perhaps it is better to view them as forces, do not feature in Dee's material, though their names are derived from

64 Benjamin Rowe, *The Book of the Seniors.*

the outer ring of the Sigillum Dei Aemeth, starting with the letters and numbers found in their sigils or emblems (which are indeed found in Dee's diaries).

They form part of the Golden Dawn corpus of teaching on Enochian matters, and so Dee purists may wish to ignore this aspect. I would say, however, that there are many mysteries in the material received by Dee, and following the hints and clues can unearth some intriguing and potent aspects, just like these particular forces.

In the OSDL, there were four officers in charge of the elements called Sentinels (which were very different to the office of the same name in the Golden Dawn system), and part of the work taken on by these officers involved the Overseers. It was quickly discovered that the Golden Dawn's warnings about these were not exaggerated at all.

Vengeance: Kings (Severe)

The name derived from the central whorl of each Watchtower, with the right-hand central square, is the severe form of the King, who is suitable for matters of "extreme judgement," including punishment for crimes and vengeance for evil acts.

The Golden Dawn employed both central letters, likely due to its emphasis on balance.

Forgiveness: Kings (Mercy)

The name derived from the central whorl of each Watchtower, with the left-hand central square, is the merciful form of the King, who is suitable for "general" matters, but is often experienced as a more affable and understanding figure, more prone to forgiving, and highlighting the power of forgiveness, and choosing not to act, when acting would cause more damage than it solves.

The Golden Dawn employed both central letters, likely due to its emphasis on balance.

VIII

OPENING THE SIGILLUM DEI AEMETH

For most, the Sigillum Dei Aemeth is simply placed upon the Table of Practice, left as a kind of passive object that is naturally empowered by the material and symbolism. There are no specific prayers or invocations for opening or unlocking the power of this device, but there are some fairly simply procedures for achieving this.

We must first recognise that the Sigillum Dei Aemeth is made up of the names of numerous angels, arrayed around the figure in a variety of ways (see Chapter VI of *Enochian Magic in Theory* for how the Seal is constructed). These angelic forms, therefore, clearly have some influence over this pantacle, and provide the very essence of its potency.

Recognising this, if we call upon those same angels, we can more fully tap into the power of the Sigillum. If we follow these names in order from the outer rim through the various rings, heptagons, heptagrams, and pentagram, we can gradually empower our workings, granting additional protection, and, perhaps more importantly for skrying work, access what I have found to be one of the primary purposes of the Sigillum: the ability to ensure true and accurate visions, with each layer of the Sigillum acting as a kind of filter to illusory forces, even the misleading aspects of our own minds.

This is largely why I consider the Sigillum indispensable in skrying work of any kind, whether it is working with the Enochian letters or the Aethyrs. The potential for self-delusion, and the very real threat of deception by spirits (good, bad, and neutral), make this a powerful tool, made all the more powerful with an appropriate invocation.

I developed the following invocation while in the OSDL, amending it slightly over the years, and it has served me well for close to a decade.

> "In the Names of God borne upon this Seal, I now declare the Sigillum Dei Aemeth duly open! By the opening of this Seal of God, this Seal of Truth, may the blessings of God, the Christos, his good angels, my own Holy Guardian Angel, my Higher Self, and all other beneficent forces be upon me and this ceremony.
>
> Lord God, thou who art called Truth, give me eyes to see, and ears to hear. Grant me a true sight, a clear vision, that I may more fully come to know thy mysteries. Help my ears distinguish between what is true and false, and let no spirit deceive me, either by thought, word, or deed, or any other means whatsoever. If they should try, cast them out, as if from the circle of this Seal, which shall ever be a barrier unto them, blocking out the deceivers, and blotting out their lies.
>
> I call upon the forces of the Sigillum Dei Aemeth to aid me in ensuring truth, accuracy, and veracity in this work, and to dispel all lies, illusions, preconceptions, falsities, deceptions, and illuding spirits.
>
> I do this now in the Names of the Seven who bear witness to Truth: Galas, Gethog, Thaoth, Horlwn, Innon, Aaoth, and Galethog; in the Names of the Seven

> Archangels Before God: Zaphkiel, Zadkiel, Cumael, Raphael, Haniel, Michael, and Gabriel; in the Names of the Seven Angels of Light: Sabathiel, Zedekiel, Madimiel, Semeliel, Nogahel, Corabiel, and Levanael; in the Names of the Sons and Daughters of Light, and the Sons of the Sons and the Daughters of the Daughters, and by the everlasting virtue of Emeth, Herald of Truth. May they all watch over this ceremony and keep it within the sanctity of verity. AGLA! Ateh Gibor Le-Olahm, Adonai! Amen."

Variations can be used, but the two essential ingredients are as follows: 1) calling upon all of the names that make up the Sigillum, either overtly or in summary; and 2) asking specifically for truth and accuracy in the ensuing working. "Ask and it will be given to you." If one does not specify the purpose of the invocation, it is essentially wasted.

Obviously the inclusion of the Hebrew word *Emeth* (אמת), alternatively transliterated *Aemeth*, meaning "Truth," is important. The use of AGLA here to end the invocation relates to these letters on the reverse side of the Sigillum, which effectively grounds and seals it, and thus grounds and seals the invocation, making a perfect ending.

Indeed, one could even trace the Hebrew letters Aleph, Mem, and Tav over the Seal while speaking this invocation, to further empower it and its filtering effect.

Similar invocations for truth were used by seers in the past, beginning with the recitation of several Divine Names. One such invocation can be found in Sloane 3851, the *Grimoire of Arthur Gauntlet*, an important 17th Century magical text, which includes the following wording:

> "... let them [the angels] make true answers, true judgement, and true appearance, revealing unto us all things doubtful and uncertain, without all falsehood, fraud, or deceit."[65]

I have found that approaching such an invocation almost like a legal

65 Sloane 3851 (via Christopher Whitby, *John Dee's Actions With Spirits*, p. 89.)

contract, including alternate wording to cover different forms of deception, helps ensure no spirit effectively employs a "loophole" to bypass it. Not every variation can be accounted for, but the more clauses covered, the more protected one will be from those illuding forces. This will also lead to a longer invocation, and this can be important in terms of affording the necessary time to fully infuse it with the magician's will and emotion.

I have found from experience that the First Call works really well with the Sigillum, helping to open it, so it has largely become standard practice to use them, along with the above invocation, together.

Another point I think is worth making here: if one is to cover the Sigillum Dei Aemeth with a cloth, as prescribed by the angels, it should be covered fully. If it is only partially covered, it will negatively affect its use. Indeed, I have found that not covering the Seal can make it a major distraction while attempting to focus one's attention on the shewstone. Yet when performing an invocation related to this Seal, it may be uncovered, then recovered immediately after.

IX

SKRYING THE LETTERS

The letters of the Enochian alphabet are powerful, so much so that they are forces in their own right, and it is essentially the combination of these forces that create specific angelic forms. It follows, therefore, that working with these letters, and attempting to come to a better understanding of them, will in turn award a better understanding of the angels themselves.

The significance of the Enochian alphabet for magical use is highlighted by the Golden Dawn in a passage from one of the Order's official papers on the subject:

> "These special Angelical Language letters have more magical virtue than common Hebrew, or English letters, especially in respect to the working of the Squares of the Tablet in Spirit Vision or the so-called method of Skrying in the Spirit Vision. They are therefore more sigils than simply letters."[66]

This concept is important, and something that has been validated

66 Ritual X, *The Book of the Concourse of the Forces* (Private Collection)

by my own experience. The shape of the letters is not arbitrary, and one may find that this sigil-like nature makes for powerful talismans. Indeed, when the Great Table is converted from English to Enochian lettering, the entire thing comes to life, for these are living forces. As one of the OSDL ceremonies stated: "The Letters, expressions of a Living Fire, join into Words, expressions of a Living Being."[67]

In the OSDL, I began skrying the letters independently of the leader of that group, and found the experiences revelatory in nature, and initiatory in feel. We compiled our findings separately, and shared and compared them later. I recommend following suit, because reading other people's experiences before conducting one's own is likely to lead to preconceptions.

THE SPHERE GROUP

While I conducted my skrying sessions based on an intuitive urge, not knowing that anyone else had done this before me, and then thinking that it was a relatively recent practice, it seems that skrying the Enochian letters goes as far back as the late 19th Century, when a group of Adepts in the Order of the Golden Dawn established the Sphere Group.

This was an unofficial consortium of higher grade members, most notably Florence Farr (or rather Florence Emery at the time) and R.W. Felkin, who conducted skrying experiments and attracted the wrath of Annie Horniman, the criticism of W.B. Yeats, and the approval of Mathers (according to a letter sent by Farr to Theorici Adepti Minores on 17 January 1901).[68] Two versions of this group existed, the first from 1898 to 1901, and the second from 1901 to 1902, making up some of the more interesting explorations of the Enochian system beyond the Zelator Adeptus Minor and Theoricus Adeptus Minor grade work.

The skrying of the Enochian letters appears to have been a major focus of the Sphere Group, with detailed recordings of sessions in July and August of 1901. It is not surprising that these letters were chosen, given the appeal of the Enochian system and the general

67 OSDL Aspirant Ceremony (Unpublished).

68 Darcy Küntz, ed. *Enochian Experiments of the Golden Dawn*, p. 32.

mystery surrounding the letters of its alphabet.

Interestingly, membership of the Sphere Group was originally reserved for Zelatores Adepti Minores, but was then increased to Theorici Adepti Minores when many of them had been thus advanced. I believe it fair to say that had they made it to Practicus Adeptus Minor, the Sphere Group would have been further bumped up so that it remained open to only the most advanced members of the Inner Order.

While so little is known about the higher sub-grades of Adeptus Minor, the jewel of the Practicus Adeptus Minor grade was a "crystal orb,"[69] the equivalent magical implement of which was almost certainly a shewstone or crystal ball. Chances are that Mathers and Westcott intended to employ this for more intense skrying sessions, perhaps even reminiscent of that of Dee and Kelley. The Enochian letters would have made a perfect set of symbols on which to practise. This would have also been a good way to placate any unrest caused by the Sphere Group and its detractors by making much of its work part of the syllabus for one of the sub-grades, and thus "official" Order teaching, especially given that Mathers seemed to recognise Farr's claim to have contacted a member of the Third Order, of a grade equivalent to 8=3, called the "Egyptian Adept."

Farr also pointed out the connection of the Enochian system to the Moon. "The Tablets are purely Luna," she wrote in a diary entry dated 17 August 1901.[70] She argued that the Tablets represent the days of the Lunar month, and the 21 letters represent the 19 years of the North Node's revolution in the Zodiac, with the remaining two letters attributed to Caput Draconis and Cauda Draconis. She also noted that there was very little solar influence, apart from the Kings that form the central whorl of each Tablet. This might have been a concern for the use of such Tablets in what is otherwise a solar order, though it may be argued that this lunar connection helps balance things within the system.

What is interesting about the connection to the Moon is that there is some evidence of this in Dee's diaries, as outlined in my book *Enochian Magic in Theory*.[71] For example, the central name on the

69 *Second Order Insignia*, by William Wynn Westcott, 1892. Private Collection.

70 Darcy Kuntz, ed. *Enochian Experiments of the Golden Dawn*, p. 29.

71 Frater Yechidah, *Enochian Magic in Theory*, pp. 70-71.

Sigillum Dei Aemeth is Lavanael, an angel linked with Levanah, the Hebrew name for the Moon. The special holy day suggested by the angels to Dee and Kelley was Monday, the day of the Moon. It is not clear if Farr knew about these links, but it is interesting to see that what she was picking up on in her own magical work matches up.

PROCEDURE

Since skrying the letters was new for me, and I was doing this of my own volition (as opposed to it being in the grade syllabus of the OSDL, though it was later adopted there), I had very little to go on, starting small and gradually building up an effective method through trial and error, and a healthy dose of common sense.

From my study of Dee's diaries, I knew that the letters were divided into three groups of seven. I felt instinctively that I should work these in a similar manner, presuming each group of letters may have some important relationship.

At this point I must highlight the importance of: a) following the Enochian alphabet as is (i.e. do not started with A [Veh], as in English, as this is not the first letter of the Enochian alphabet—B [Pa] is); and b) completing each group of seven letters, as they are, in my experience, an initiation in and of themselves, and to leave a set incomplete is to leave oneself imbalanced. A rule of thumb in magic is to always complete what one has started.

For my initial procedure, I used the Lesser Banishing Ritual of the Pentagram to remove any existing energy or influences, then recited the First Call, in English and Enochian, to give me a "blank slate," and put me in tune with the Enochian forces. I then imagined the Enochian letter before me, and vibrated the name repeatedly, until it felt like I was ready to proceed, at which point I imagined myself giving the Golden Dawn's Sign of the Enterer, otherwise known as the Sign of Projection, and imagined myself passing through the symbol of the letter. Then I paid close attention to what unfolded. When ready to close, I imagined passing back through the letter and giving the Sign of Silence.

My approach changed over time, as I learned more about what

worked and what did not. When I found I could not test with some of what I had been using with Watchtower work, I began incorporating other tests, such as drawing the letter before an entity, while simultaneously pronouncing it. Later sessions included some of the Heptarchic tools, such as the Sigillum Dei Aemeth, to make the workings safer, and also help ensure the accuracy of the vision.

My intent with these initial sessions was to find the meaning of the letter, if there was any, not to communicate with any angelic forces, but in time I began to ask for a representative of the letter to be shown, while in some later workings I asked for the letter to manifest as a being, so that I could communicate with it. These were often difficult forms to communicate with, being somewhat primal, so I recommend leaving this latter approach for subsequent rounds of skrying.

I also learned over time that not having a physical object or symbol to ground the experience can be quite taxing. I printed some of the letters, then felt as though I was being scolded for this "short cut," so decided then to print only the outlines and fill them in, to ensure the shape of the letters was as exact as possible. In a way this also mirrored somewhat the transmission of the letters, where Kelley traced over the forms shown in yellow, before the yellow disappeared. One can also draw the letters from scratch, but care must be employed to ensure the shape is correct, as any variances (like those popularised in Regardie's *The Golden Dawn*) will significantly alter the vision. This is why I opted for a printed outline, as a kind of middle-ground. I have included outlines of the letters at the end of this chapter for anyone who wishes to trace over them or scan and print them.

Those with little or no magical experience may consider skrying the Hebrew letters first, which, while potent, will still be tamer than the Enochian alphabet. The procedure for both is largely the same, though Hebrew can be divided into groups of three, seven and twelve, based on the division of the Mother Letters, Double Letters, and Simple Letters. With such a division, I would start with the Simples, then Doubles, then Mothers. Alternatively, one could work with them as they are assigned by the Golden Dawn to the Tree of Life, working backwards from Tav to Aleph.

Once a full set of Enochian letter skrying has been conducted, the magician may then decide to compare with others, to see if anything matches. This approach may, in time, result in enough people with similar experiences that we can reliably appoint meanings and correspondences to the letters, and perhaps expand our understanding, and maybe even our vocabulary.

When I finished each set of seven letters, I went over my diary entries and condensed and compiled the information into a chart of correspondences, including the primary meaning/s, planetary or zodiacal associations, related Tarot cards, and possible Hebrew associations (noting that the latter was said to be a corrupted form of the Angelical tongue). I was also interested in verifying the OSDL's gematria, or finding the true gematria (if any existed) for these letters.

In some cases I found that experiences overlapped, leading to conflicting correspondences, but subsequent skrying sessions helped clarify these, especially when I began asking for answers to these riddles by the angelic "governors" of the letters.

SAMPLE LETTER SKRYING SESSIONS

In order to get a better idea of how a skrying session of one of the Enochian letters might work, I have decided to share the accounts of my initial skrying sessions of the first two Enochian letters, *Pa* (English B), and *Veh* (English C/K). These sessions are dated 11 July 2006 and 21 July 2006 respectively. I have made no alterations to the text, though I have updated the images (the originals were very crudely drawn).

Let me stress that what follows are merely examples, and one may experience something completely different for these letters.

Skrying Session 1 - Pa - [11/07/06]

Basic Procedure: LBRP; First Call; Vibrate name of Letter with visualisations; Pass through letter with Projection Sign, etc.

A small white square appeared, and I felt as if I was being drawn towards it, so it became larger, until it became a truncated pyramid, and there was a wisp of cloud that formed into a shell, standing upon the central square of the truncated pyramid (my view had now wrapped round so I was seeing it from the side). Then the word "cocoon" came into my head, and I saw that this shell was also a cocoon, and represented or contained a Being of some kind.

Then the vision changed, so that I saw what appeared to be a stained-glass image of Mother and Child, both with stained-glass style halos. The child was being held close to the mother's chest, in a protective manner. Then this was superimposed upon another stained-glass image of a person holding a Book. This changed to laying down the Book and the Child at the same time (The Book is the Child? The Word? Logos?) by a river. There was a Baptism about to take place. The mother or the person with the book (or both?) took a jug of water to baptise the child.

Then the vision changed again, to explore another area of the Letter. The word "hook" came into my head, relating to the "hook-shape" at the end of the V-shape of the letter Pa. Then I saw that this hook was a P, which began the name of the letter, somewhat like the following:

Then the "V" also spelled "Vessel," which was the Jug. My vision swept round so that I was looking down on the V as if it were a landscape, and it was a river (perhaps the same river as earlier?). Then I saw a stack of "containers" of some kind (paint cans, perhaps?), forming in a pyramid, and this pyramid was an upside-down V-shape.

Then I explored the English letter equivalent in context, and saw the letter B before me, which tilted until the curved area was down, and appeared to act as either a set of eyes themselves or glasses for those eyes. Then the same shape was a wooden log container "opening-out"—it closed before me to illustrate this, like the following:

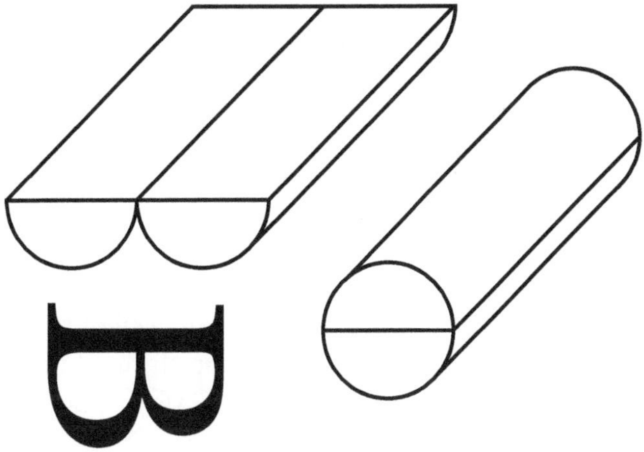

I also received an important thought that in regards to the Bonorum, the predominance of the letter B related to this letter acting as a container for the force exemplified through the other letters.

Then the B switched to the other way round, to represent a woman's breasts, the containers of milk (also linking back to the "Mother and Child" earlier). I also received the thought of these breasts being "jugs" (pardon the pun), particularly the jugs/cups in the Temperance card.

Then I saw a woman in robes standing up a few steps within a temple doorway. She had a round container, like a bowl, and drank from it. In fact, it seemed as if she was drinking to me, so I gave a mental "nod" and felt that I would get little more out of this Session, so ended the vision by retracing [my steps] and banishing, etc.

Main Derived Meaning: Container

P.S. Originally I had, via intuition, attributed Luna to this letter. Given the "receptive" nature of both a container and Luna's energies, I feel this might be an accurate link.

Skrying Session 2 - Veh - [21/07/06]

Basic Procedure: Same as last time, except with an Enochian LBRP, then First Call, vibrating letter name, etc.

I imagined the letter before me, stepped through it with the Projection Sign, then saw it before me from an isometric view. In the top part of the letter was a well of fire, spouting forth flame. The energy of this flame then travelled up, around, and down through the other side of the letter, which had a downward-pointing well of fire, which, in turn, sent its energy down, around, and up through the first well. With this came the distinct thought of a *transfer of power*, as well as the word "conduit," equally relating to a transferal.

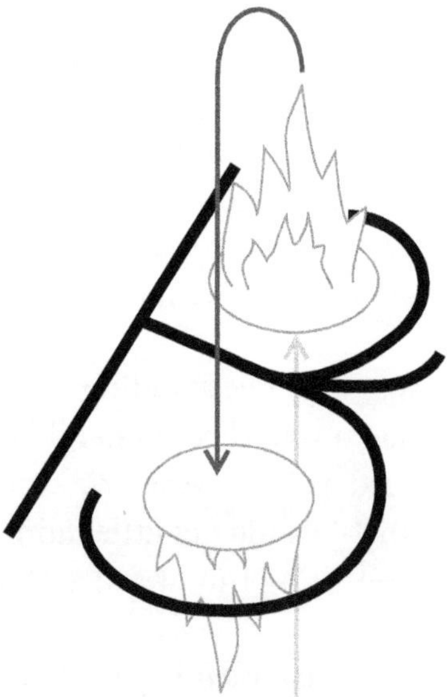

Next I saw the winged element of the caduceus wand, and thought of the "phoenix wand," which then appeared. Given previously working with images of the caduceus wand, I have decided to cast a great deal of doubt over the validity of this segment of the vision, so discarded it and began afresh with a new section.

I saw what appeared to be a rose, which was also a chalice, and the petals formed what was like a crowned-ridge around the edge of the chalice. This reminded me of the container/vessel mentioned in the "Pa" visions, so when I thought of this, there was a huge expansion of power in the form of an outward explosion—the Big Bang. I saw this energy travel outwards and form new rose-crown chalices (i.e. new vessels), which again related to the transfer of power from one area to another (kind of like the Sephiroth pouring forth into the next in the original process of coming into being).

Then, very suddenly a new and important (to my intuition) piece of information came along. The letter Veh stood before me as an hour-glass—you will notice their similarity in shape in the following image:

This, as you can clearly tell, also relates to transferral, given the hourglass transfers sand from one side to the other (I got the distinct impression that "time" had very little to do with this, that the hourglass symbol was merely representing transferral). In the above image you will also see the original character and the slightly flawed edit of the character where it is in two parts. I have used the latter but joined the middle line back to the other part of the letter, so that it is one whole unit, which I feel it *must* be for the transferral of power to take place.

Then I saw the letter on its side, and the line represented a base, with the three "prongs" from this line acting as the bursting forth of energies from a fountain. With this came the thought of "continuous transfer," as the outbursts from the fountain curve back in on themselves, so that the water (or whatever energy is being used) returns to the base to be reused in another outburst from the fountain:

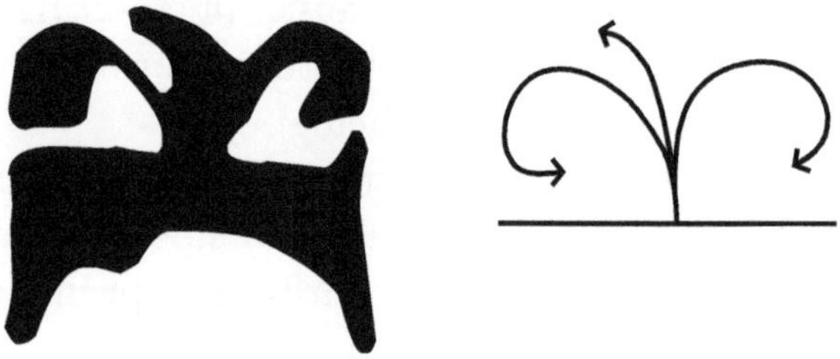

Then, the letter upright represented a wall and energy springing forth from the wall, from the stable to the energetic. With this also came the thought of milk from a woman's breasts (harking back to the same imagery used in the Pa visions), which is the transfer of life-force from the mother to a child. If you put the letter on its side, you also get the same "breasts" shape as the English B part of the Pa vision. A thought with this was: transformation, which shares the same stem (trans) as transferral.

Then I saw a cauldron on a stand in the following manner:

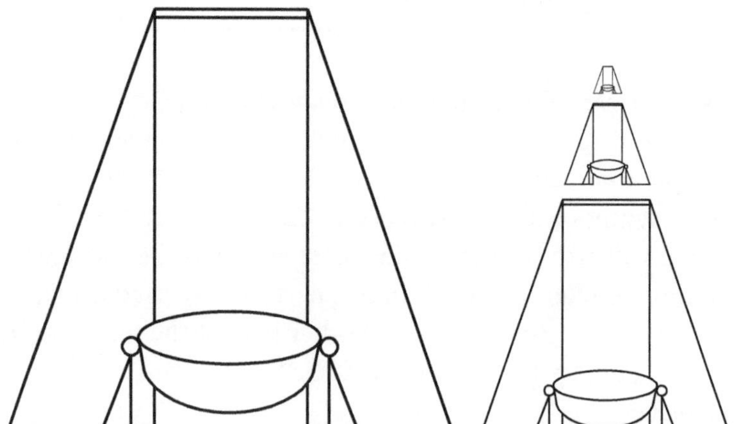

There was a fire in this cauldron like that of the well of fire earlier. This cauldron tipped forth, pouring out a molten liquid (I get the impression of a process of alchemy here, which relates to "transformation"). The liquid pours onto the ground, which is then in turn the roof/top beam of the next cauldron piece, and this continues to "pour forth" in this manner, so that there is a pyramid shape forming from the multiple cauldrons, relating, to my thought, to Kether pouring forth continuously until one gets to Malkuth, which is larger and at the bottom of the "pyramid," because it is denser and more "manifest."

Next, tying in with the above, was a vision of the heavens pouring forth continuously into/onto the earth. Then the entire image flipped, so that the earth was pouring forth continuously into/onto the heavens. This continues eternally, and reflects a rotating universe (and also "As Above, So Below"), as well as harking back to the hourglass, which flips so that the transfer of sand reverses from one side to the other.

I also briefly inspected the letters C and K in their shape and form, and came up with the same "spring forth" of power—i.e. a fountain.

Next I became aware of a presence, and saw then that the 24 Seniors had gathered around me in a circle and were watching my work with great interest. I then decided to openly invite a being relating to the letter in question to come forth, which they did (seemingly through the circle of the seniors, again as if they were acting as a conduit for the being to manifest through). This being was robed and cowled and held up their right hand in a gesture of boon, which I returned (I felt it would be foolish to try to test with elemental or planetary signs, etc., since that might influence the vision). In the same hand they held what appeared to be a small round object, between their thumb and index finger. I asked what this was, which they showed me was a globe—the globe of the earth. This was divided in two halves, almost like a marble, and this being was showing me that the rotation of the earth includes this constant transferral of power, in the form of one half getting night, one half getting day, but changing constantly, etc.

Next this being traced the number 3 in a stylised form before me. I asked if this was a number, and they said "yes and no". I asked what planet was related to this letter, to which they answered Jupiter. I asked why, and they said that Jupiter transferred Power to Saturn (Saturn being the number 3). Next I asked what the gematria of the letter was, to which I got the number 8. I thought immediately then of the infinity loop, which again echoes a continuous transferral of power, and the shape also is similar to that of the aforementioned hourglass.

Then I asked if there was anything else they wanted to show me, which in return I got a mental "no". I then gave the Sign of Boon, to which they returned it and ended the vision.

Main Derived Meaning: Transferral Of Power/Energy

DRAWING THE CURTAIN

It is quite common for a symbolic "drawing of a curtain" to occur to precede the vision. This may take the form of an actual curtain seen in the crystal or imagined in the head, or may take another similar form, such as the clearing of smoke or fog, the dispersing of a cloud, the opening of an egg, or a blinding light that steadily dissipates to reveal a scene.

This kind of "introduction" to a vision is not a requirement for the vision to be deemed valid, but I point it out as many people experience something of this nature. Indeed, a large number of Kelley's visions were introduced in this manner, with the drawing of a black cloth or veil, or a white curtain, and many of them also ended with the cloth, veil or curtain covering the scene.

I should point out that there tends to be a very distinct feeling or impression when this happens, which is difficult to describe, but is a good sign that something significant is about to occur. At times it may seem like nothing is happening, like the magician is sitting in the audience, waiting for the act to start—and then the lights dim, and the curtains are drawn open.

CAUTIONS

Before experimenting with this line of work, or any magical work in general, it is a good idea to be aware of some possible risks. I include some caveats here.

It is generally unwise to employ a symbol on the body (such as taped to the forehead) for skrying work. Such an approach is likely to cause strain, exhaustion, or illness, and is more likely to mix the magician's own energies with that of the symbol, and so increase the likelihood of self-delusion. For this reason I also caution against putting symbols under one's pillow at night. This is especially dangerous for the beginner, who is more open to influence in dream, and may have poor protective means in place.

While the symbol can be visualised, it is generally a good idea to have a physical object in magical work, which helps ground the experience, and reduce the potential astral strain experienced. These should be made by yourself alone, and not touched by another, which may contaminate them. If you feel there to be the influence of another over the materials you employ in your symbols, then you can banish those energies by appropriate means.

The skryer should avoid falling into an entirely passive state. The aim is not to become entranced or obsessed by a symbol, and self-hypnosis by means of the symbol should be avoided. A careful balance should be maintained between the receptive condition required and the active control of the magician, and the latter should never be relinquished, either voluntarily or by means of deception. If you find yourself being lulled into a trance, or seduced by sleep, the working should be ended immediately. Some means of banishing should then ideally be performed before retiring to bed.

Should a spirit attack the magician during one of these workings, various protective symbols (the pentagram, etc.) may be drawn, and Divine Names may be employed against them. Should a spirit attempt to capture one's gaze, and so cause a kind of hypnosis, the magician should assert his or her authority and banish the entity. It is also possible for the environment to provide such a risk, such as a mire or river, which may act like a mirror. In this line of working, the line between entities and the environment itself can be very blurred.

These cautions should not discourage the magician from attempting these exercises when ready. Fear must be overcome, and the magician, once armed with knowledge, must then dare to walk the path and employ that knowledge practically. Otherwise it is useless to him or her. Yet the theory is a natural prerequisite to safe practice, and all means of protection and safety protocol should be employed.

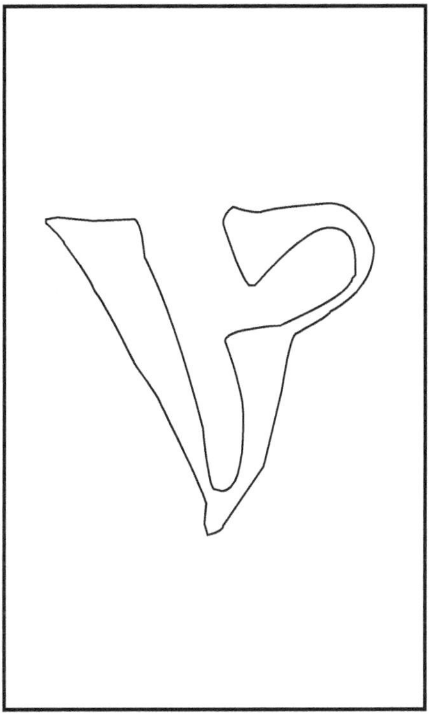

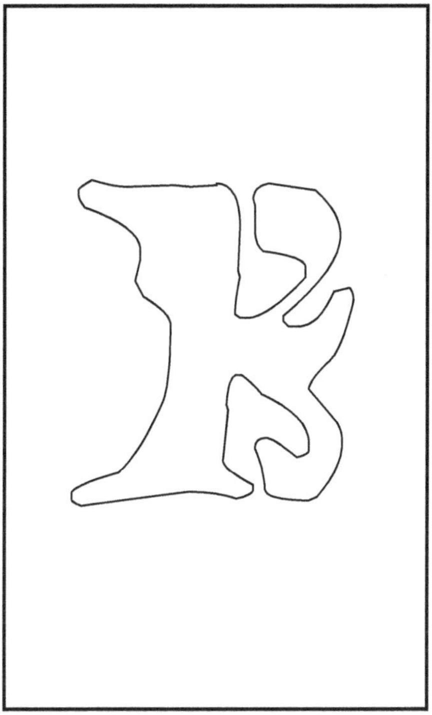

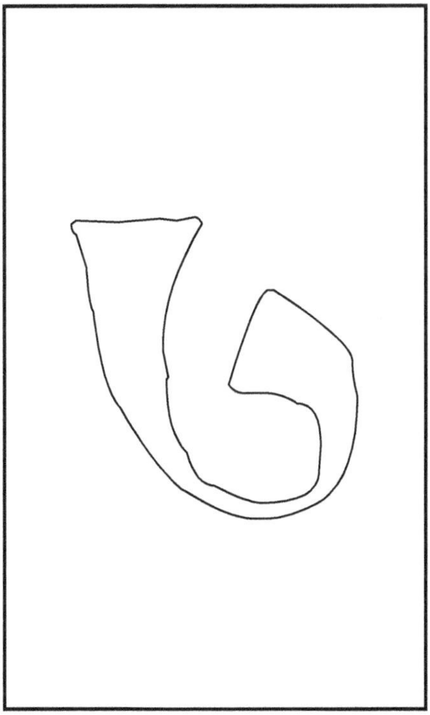

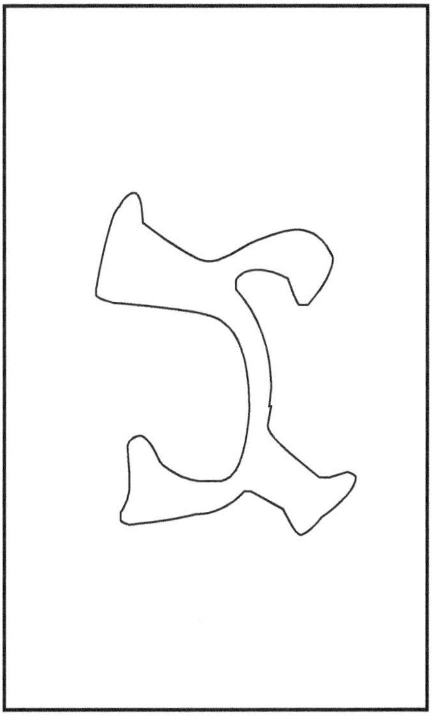

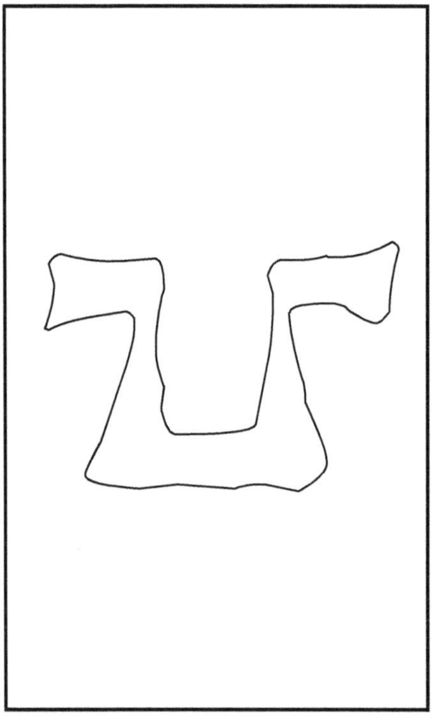

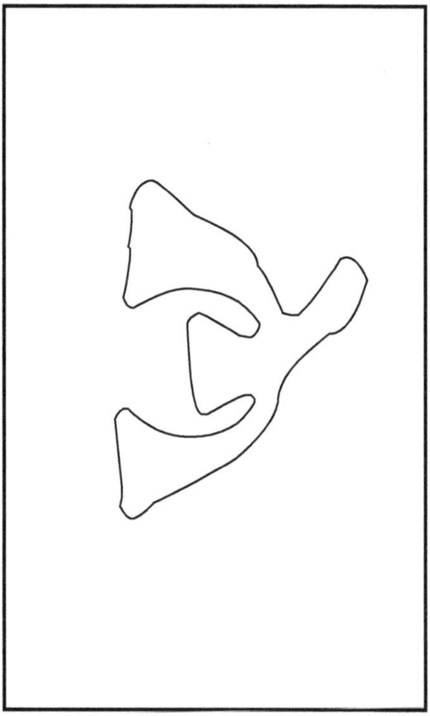

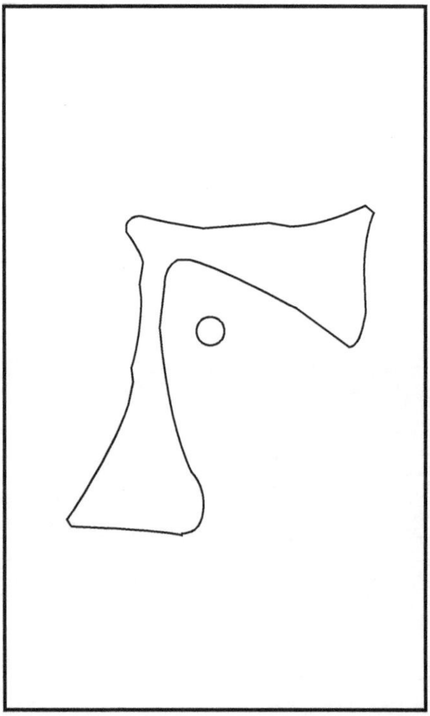

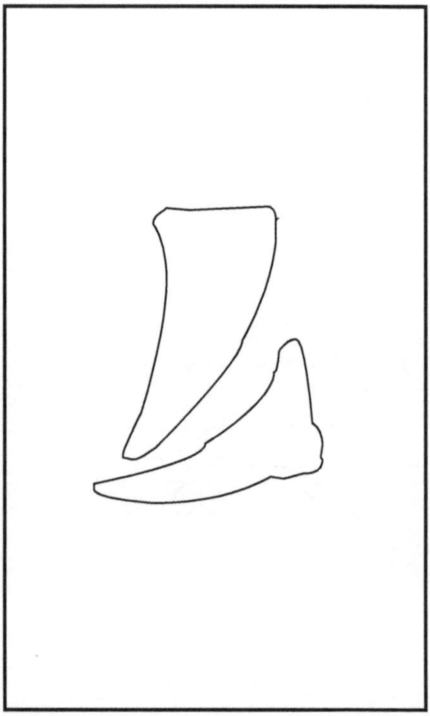

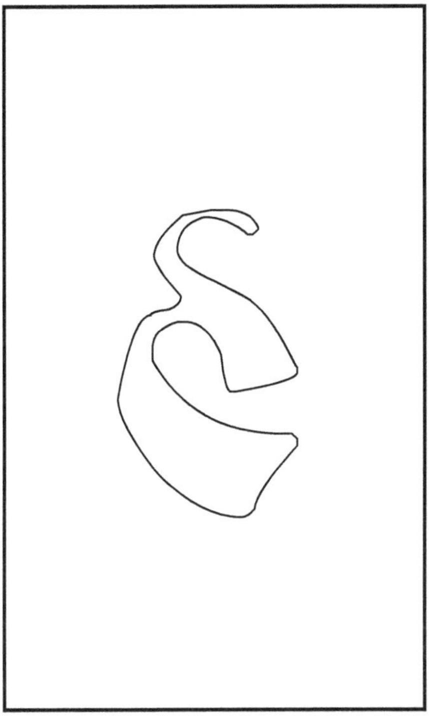

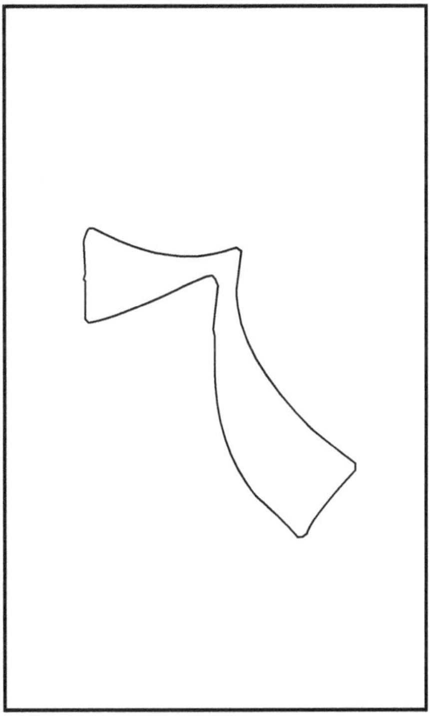

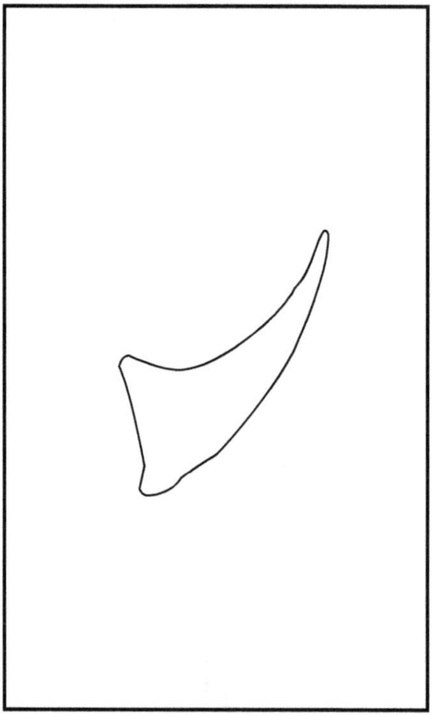

X

OPENING THE WATCHTOWERS

The Great Table, more popularly known as the Watchtowers when split into the four individual Tablets, is the section of Enochian magic that receives the most attention, so there have been a number of methods shared for "opening" these and working with the spirits dwelling inside.

THE DEE METHOD

From a Dee purist perspective, the 19-Day working (covered in Chapter XVI), is the only approach required to working with these entities, as they should then come when called, even without the need for a proper ceremony.

To briefly summarise this method, it involves calling forth all of the angels from the Watchtowers in turn, and enjoining them, in the Name of God, to work with the magician. The Cacodaemons, however, are not to be called.

This approach is fairly basic in that it relies completely on invocations, many of which follow a set pattern. There are no specific techniques to open the Watchtowers. The spirits are simply called forth, and do not actually appear until the final day.

The challenge is, therefore, more in committing to a certain number of days, for no day can be missed or skipped, and it is very unwise to abandon the operation midway through. Unlike most of the techniques that follow, this is a one-off procedure.

THE REGARDIE METHOD

Israel Regardie, who gained popularity and notoriety for publishing a large amount of Golden Dawn (or technically Stella Matutina) teachings, developed a technique called Opening by Watchtower, which has become a stapel of some magicians' ritual routines.

This procedure is based upon the Golden Dawn's ceremony for the Consecration of the Vault of the Adepti, otherwise known as Ritual K (or rather the Stella Matutina redaction of this, which has some small variances). This technique is obviously heavily reliant on other Golden Dawn teachings, and requires knowledge of some basic rituals employed by the Order, which can be found elsewhere.

It is worth noting that for the Consecration Ceremony, the angels are called forth as protective forces, to purify and consecrate the Vault for the year ahead. As a personal ceremony, it still retains these elements, but they are somewhat lacking in purpose, barring general warding, for which there are numerous other appropriate rituals.

To call forth specific angels, and not all of them at once (as this does), would require extensive editing of the ritual, so much so that it would be largely unrecognisable afterwards. Therefore, I would argue that there are better approaches than this.

Opening by Watchtower[72]

The Temple should be prepared as follows:

- *A central Altar, with Tablet of Union, a rose, and the Magician's Wand and Dagger.*
- *A Fire altar in the South, with appropriate tablet and weapon.*
- *A Water altar in the West, with appropriate tablet and weapon.*
- *An Air altar in the East, with appropriate tablet and weapon.*
- *An Earth altar in the North, with appropriate tablet and weapon.*
- *Incense, appropriate to the working being done, may be burned, as well appropriate music should be played if so desired.*

I. *Stand at Altar, facing East, and announce:*

> HEKAS, HEKAS, ESTE BEBELOI!
> (hay-kahs, hay-kahs, ess-tee bee-ba-loy!)

II. *Perform the Banishing Ritual of the Pentagram.*

III. *Perform the Banishing Ritual of the Hexagram.*

IV. *Go to Fire altar. Pick up Fire Wand and shake it three times in front of Tablet.*

V. *Holding Fire Wand above head, walk slowly deosil around perimeter, saying:*

> And when, after all the phantoms have vanished, thou shalt see that holy and formless fire, that fire which darts and flashes through the hidden depths of the Universe, hear thou the Voice of Fire.

VI. *On returning to the Fire altar, shake the Fire Wand three times in front of Tablet.*

VII. *With Fire Wand, trace a large circle in front of the Tablet, then an*

72 From *Ceremonial Magic* by Israel Regardie.

invoking Pentagram of Fire within it, then the Fire Kerub (sign of Leo) in the center, saying:

> OIP TEAA PEDOCE (oh-ee-pay tay-ah-ah pay-doh-kay). In the names and letters of the Great Southern Quadrangle, I invoke ye, ye Angels of the Watchtower of the South.

Replace Fire Wand.

VIII. *Walk deosil to the Water altar. Pick up Water Cup and sprinkle a few drops three times in front of Tablet.*

IX. *Holding Water Cup above head, walk slowly deosil around perimeter, saying:*

> So therefore first, the priest who governeth the works of fire must sprinkle with the lustral water of the loud resounding sea.

X. *On returning to the Water altar, sprinkle a few drops three times in front of Tablet.*

XI. *With Water Cup, trace a large circle in front of the Tablet, then an invoking Pentagram of Water within it, then the Water Kerub (eagle's head) in the center, saying:*

> EMPEH ARSEL GAIOL (em-pay-hay ar-sel gah-ee-ohl). In the names and letters of the Great Western Quadrangle, I invoke ye, ye angels of the Watchtower of the West.

Replace Water Cup.

XII. *Walk deosil to the Air altar. Pick up Air Dagger and shake it three times in front of Tablet.*

XIII. *Holding Air Dagger above head, walk slowly deosil around perimeter, saying:*

> Such a fire existeth, extending through the rushing of Air. Or even a fire formless, whence cometh the image of a voice. Or even a flashing light, abounding, revolving, whirling forth, crying aloud.

XIV. *On returning to the Air altar, shake the Air Dagger three times in front of Tablet.*

XV. *With Air Dagger, trace a large circle in front of the Tablet, then an invoking Pentagram of Air within it, then the Air Kerub (sign of Aquarius) in the center, saying:*

> ORO IBAH AOZPI (eh-roh ee-bah-hay ah-oh-zohd-pee). In the names and letters of the Great Eastern Quadrangle, I invoke ye, ye Angels of the Watchtower of the East.

Replace Air Dagger.

XVI. *Walk deosil to the Earth altar. Pick up Earth Pentacle and shake it three times in front of Tablet.*

XVII. *Holding Earth Pentacle above head, walk slowly deosil around perimeter, saying:*

> Stoop not down into that darkly splendid world wherein continually lieth a faithless depth and Hades wrapped in gloom, delighting in unintelligible images, precipitous, winding; a black ever-rolling abyss, ever espousing a body unluminous, formless and void.

XVIII. *On returning to the Earth altar, shake the Earth Pentacle three times in front of Tablet.*

XIX. *With Earth Pantacle, trace a large circle in front of the Tablet, then an invoking Pentagram of Earth within it, then the Earth Kerub (sign of Taurus) in the center, saying:*

> EMOR DIAL HECTEGA (ee-mor dee-ahl hec-tay-gah). In the names and letters of the Great Northern Quadrangle, I invoke ye, ye Angels of the Watchtower of the North.

Replace Earth Pentacle.

XX. *Walk deosil around Altar to the West and then face East. Pick up rose and trace a large circle over Altar, then the invoking Pentagrams of Spirit (active and passive), saying:*

> EXARP (ex-ar-pay). BITOM (bay-ee-toh-em). NANTA (en-ah-en-tah). HCOMA (hay-coh-mah). In the names and letters of the mystical Tablet of Union, I invoke ye, ye divine forces of the Spirit of Life.

Replace rose.

XXI. *Making the Portal Sign of the Rending of the Veil, say:*

> I invoke ye, ye Angels of the celestial spheres, whose dwelling is in the invisible. Ye are the guardians of the gates of the Universe, be ye also the guardians of this mystic sphere. Keep far removed the evil and the unbalanced. Strengthen and inspire me so that I may preserve unsullied this abode of the mysteries of the eternal Gods. Let my sphere be pure and holy so that I may enter in and become a partaker of the secrets of the Light Divine.

XXII. *Go to the North-east, and say:*

> The visible Sun is the dispenser of Light to the Earth.

> Let me therefore form a vortex in this chamber that the Invisible Sun of the Spirit may shine therein from above.

XXIII. *Circumambulate three times deosil beginning in the East. Make the Sign of the Enterer each time you pass the East.*

XXIV. *Return to the West of the Altar, face East, and say the following Adoration, making the Sign of the Enterer at the end of the first three lines, and the Sign of Silence after the fourth line:*

> Holy art thou, Lord of the Universe.
> Holy art thou, whom Nature hath not formed.
> Holy art thou, the Vast and the Mighty One.
> Lord of the Light and the Darkness.

XXV. *Stand in stillness, feeling the forces around you.*

XXVI. *Perform desired Working.*

XXVII. *When ready, close the Temple by reversing the circumambulations (widdershins), making the Sign of the Enterer each time you pass the East.*

XXVIII. *Perform the Banishing Ritual of the Pentagram.*

XXIX. *Perform the Banishing Ritual of the Hexagram.*

XXX. *Stand at Altar, facing East, and say:*

> I now release any spirits that may have been imprisoned by this ceremony. Depart in peace to your abodes and habitations, and go with the blessing of YEHESHUAH YEHOVASHAH (yuh-hesh-you-ah yuh-hoh-vah-shah).

XXXI. *Pause, then say:*

> I now declare this Temple duly closed.

THE GOLDEN DAWN METHOD

The Golden Dawn assigned the first 18 Calls to the Watchtowers, with 1 and 2 relating to the Tablet of Union, and 3-18 relating to the 16 sub-angles of the Watchtowers themselves.

The Golden Dawn employed some rules for the use of these Calls with the Watchtowers, which are worth considering here for anyone wishing to follow that particular system.

Calls 1-6 are employed for calling the angelic forces of the Tablet of Union. The First Call governs the Tablet of Union as a whole (which may explain why it gives a general "clean slate" feeling when employed). The Second Call governs the letters EHNB, the first letters of each horizontal name, being those related to Spirit. Calls 3-6 relate to the horizontal names themselves, in turn: EXARP, HCOMA, NANTA, and BITOM respectively.

These latter four Calls also relate to their respective Watchtowers, and more specifically to the "purest" sub-angle (for example, Air of Air, in the case of the ORO Tablet, or Water of Water, in the case of the MPH Tablet). The First and Second Calls, however, are only to be used with the Tablet of Union, and not at all with the Elemental Tablets.

At this point it is perhaps worth noting that, while Dee used the Black Cross as opposed to the Tablet of Union, the Golden Dawn did not invent the Tablet of Union, and it has a definite precedence in Dee's diaries, for he was instructed to assemble the names into a table matching exactly what was later employed by Mathers and Westcott. The names were then taken from this tablet and used in the central cross that "bindeth the four angles of the [Great] Tablet together"[73] (in the words of Ave), described soon afterwards as a "cross of union"[74] (in the words of Dee). While clearly the angels did not intend for the names to remain in the 4x5 table, such tables that were used as a means to an end elsewhere turned out to have their own purpose, and Dee's description of the cross shows that the appellation given to the Tablet of Union is not plucked from thin air.

When working with very specific forces, the respective Calls

73 *A True and Faithful Relation*, p. 179.

74 Ibid., p. 180

would be used in succession. Thus, when calling forth any of the angels of the EXARP line, the First Call would be read (since it relates to the Tablet of Union), followed by the Second Call (since it includes E of EHNB), followed by the Third Call (which relates both to EXARP and the ORO Tablet). Since the latter Call also taps into the Watchtower itself, we see how the use of the first two Calls helps focus the experience to the Tablet of Union instead.

Likewise, when working with a specific sub-angle, such as Air of Water, two Calls will be employed, one after the other. In this example, neither the First nor the Second Calls would be used (for they would redirect our attention to the Tablet of Union, making any of the next four Calls select a line from there). Instead, we select the Call for Water, which is the Fourth Call, and we then select the Call for the sub-angle of Air from the Water Tablet, which is the Tenth Call.

If we instead want to access one of the "purer" sub-angles, such as Water of Water, we would only need to use a single Call (in this case the Fourth). In the OSDL we had some debate over whether we should repeat the same Call, so that the first use is for the Tablet as a whole, and the second for the sub-angle, but this is not really necessary.

While the link between the Calls and the Watchtowers has been called into question by some, we do know that the Calls can serve multiple functions, such as the Call of the Aethyrs, which is employed both for the Parts of the Earth (which are, in fact, in the Watchtowers) and the Gebofal operation (covered in Chapter XVII). If the last 30 Calls have a dual purpose, it follows that the first 18 likely have a dual purpose too.

Indeed, the Golden Dawn applies these Calls to more than just the angels of the Watchtowers. They can also be used to summon the Chiefs of the Elementals described in the Golden Dawn's Tarot instructions. However, in this case, the angels Michael and Raphael are recommended as ruling forces.

On the use of these Calls in general, it is worth taking into consideration the following warning from one Golden Dawn paper on the subject:

> "These Calls or Keys are only to be made use of with the greatest care and solemnity, especially if they be pronounced in the Angelical Language as given. And anyone profaning them, by them with an impure mind, and without a due knowledge of their attribution and application, shall be liable to bring serious spiritual and physical harm unto himself."[75]

THE OSDL METHOD

The OSDL method is very similar to the Golden Dawn approach, in that the Calls are employed to open the Watchtowers, but there were a few additional elements employed, mostly to enhance the idea of opening and closing a gate, so that there is a greater divide between the magical experience and the mundane world.

The first thing we employed is a Bell, which is rung at the beginning and end, similar to the knocks employed in Golden Dawn ceremonies. The second thing is the Sign of the Rending of the Veil and the Sign of the Closing of the Veil, which have a natural opening and closing effect.

We also tended to include some kind of acknowledgement that the Watchtower is opened, then the same for a particular sub-angle, and so forth, before proceeding to call any of the particular forces of the Tablet.

75 Ritual T, *The Book of the 48 Angelical Keys or Calls* (Private Collection).

XI

SKRYING THE WATCHTOWER SQUARES

Perhaps the most widely known Enochian practice within the Golden Dawn variant is skrying the Watchtower squares. Instructions for this were given in detail, along with several examples of visions experienced by original Order members.

To fully appreciate the Golden Dawn approach to Enochian requires full immersion in the Golden Dawn system in general, especially considering pretty much every part relates to another. Therefore, approaching a particular subject in isolation is difficult, much more so for Enochian, where the correspondences really come together. So, please bear in mind that what is presented here is not, and cannot be, an accurate representation of the full approach the Golden Dawn takes to this subject.

Caveats aside, this particular approach provides a slew of options, and allows us to engage with the Tablets in a way that goes far beyond what Dee and Kelley received.

PYRAMIDS AND ATTRIBUTIONS

The Golden Dawn introduced a novel approach to the Squares by viewing them as truncated pyramids, with the four sides showing the numerous correspondences of that particular Square, and the flattened top showing the letter in question.

This not only acted as a way to store the significant volume of data related to these Squares, but was employed magically to gain access to the secrets and mysteries of each particular Square. The Squares are coloured based on these attributions, so that, for example, one side of every Square in the Earth Tablet will be coloured black, relating to the Earth Element.

However, the manner of attribution is different for different types of Squares, so it is not a "one glove fits all" system. These are the particular layouts used for the different style of Squares, with an explanatory note of how they may be read in the third column:

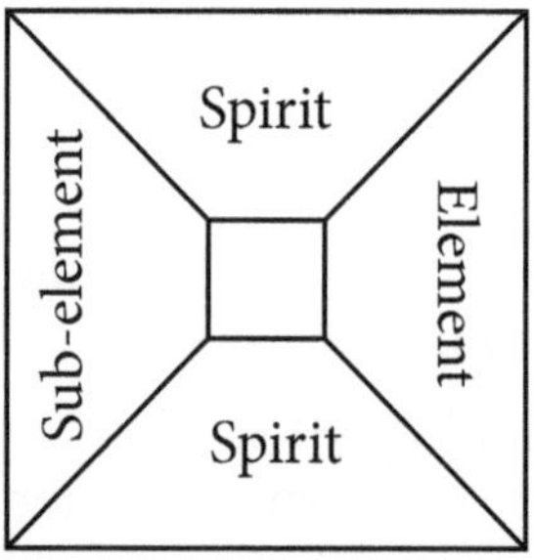	Tablet of Union Squares	Sub-element of Element of Spirit of Spirit
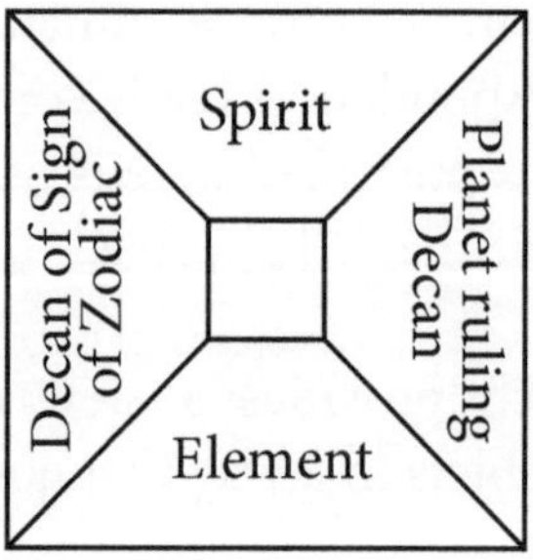	Great Cross Squares	Decan of Planet of Spirit of Element

<table>
<tr><td>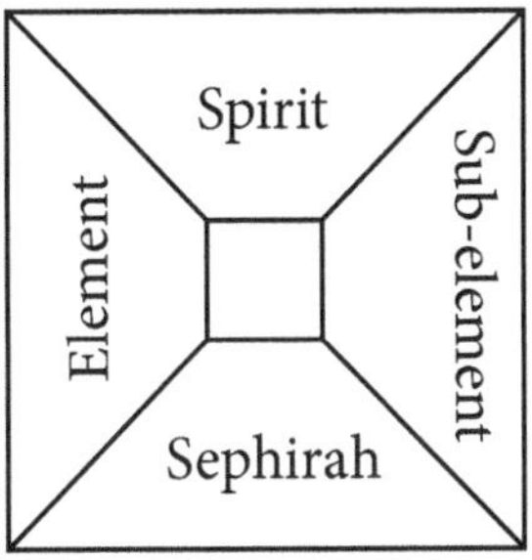
</td><td>Calvary Cross Squares</td><td>Sephirah of Spirit of Sub-element of Element</td></tr>
<tr><td>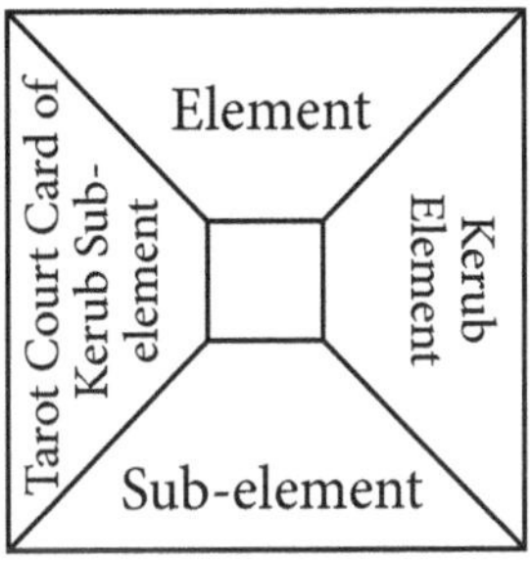
</td><td>Kerubic Squares</td><td>Tarot of Kerub of Sub-element of Element</td></tr>
<tr><td>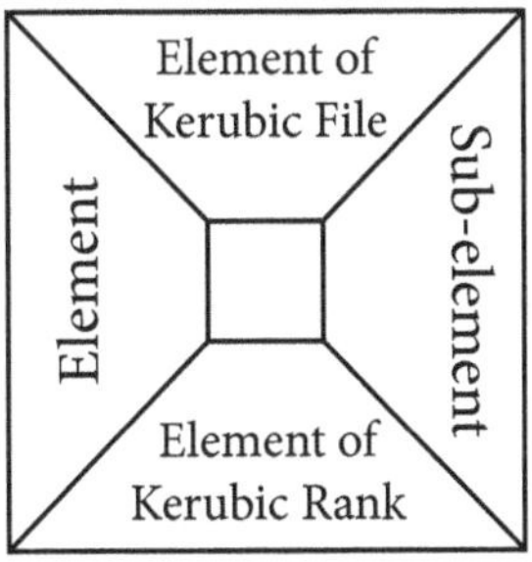
</td><td>Servient Squares</td><td>Rank of File of Sub-element of Element</td></tr>
</table>

Of course, the above is actually somewhat of a simplification, for the correspondences go beyond those listed, but this is a good level with which to start, and sufficient for initial skrying work (and identifying Cacodaemons).

The specific rules for ascribing all of these correspondences would require a book in and of itself, and some of these have been explained, in somewhat incomplete form, elsewhere (in, for example, Israel Regardie's *The Golden Dawn*). They are beyond the scope of this book, but I have supplied completed Watchtower diagrams online containing the full correspondences so that they may be employed practically.

The OSDL adopted a simplified attribution scheme, which applied across the entire Watchtower, regardless of whether it was Kerubic, Servient, or Calvary Cross squares. It followed the model of Rank of File of Sub-element of Element, essentially matching the Servient Squares. It created a much more streamlined system, but presents problems for the Great Cross. Indeed, since this entire approach of attributions is derived from the Golden Dawn, I think it better to employ the full Golden Dawn approach, because the mode of attribution is different for different types of Square for a reason.

While Dee obviously did not work with such an appropriate, the *different nature* of the various types of Square is indicated in his diaries (above and below the cross in each sub-angle, for example).

ANALYSING THE SQUARES

The interaction of the various forces within a Square, following some rules set forth by the Golden Dawn, provides for a unique interpretation of the nature of that Square, and can help in selecting a particular one consonant with the desired outcome the magician is seeking.

For example, if the magician wishes to work on his or her emotions, then the Water Tablet should be employed. Yet, this should be further narrowed down, so that, for example, the emotion of anger would relate to the Fire of Water sub-angle. It can be pinpointed further by delving into the two remaining associations of each Square, be it Element, sub-Element, Spirit, Planet, Sephirah, Tarot card, or so forth. The more specific the magician can be, the more likely they are to find a Square that relates to the issue at hand, and so be able to visit it to learn more, or work with the relevant angel to resolve that particular problem.

A certain amount of leeway is allowed here in terms of how each Square is interpreted, and this will largely depend on the context of the question or working involved. Someone looking to the Earth Tablet for improving their physical health will likely look at the Squares differently than someone working with the same Tablet in order to forge a better relationship with the land around them.

Yet there are some guidelines, as well as some examples, which will highlight how this process works. The primary key to this is knowing where the Elements are strongest on the sides of the Pyramid Squares. This is summed up in the following diagram:

We see, therefore, that the two active Elements (Fire and Air) operate on a vertical plane, Fire ascending, and Air descending; meanwhile, the two passive Elements (Water and Earth) operate on a horizontal plane, Water moving from right to left, and Earth moving from left to right.

So, if a particular Square has Water attributed to the right-hand triangle of the Pyramid, Water is in its strongest position, and is thus strengthened by that placement. If it was in the left-hand triangle, it would be in its weakest position, and so any reading of that Element must account for its subdued nature.

There are also some other things to bear in mind. Each Element has its natural opposite (Water opposing Fire, and Air opposing Earth), and so if Water appears in the strongest place of Fire, it is also weakened by that position. Spirit is strong in any position, and often tempers the potentially volatile forces of a Square.

Mathers provided several sample analyses of Squares, some of which I include on the following pages:

The Square a of e x a r p in the Tablet of Union

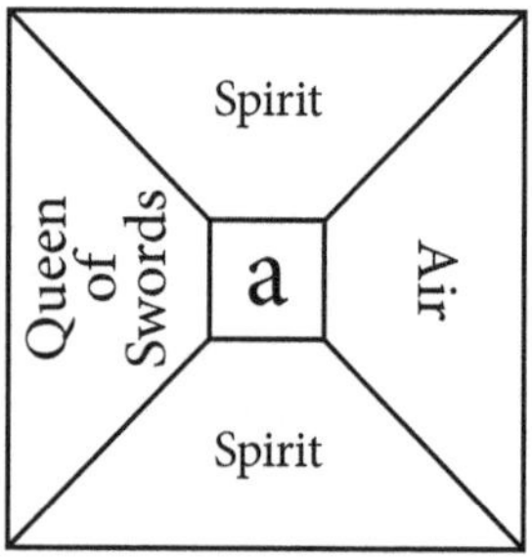

Nearly all the Squares in this Tablet represent some combined effect of Light and Life.

Here Spirit acts both downwards and upwards. Air is not very strong in action when it is here placed, and the Queen of Swords represents the moist Force of Air, ה of ו, therefore the terrestrial effect would be that (if one could attribute a direct material action unto the Squares of the Tablet of Union) of a moist and gentle scarcely moving breeze, with a soft vibrating Light playing through it like the most gentle sheet lighting in Summer.

The Square h of m p h in the Great Central Cross of the Tablet of Water

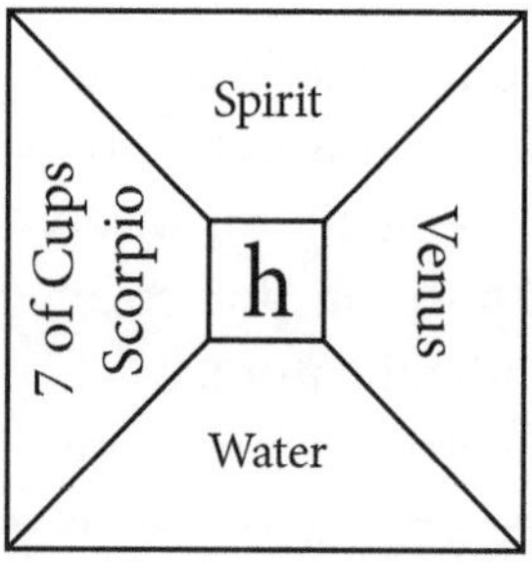

Here the action of Water is extremely passive, Scorpio representing especially still water, and Venus having her quiet action still more intensified, therefore were it not for the action of Spirit, the effect would be rather evil than good, representing Deception, and well summed up in the 7 of Cups, the "Lord of Illusionary Success." But the action of the Spirit makes it mild and beneficent, a gentle peaceful force.

The Square O of O m e b b in the Calvary Cross of the Lesser Angle of Water of the Tablet of Water

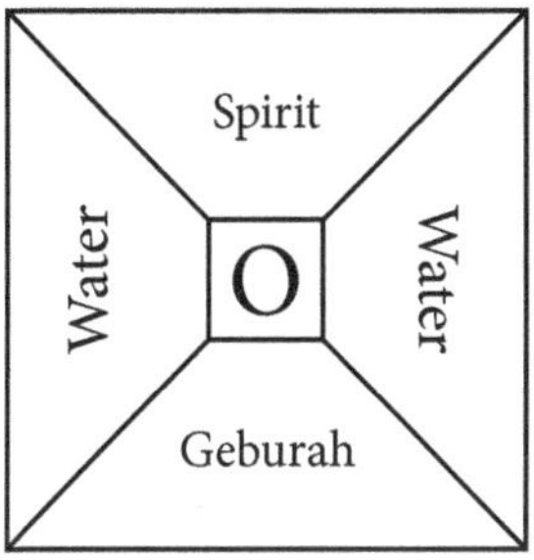

Here Water is extremely strong and is stirred to action by the energy of Geburah, and were it not for the Spirit it would be the destroying energy of a flood, but the latter renders its effect more gentle and benificent, promoting the solution and nourishment of matter.

It can be useful, therefore, when picking a particular Square to work with, to perform an analysis like the above to ensure the Square fits, before then skrying it, or calling forth the angel whose name begins with the letter of that Square, or performing a binding ceremony on the Cacodaemon whose name starts there.

GODS AND SPHYNXES

The Golden Dawn extends its approach to the Squares further by assigning to them the symbolic form of a Sphynx, as well as an Egyptian deity. These are particularly useful for magical work.

Ritual X tells us:

> "This small square at the apex maketh of the Pyramid a certain Throne or Shrine. On this Throne a Ruling Force is seated. Within the Shrine is a Sacred Symbol. Place then its Sphynx within each Pyramid and the Image of its God above.
>
> Take then the Pyramid as the Key of the nature of each Tablet Square."[76]

The specific Egyptian gods in question, acting as "the Symbol of the Power of the Light" acting on that particular Square, are given in detail for the Servient Squares, while instructions on the gods of the Kerubic Squares was reserved for those who attained the grade of Theoricus Adeptus Minor. Gods for the other squares, such as the Sephirothic Cross and Great Cross, were presumably planned for higher sub-grades in the Golden Dawn system, but the system appears to have not been finished. Regardless, the surviving instructions are detailed, and give us plenty to work with.

The Sphynxes are created by combining parts of the four traditional Kerubic creatures: the Bull, the Eagle or Hawk, the Angel (or Man), and the Lion. The Eagle and Angel are winged, while the Bull and Lion are wingless. These relate to the elements in the following way:

Lion	Fire
Eagle	Water
Angel	Air
Bull	Earth

However, the forms co-mingle, creating a kind of mutated form, depending on the particular elemental makeup of the square in question (except in the cases where only a single element is present, which means only the form of a single creature is employed). The element attributed to the top triangle of the truncated pyramid tells us what the head will look like. The bottom triangle tells us what the feet, lower limbs and (in the case of the Bull, Hawk and Lion) tail will look like. The triangles on the right and left sides will show us what the trunk and fore limbs will look like.

76 Ritual X, *The Book of the Concourse of the Forces* (Private Collection).

While these might initially appear as a kind of Frankenstein's monster, they provide a potent visual representation of the combined forces of the Square in question. Some examples will be provided later.

As to whether the figure is male or female, it depends on which elements are dominant. If there is more Fire and Air (the active elements), the figure will have a male tendency. If there is more Water and Earth, the form will be more feminine. In cases where the elemental makeup is evenly distributed, we can presume a certain hermaphroditic quality.

The Golden Dawn provided a diagram showing an example of all of the above in action:

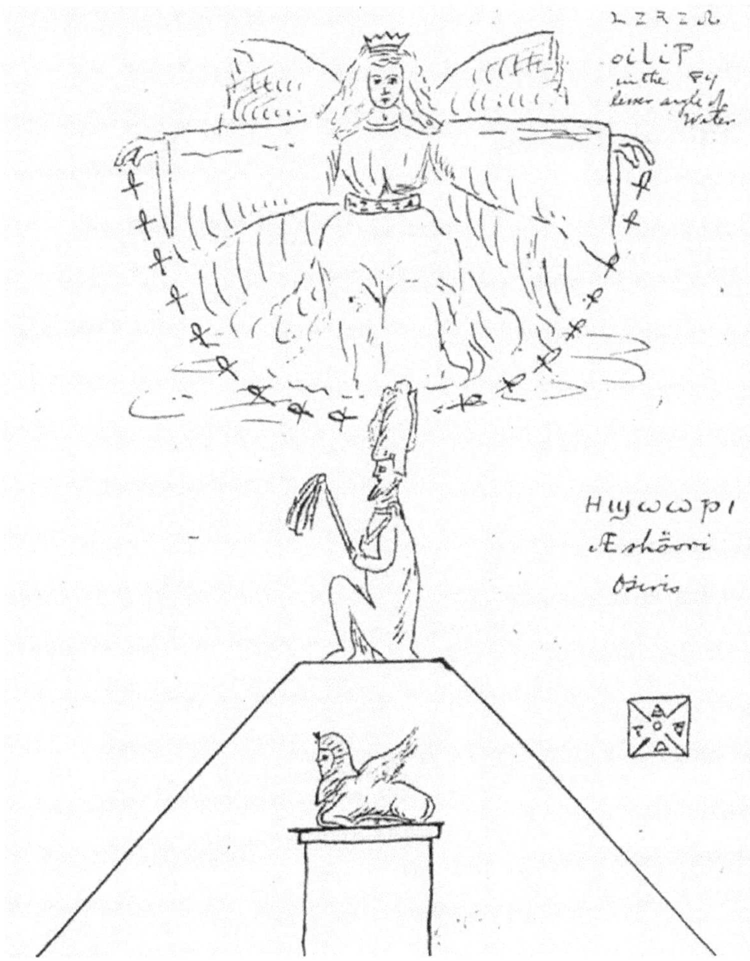

In the example on the previous page, we see the Square O of OILIP (or oiliP if we employ the proper capitalisation from the Tablet) from the "Earthy lesser angle of Water" (or, more simply, Earth of Water), with its appropriate god, Osiris (sitting on the truncated platform of the pyramid), Sphynx (inside the pyramid on a plinth), and Angel (OILIP herself, extending over the entire form).

We see that the elemental makeup of the Square creates the form of the Sphynx. The top triangle is Air, so the head is that of an Angel (or Man). The bottom triangle is Fire, so the tail and hind legs are that of a Lion. The triangles on the right and left are Earth and Water, creating a combined trunk and fore limbs of Bull and Eagle (the limbs being of the former, the wings of the latter).

As for which god is attributed to each Square, there is the following formula based on the elemental makeup of the Square in question:

Four different elements	Osiris
3 or 4 are Water	Isis
3 or 4 are Earth	Earth
3 or 4 are Fire	Horus
3 or 4 are Air	Aroueris
2 are Water, 2 are Earth	Athor
2 are Water, 2 are Fire	Sothis
2 are Water, 2 are Air	Harpocrates
2 are Earth, 2 are Fire	Apis
2 are Earth, 2 are Air	Anubis
2 are Fire, 2 are Air	Tefnu or Pasht
1 of Fire, 1 of Water, 1 of Earth	Amset or Emsta
1 of Fire, 1 of Water, 1 of Air	Hapi
1 of Water, 1 of Air, 1 of Earth	Taioumatf
1 of Fire, 1 of Air, 1 of Earth	Kabsenuf

In the latter cases, it does not matter what the fourth element is (providing it is a duplicate of one of the other three, or otherwise Osiris would be used). So, we could have 2 of Fire, 1 of Water, and 1 of Air, and it would be Hapi. Likewise if we had 2 Water or 2 Air in that combination.

It should be noted that these forms have special governance

over the Servient Squares. There are additional forms given for the Kerubic Squares, but they are beyond the scope of this book.

I have included diagrams of all 15 gods in question, exactly as they are given in Ritual X. They are all shown standing, even though the example of Osiris in the earlier diagram is given seated. The brief description of their shape, also drawn from that document, is included, as is their names in Coptic (both transliterated and in Coptic lettering). You can find some alternative depictions of these gods in *The Essential Enochian Grimoire* by Aaron Leitch.

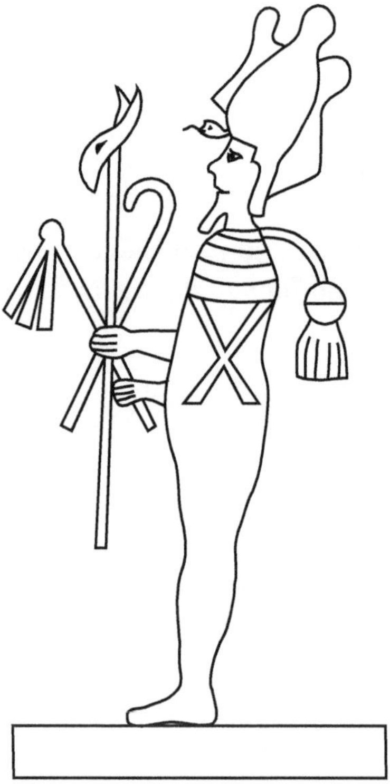

Osiris

Æshöori

Ⲏϣⲱⲱⲣⲓ

A mummied God with winged Mitre,
Crook and Scourge, and a Phoenix Wand.

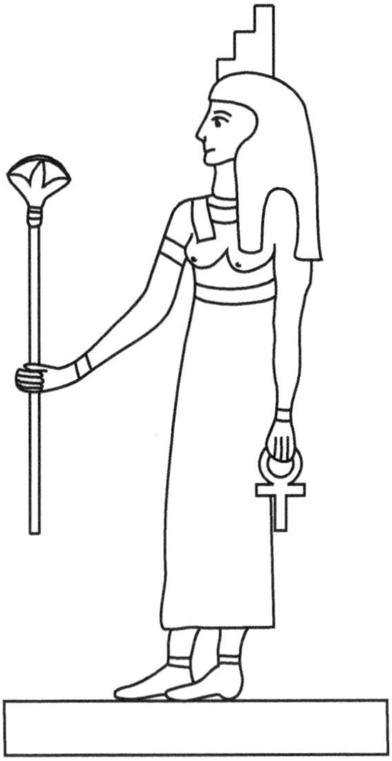

Isis

Æiseh

HICE

Goddess with Throne head-dress,
Lotus Wand and Crux Ansata.

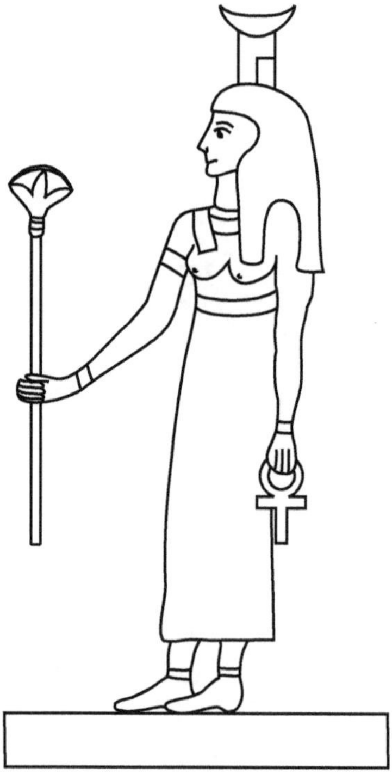

Nephthys

Neuphthuseh

ⲚⲈⲨⲪⲐⲨⲤⲈ

Goddess on an Altar with Altar Head-dress surmounted by a Bowl, bears Lotus Wand and Crux Ansata.

Horus

Höor

ϩωωρ

God with Hawk’s head and double mitre,
Phoenix Wand, and Crux Ansata.

Aroueris

Araöweri

ⲁⲣⲏⲱⲩⲉⲣⲓ

A God with double mitre, bearing a Phoenix Wand and Crux Ansata.

Athor

Ahathöor

ⲁϩⲁⲑⲱⲱⲣ

A Goddess, with disk and plumes between horns surmounting the head-dress. Bears Lotus Wand and Crux Ansata.

Sothis

Shaöeu

ϣⲏⲱⲉⲩ

Goddess with a Cow's Head, disk and plumes between horns, Lotus Wand and Crux Ansata.

Harpocrates

Höorpökrati

ϩⲱⲱⲣⲡⲟⲕⲣⲁⲑϯⲓ

Youthful God with double Mitre, long curling tress of hair, with left forefinger on lip.

Apis

Ahapshi

ⲁϩⲁⲡϣⲓ

God with Head of Bull and disk between Horns.
Crook and Scourge in hands.

Anubis

Anöubi

ⲁⲛⲱⲩⲃⲓ

God with head of dog or jackal, bearing
Phoenix Wand and Crux Ansata.

Tefnu or *Pasht*

Tharphesh

θαρφεϣ

Goddess with Lioness' head crowned with disk and with Lotus Wand and Crux Ansata.

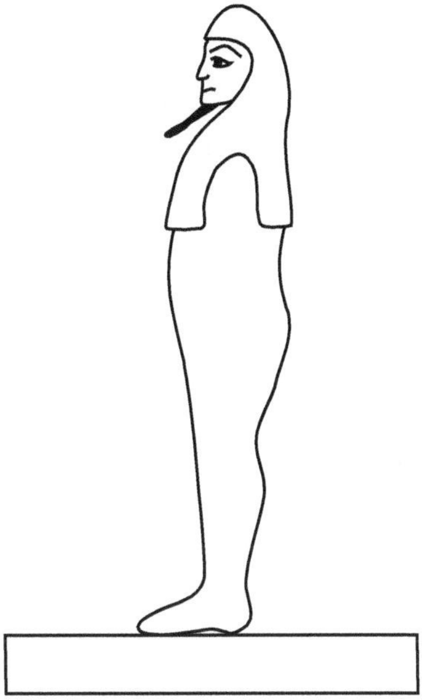

Amset or *Emsta*

Ameshet

ⲁⲙⲉϣⲉϯ

A God mummied, with human head.

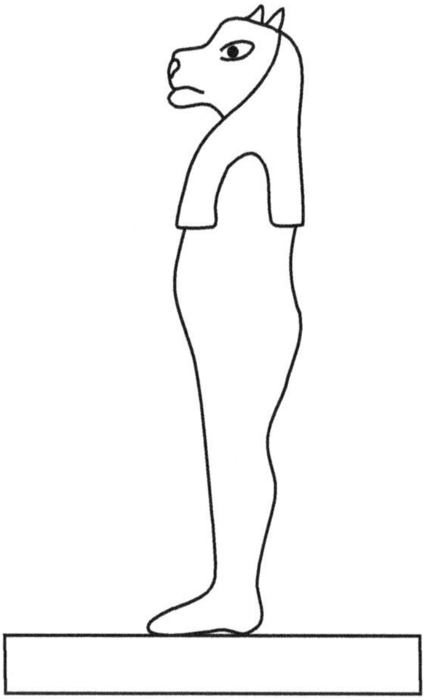

Hapi

Ahephi

ⲁϩⲉⲫⲓ

A God mummied, with Ape's head.

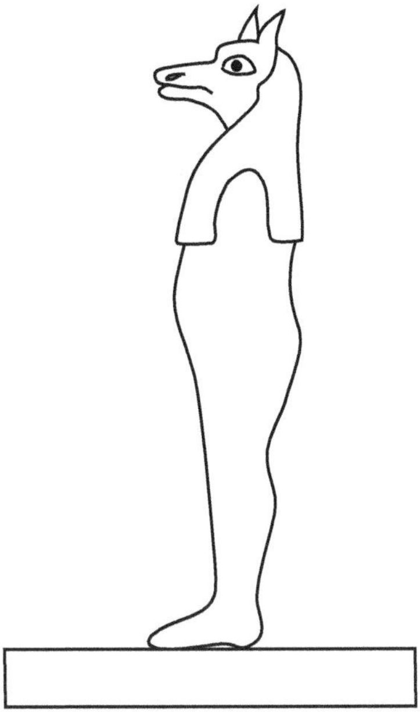

Tiaoumatf

Toumathph

ϯⲱⲩⲙⲁⲑⲫ

A God mummied, with head of Dog or Jackal.

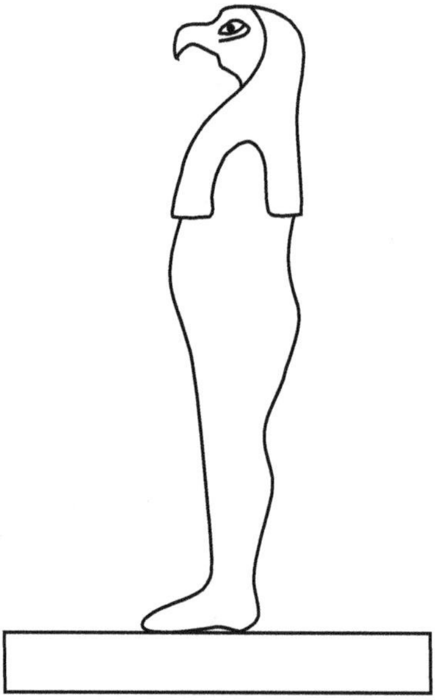

Kabsenuf

Kabexnuf

ⲔⲀⲂⲈⲜⲚⲨϤ

A God mummied, with a Hawk's head.

PHYSICAL REPRESENTATIONS

One of the best ways to really see how the truncated pyramids, and their Gods and Sphynxes, work in action is to make physical representations of them. This not only helps with understanding the principles and procedures, but acts as a visual aid, and can significantly enhance a magical operation, not to mention ground the experience.

A note by Mathers shows one way to approach this:

> "I have found it convenient for building the symbol for the Square to have 16 coloured Triangles, truncated at the apex: 4 RED; 4 BLUE; 4 YELLOW; 4 BLACK—and with four of these to build in front of you a shallow Pyramid of the Square required, by leaning them against the sides of a small shallow cardboard Pyramid, (because if the Pyramid is too deep, you cannot look down sufficiently at once on all four sides).
>
> By having a Red Lion, a Black Bull, Blue Eagle and Yellow Angel, each divided into three parts, the central part again being halved, you can similarly build up any Sphinx required and lay it within the Pyramid.
>
> And you can have little cardboard Figures of the Egyptian GODS cut out and fixed into bits of cork for stands, to put above the Pyramid.
>
> Which altogether makes a very complete magical apparatus for study of the Squares."[77]

All of the above is quite simple to make, and it makes a world of difference to working with the Squares. As an aid, I provide some diagrams of the Sphynxes, divided into four parts. The designs are admittedly somewhat crude, but for this kind of exercise basic is good. At the very least, it demonstrates how the heads can be interchanged, or the wings of the Eagle added to the Bull, and so on. An alternative take on these can be found in *The Golden Dawn Enochian Skrying Tarot* by the Genaws and Ciceros.

77 Ibid.

Some people go much further, creating entire sets of truncated pyramids for all four Watchtowers, keeping them loose so that a specific one can be taken for use in skrying later. Indeed, it is even possible to create a huge human-sized truncated pyramid, which can be physically entered, but this might be going a little overboard, and may cause the magician to lose sight of the fact that the pyramids in question are merely symbolic of the combined forces of the Square.

I personally prefer the approach Mathers gives, largely because laying out the appropriately coloured triangles on the sides of the pyramid is a kind of preliminary process in its own right. They may be laid in a particular order, starting first with the side of the Watchtower, then the side of the sub-angle, then the file, then the rank. This therefore marks the process of gradually descending into the depths of the Watchtower until the magician arrives in the particular Square. This approach also means it can be stored and transported more easily than a full set of ready-made pyramids.

While it is possible to work with a flat 2D design and still get appropriate visions, I strongly recommend that a 3D prop is used. The vision is likely to be stronger, more vibrant, and more accurate.

SKRYING INSTRUCTIONS

The basic procedure for these visions is as follows:

1. Prepare appropriate Implements and Insignia and have them at hand.
2. Prepare the symbol of the Pyramid.
3. Read the appropriate Enochian Calls.
4. Recite the appropriate Divine Names.
5. Imagine yourself enclosed or standing within an atmosphere related to the elemental makeup of the Square.
6. Find yourself in a landscape or region consonant to the elemental makeup of the Square.
7. Invoke the Egyptian god who rules the Pyramid by the power of the Angel of the Square.
8. Test the figure that appears.
9. If it passes, ask it to manifest the form of the Sphynx related to the Square.
10. Test the form that appears.
11. Ask it to share the knowledge of that Square.
12. Once complete, retrace your steps and close the working.

There were a particular series of points Mathers suggested that the magician should ask about:

> "Regarding the special attributes of that vast portion of
> the confines of the Universe included in that Sphere;
> Of its varying Natures;
> Of its Elemental Nature;
> Of its Inhabitants, Elemental and Spiritual, etc.;
> Of its influence upon this particular Planet;
> Upon Animals, Planets, Minerals;
> and lastly upon Man the Microcosm."[78]

He also made sure to point out that even after obtaining such knowledge, one should recognise that this is only a small part of the

78 Ibid.

knowledge and wisdom related to just that one particular Square. This deserves special note, as it can be easy to think one has "seen it all" after a single trip, or even multiple visits, to a particular Square.

SAMPLE VISIONS

One of the Golden Dawn Flying Rolls, number XXXIII, provided several examples of visions that Adepts had of particular Servient Squares. These are very useful, as they show the method put into action, and the possible results that may occur. I give three of the seven sample visions below:

A Vision of the n Square in the Airy Lesser Angle of the Tablet of Water

The Pyramid God is Ahephi = 

n.h.d.D.

Having recited the Calls 4 and 10, and invoked the Angelic Names of the Tablet of Water, and the Airy Angle, I was carried up by the gently moving waves of warm moist Air, through which I could see bright blue sky with greyish white clouds moving across rapidly.

I rose in the Air till I found myself on a vast sandy plain; on the right little vegetation, on the left a broad river, with trees and grass on its banks.

A cool breeze blowing from the river across the plain, and seemed to refresh the Green after the heat of the day.

I called on Ahephi to appear and the Form gradually filled the place until the scene disappeared altogether. Tested by the letters, it grew immensely larger, and seemed to have a Yellow and Blue striped Nemess, whitish wrappings, with broad bands round it—and a greenish yellow light shown round it.

I gave the 5=6 Signs and asked to be shown the Sphynx of its power. This gradually appeared through the Yellow Light behind the God form—human head, very fair and bright face; Wings, Yellow and Blue Nemess; Claws of Eagle extended in front, and hind legs and tail of Lion in lying position.

On asking for the Action of the Force of the Square, was shown a bubble of Water, into which Air was continually pouring, and expanding it till it burst and disappeared, the energy then seeming to pass into other forms and come under the rule of another Square.

It seemed a transitory action, more the initiator of fresh conditions than an end in itself. I asked its effect on the Earth and was taken to the scene I had left, and saw again how the moist breeze from the river gave fresh life to the vegetation, which had flagged during the day.

Asking its effect on the Animal World, was shown a Deer standing by a Lake—a current of this force passing over it—seemed to bring the dawn of reason and glimmering of consciousness, the first conscious stirrings of an Animal.

Acting on Man, it seemed to affect the brain, producing a vague waving motion which prevented fixity of thought and definiteness of idea, loss of the power of concentration.

I then asked to see the Elementalsof the plane, and saw numbers of small-sized human figures, fair, active expression on face—bodies rather solid-looking compared to the head—large wings like dragon-flies, which were irridescent and seemed to reflect the colouring of things about them.

I gave the 5=6 Signs to Sphynx and then called on the Angel of the Square. I saw above the God the figure I had drawn, the wings on the Crown were blue, the cuirass bright steel, with the Eagle Symbol on the breast in Gold, the drapery below was a yellowish green, and the feet blue.

Signed = Vigilate

A Vision of the Square A of the Airy Lesser Angle of the Tablet of Water

A.x.p.a. Ahephi

After vibrating the Names of Airy Angle of Water and reading the Call, I seemed to be in the Air, ascending in a current of tiny drops of Water, which darted upwards in every direction, and were of every colour of the rainbow, very minute and light.

On looking about for the cause, I saw below a tremendous volume of Water falling to a great depth, and this atmosphere in which I was, was the spray rising from it.

Called on Ahephi to appear and gradually got the God form, as before, but standing above a pyramid composed of the living Elements. The Water sides of the Square were like two greenish blue waves, always rising and falling, and on all sides were in continual motion, and gave the idea of intense restlessness. Gave the 5=6 Signs, tested it, and asked to be shown the Sphynx. This appeared in a greenish yellow mist behind Ahephi in a crouching position, with the human arms stretched out in front. A silver crown on the Lion's head set with sapphires. I saluted with the Signs, which were returned.

I asked for the explanation of the force of the Square, but could not get it clearly. It seemed an ever-moving subtle force, which working imperceptibly brought purification and cleansing with it.

The Elementals I got were something like those of the n Square, but smaller and in rainbow colours, and they moved more quickly. They carried cups in their hands, shaped like lotuses in which they caught drops of water and darted into the air with them.

On the Earth their work seemed to be the purifying of the magnetism.

I could not get anything clearer although I tried for a long time.

Signed Vigilate

A Vision of the x Square in the Watery Lesser Angle of the Fire Tablet

Ruler Amset = Amesheth

△ ▽ 🜃 ⲁⲙⲉϣⲉϯ

I rose through the Pyramid with the White light, which streamed down from the Apex, and came into the Sky, where the same Colours are repeated like sunrise, etc. The colossal Pyramid with Ameset on it, a mummified figure in white, bands of colour like the Pyramid and a blue human face (the same blue as I have seen in Egyptian paintings). I made the Signs and called on the Names and begged to be allowed to see the Angel. She appeared with a blue ◡ on her head, brown hair very long. Robe pale blue with black border and a ☆ in red on her breast; her wings were blue also, and so was the Cup in her left hand; in her right hand she bore a red torch.

Around her was a ◇ of red yods. She told me her office was "Change and Purification through suffering such as spiritualises the material nature." I told her that her pale face and blue eyes had a sad and tender expression as she spoke. The subs were similar but smaller and not all of them winged.

The Elementals were like blue naiads bearing flames and their robes were black bordered. Some wore blue winged helmets and cloaks, red breast plates and Swords and black leg armour.

I was told that only through my Knowledge of ⲁⲙⲉϣⲉϯ was all

this shown unto me.

Then I saw the Sphynx. The head was that of a blue Eagle, and so were the back and wings, the tail and hind legs were black like a Bull and the fore legs and chest those of a Red Lion. The creature lay on a black marble pedestal.

I saluted it and called on it by the names to tell me its nature and office. Its universal quality, it said "To change and development, not apparently harmonious, but growing stable after the first efforts."

In the Elements (weather) floods of rain and lightning refreshing the Earth.

The Elementals and Angels are above described. The general effect of this Square upon the Earth is the partly unbalanced efforts of the material Universe towards perfection—which efforts are all towards the Spirit and are all necessary—as taken all together they are balanced.

In the Tablets there are equal numbers of Triangles of each Element.

On this World the effect is that of the floods of water mingling with submarine volcanoes, and so disturbing the Earth under the Sea.

The Animal Life is that represented by the fish who rest hidden among the rocks in warm climates. I seemed to see them, blue with black or red spots.

The Plants are Water Lillys, a root in the black mud, the leaves resting on the surface of the water, loving the Sun.

In regard to minerals I saw a great bluish opal with red lights playing in it; it rested in a black marble basin, and from it radiated a lovely light.

On Man the effect of the Square is restlessness, like waves of the Sea carrying him on with enthusiasm to some completed work. I seemed to see a nervous highly strung person with a pale face, dark deep set eyes, and thin white hands, making a great effort, willing to pass through fire to reach his goal, a solid black pedestal from which I knew that he could begin to rise to the Higher. But hot Clouds of Steam and great waves of water tried to hinder him from even reaching the fire.

The lesson seemed to me that—severe criticism, social

difficulties, and heredity must all be overcome before we can reach the purifying fire of Initiation, and through that the solid ground of Spiritual Knowledge.

Signed F.E.R.

XII

EVOCATION

Evocation, or summoning of a spirit, is an integral part of magical tradition, and appears time and time again in ancient grimoires. These beings are conjured for a variety of reasons, including answering questions, finding lost objects, fulfilling tasks, and even—in the case of evil spirits—just to bind them, which may be seen as part of a larger work in the redemption of evil.

Dee encountered a wide variety of spirits in his workings, and was given the names, descriptions, and seals of numerous others. He was also given some instructions on how to call them forth, and was sometimes cautioned not to call certain entities at all (see Chapter XIII on Cacodaemons).

Although Dee wrote a book of conjurations for this work, it is not clear if he ever actually employed it in practice. In many cases he did not need to, for numerous Enochian entities came to him, but they very rarely fulfilled his requests, focusing instead on the delivery of the system.

It is also worth noting that Dee's conjurations are only examples and should not be held as the one and only way to call these spirits. He was instructed to write his own conjurations, so they are not the specific wording given by the angels. It can be argued that each magician should create his or her own book of conjurations, rather than simply replicating those of another.

EVOCATION PROCEDURE

There are several key elements to traditional grimoire-style evocation. These are:

1. Preparation
2. Opening
3. Prayer
4. Conjuration
5. Orders and/or Questions
6. License to Depart
7. Closing

Each of these elements or stages will be explored in detail below.

PREPARATION

This stage is where the Temple is set up and the furniture is properly arranged. In other forms of magic it may involve establishing a circle for the magician and a place for the spirit to be called forth (most notably, the Triangle of Art).

In Enochian, this preliminary step would involve the tools from the Heptarchic system being put in place. This includes the Table of Practice, the four Sigillum Dei Aemeth beneath its feet, and the larger Sigillum upon the Table itself. The cloth would be placed over this, and then the shewstone on top of the covered Sigillum.

The magician would then prepare him or herself. While Dee's records do not record a cleansing procedure, such as a ritual bath, this was common in similar systems. Typically a white robe would be worn, reserved just for magical use. Some instructions on this were given for the 19-Day working (see Chapter XVI).

Finally, the Lamen would be placed around the magician's neck, and the Ring would be worn, and he or she would enter the prepared chamber to begin the ritual.

In cases where a dedicated Seer or Skryer is employed, a similar cleansing and robing may be employed for him or her.

OPENING

Some manner of Opening ceremony, no matter how basic, is a good way to start the working in earnest, dividing the experience from the mundane world, and telling the mind that the working has begun in earnest.

This can be as simple as ringing a bell and speaking a brief declaration, such as "In the Names of [*divine names*], I open this Temple for the work of evocation."

Or it could be a much more elaborate ceremony, including particular invocations of elemental or planetary forces, or even replicating the Opening of one of the Golden Dawn initiation ceremonies, which act as a pattern for magical work.

Another option is to turn the whole preparation into part of the Opening, where, for example, the magician would don the Ring, saying "By this Ring, which was given by Michael to Solomon, I shall work wonders." Then setting the Tablet of Practice, the magician might say, "Upon this Table, I shall practice my work." Then setting the Sigillum Dei Aemeth upon the Table, the magician might say, "By this Seal, I ensure the blessings of God and Truth upon this ceremony." A similar approach can be taken with every tool in one's arsenal.

If an Opening is used on a regular basis, preceding all major workings, it will help trigger the "magical mindset" of the magician, and thus make the subsequent working considerably more effective.

PRAYER

Prayer begins the process. An appeal to God, the highest power, is a natural first step in the working. It is by God's authority that the magician gains his or her own authority, and so has the right to call forth God's messengers.

This concept was exemplified in a strict rule in the Golden Dawn where the Adept must first "invoke the Highest Divine Names." This ensures that the working is properly sanctified.

The specifics of prayer, and some examples Dee used, are given in Chapter II.

CONJURATION

The conjuration, sometimes called an invocation, is different to prayer in that instead of beseeching God, it beseeches the spirit directly, typically in the name of God, whose blessing is assumed to have been granted after the preceding prayer.

As the name implies, the goal of conjuration is to conjure or call forth the spirit to visible appearance, either in the shewstone, as is typical in Enochian magic, or in incense, as is common elsewhere.

Dee's book of conjurations (Sloane MS 3191) includes a sample call to the Kings of the Heptarchic system, called by him, in typically reserved fashion, "The Devout and Pious Invitations to the Good Heptarchical Angels."

The full text of this can be found below:

The General and Common Exordium & Conclusion Appertaining to the Seven Heptarchical Kings Inviting

O Puissant and Noble King, [*name*], and by what Name elsesoever thou are called, or mayest truly and duly be called: to Whose peculiar Government, Charge, Disposition, and Kingly Office doth appertain the [*describe nature of office*].

Therefore, in the Name of the King of Kings, the Lord of Hosts, the Almighty God, Creator of Heaven and Earth, and of all things visible and invisible: O right Noble King, [*name*], Come now, and appear, with thy

> Prince and his ministers and subjects, to my perfect and sensible eye's judgement: in a goodly and friendly manner, to my comfort and help, for the advancing of the Honour and Glory of our Almighty God, by my service, as much as by Thy Wisdom and Power, in thy proper Kingly Office, and Government, I may be helped and enabled unto: Amen.
>
> Come, O right Noble King, [*name*], I say Come. Amen.[79]

This is followed by the Anglican form of the Gloria Patri prayer.

An almost identical conjuration is given for the Prince, substituting "Kingly Office" with "noble office," and closing with the Lord's Prayer (including the "For Thine is the kingdom..." doxology then used by Anglicans).

Dee also included conjurations for the Watchtowers, some of which can be found in Chapter XVI on the 19-Day Working.

IAIDA, IOIAD, IAIDON

There are many Names of God used in the Enochian system, and it is wise to use the ones appropriate to the type of angel being called. For example, the names of three letters, four letters, and five letters from the Watchtowers (MOR, DIAL, HCTGA, etc.) are the best choice for all spirits contained in that particular Tablet.

Yet there are cases where it is less clear-cut what Name of God is applicable, and this includes the Heptarchic system. Thankfully, there are a number of Names employed throughout the system, including the Calls, which have an "all-purpose" nature to them.

Perhaps the most obvious is IAD, the most basic name of God in the Enochian language, translating as "God," "Your God," or "Our Lord." This name can be found repeated in the Tablet of Nalvage.

In the OSDL we typically used three Names of God together: IAIDA, meaning "the Highest;" IOIAD, meaning "Him That Lives Forever;" and IAIDON, meaning "All-Powerful." Their similar form makes them work together really well, and the sounds simply roll

79 Sloane MS 3191.

off the tongue. I have personally found them to be powerful in invocations and conjurations of spirits.

Additional Divine Names include BIGLIAD, "Our Comforter;" IADOIASMOMAR, "Him That Was, Is, And Shall Be Crowned;" IAD BALTOH, "The God of Righteousness;" OIAD, "The Just;" ENAY, "The Lord;" and MAD, "God" or "Your God."

PROTECTIVE CIRCLES

In most grimoires, some form of protective circle is employed, with divine names inscribed around the border. The magician stands in this, never leaving it until the spirit has been properly banished. The spirit, on the other hand, is often summoned into its own limiting shape, typically a triangle, which contains its own divine names.

None of this is present in the Enochian system, but there are some elements which could be taken as being their equivalent. Most notably, there is the outer ring of the Sigillum Dei Aemeth, made up of 40 divisions. Of this, Uriel said, "Out of this Circle shall no Creature pass, that entereth, if it be made upon the earth."[80]

Thus, when a spirit is called forth into the shewstone, and the shewstone is placed in the centre of the Seal, that same spirit is naturally contained within that restricting circle. Not only does this help in the conjuring process in the first place by creating the "astral vessel" in which the spirit will manifest itself, it also means they will find it much more difficult, if indeed impossible, to leave it without permission, which helps for protection, but also for the overall evocation process.

Further, if the magician wants to employ a magic circle upon the floor, this serves as the perfect form. Indeed, this may even be what Uriel meant by "made upon the earth."

80 Joseph H. Peterson, ed. *John Dee's Five Books of Mystery*, p. 91.

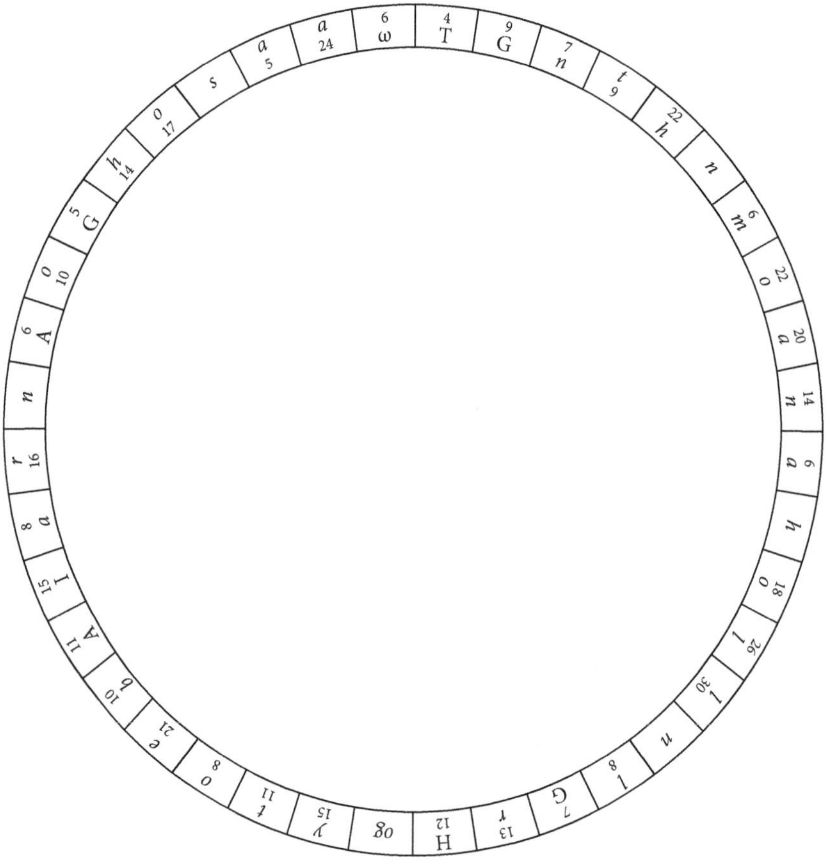

ORDERS AND/OR QUESTIONS

This stage is the meat of the operation, and occurs only when the spirit has actually manifested itself to the appearance of either the Seer, when working with another, or the Magician him or herself, when working alone. In some cases, the spirit may appear visibly to both.

A list of questions should have been prepared previously, and the Magician should allow space to document the answers. Alternatively, a tape recorder may be employed.

If the request is not for information, but rather for the spirits to take some action, such as finding treasure (a common request in grimoires, and something that even finds a place in the Enochian system), then an injunction should be prepared to be read out before the spirit, asking or ordering it to fulfil the duty asked of it. It is often a good idea to include a timeframe, as otherwise the spirit may "creatively interpret" the command and decide to deliver it at the end of time instead.

Dee never provided his own examples of this, most likely because the form largely depends on the request itself, but I include below an example I use of an injunction given to a spirit:

> "In the Name of the King of Kings, the Lord of Hosts, the Almighty God, Creator of Heaven and Earth, and of all things visible and invisible, O [*name*], [*brief reiteration of rank and office*], I do ask you to fulfil my request, to [*request*], and to do this in a timely manner, that within [*timeframe*] I may have visible confirmation of the success of this working, and that by [*timeframe*] it may be made manifest unto me; and in so doing, by the nature of thy office, by the employment of thy ministers and servants, and by the Name of God Almighty, [*divine name*], thou shalt not cause harm or injury, of any kind whatsoever, to either me or those I love; and that thou shalt act by thy good nature, sowing no evil, and so bring unto me [*request*], and unto you the blessings of God."

This may be amended for the type of spirit, and specific names of God may be employed for additional effect. This is particularly wise for the Watchtower system, where the Three Holy Names of God should be used. In some cases the magician may need to work down the ranks of the angels, so as to order each in the name of their superior. This latter process can be very effective, as each are beholden to the one above them.

Note the inclusion of a timeframe for confirmation of results, before a longer timeframe for the manifestation of these results. I find this particularly useful, as it can help determine early on if the working has been successful. It is important to afford reasonable time here and not expect big results overnight. Yet it is also wise not to let the deadline go on indefinitely.

I have also included a "do no harm" clause, which can be important in such requests, given that spirits may choose the "path of least resistance" in achieving one's aims. A classic example is a magician looking for money, so their parents die, bequeathing the magician their fortune in their will. I employ two forms to this clause, requiring that the spirit cause no harm to me or my loved ones, but also requiring that they do not work evil. While some spirits are already obliged not to do this, others may have no particular qualms in that area.

Finally, it is no harm to include a final blessing to the spirit.

LICENSE TO DEPART

While Dee was not explicitly instructed to include a License to Depart, this is standard procedure in most grimoire texts, including the ones that Dee would have read. It is also sound magical principle, and I would strongly advise that it not be omitted in any evocation.

There are several important reasons for including this step before closing. Firstly, it ensures that the spirit leaves on the magician's terms. Secondly, it gives the spirit, which has to that point been bound to appear before the magician, permission to retire. If one skips this stage and goes straight to banishing, it is essentially like slamming the door on someone before asking them to leave. Sufficed to say, this approach may not go down well with some entities. For those who do not leave voluntarily after the License to Depart, banishings can then be employed to forcefully remove them.

Here is a short example License to Depart from the Key of Solomon:

> "In the Name of Adonai, the Eternal and Everlasting One, let each of you return unto his place; be there peace between us and you, and be ye ready to come when ye are called."[81]

The Key of Solomon gives a variety of potential Licenses to Depart,

81 S. Liddell MacGregor Mathers, trans. *The Key of Solomon the King*, p. 41.

some more detailed than others. The essential ingredients are:

1. The use of a Divine Name by which the License is authorised;

2. Permission for the spirit to return to its abode;

3. An injunction for peace between the spirit and the magician;

4. A requirement that the spirit return when asked (in other words, this is not a License to Depart for good).

Additional stages can also be included, where, for example, the spirit is allowed to partake of the incense, or is given the blessings of God. In one example from the Key of Solomon, the requirement for the spirit to return is expanded so that the spirit must come even "without solemn rites and observances on our part."[82] In this sense, the magician has the permanent ear of the spirit. In some cases the License is authorised not by a Divine Name, but by the power of the Pentacles, or other sacred devices, which typically contain one or more Divine Names.

The Golden Dawn uses very similar Licenses to Depart, down to almost identical wording, so these examples are equally useful for those adopting a Golden Dawn approach, or those looking for a more traditional grimoire experience.

CLOSING

It is always a good idea to have some kind of formal Closing to a ceremony. Combined with the Opening, it will bookend the ritual and help separate it from everyday life. This separation is necessary for good progress in magic, and for retaining one's sanity.

82 Ibid., p. 43.

GOLDEN DAWN METHOD

Westcott gave some good instructions for evocation of Watchtower angels. I have summarised these below:

Requirements

The magician will need a full set of Watchtower Tablets, and the Tablet of Union, all appropriately coloured in their flashing colours; and also the four Elemental Implements (Fire Wand, Water Cup, Air Dagger, Earth Pantacle), properly consecrated.

Preliminary Rituals

Ritual of the Pentagram for angels of Spirit and the Four Elements; Ritual of the Hexagram for the King and Seniors. Banishing rituals are performed with the Sword, invoking rituals with the Elemental Implement.

Directions

The directions of the Elements change depending on whether you are summoning spirits or forces to you (in which case the attribution is directional, based on the Four Winds: East = Air, South = Fire, West = Water, North = Earth) or are visiting spirits or forces on their own plane of existence (in which case the attribution is zodiacal, based on the Kerubic Signs: East = Fire, South = Earth, West = Air, North = Water).

Modes of Working

There are two modes of working, the first subjective, the second objective. Both are useful for different purposes, the former with workings directed at change within the magician or his or her immediate environment, the latter with understanding greater concepts about the universe at large.

Subjective: Imagine yourself standing upon the Tablet of Union, in its exact centre. Imagine the Watchtowers around you, as if they were the four walls of a room.

Objective: Alternatively, imagine yourself in the centre of a sphere, with the Tablet of Union at the north and south poles (so that it is duplicated), and the sphere divided into four quarters (representing the Watchtowers). Then imagine yourself moving outside the sphere, so that you are looking at it externally.

Method

1. Choose an angel with which to work. In his example, Westcott chose OMDI, a permutation of the Servient Angel DIOM from the Earth sub-angle of the Fire Tablet.
2. Choose the Elemental Implement relevant to the Element of the Watchtower in question. In this case, the Fire Wand.
3. Perform with the Implement the relevant invoking Pentagrams in all four quarters. In this case, Active Spirit, and Fire.
4. After drawing the Pentagrams, repeat the following invocation (in all four directions), inserting the name of the angel, and its prefixed version, where applicable, and also the appropriate Elements (in the square brackets):

   > "EDLRPNAA, the Great King of the South, VOLEXDO and SIODA, I command ye in the Divine Name OIP TEAA PDOCE and BITOM that the Angel who governs the [Watery] and [Earthy] Square of [OMDI] shall obey my behest and submit to me when I utter the holy name [OOMDI]."

5. Face the East or South, depending on whether summoning spirits or visiting them.
6. Gaze upon the Tablet before you until it is imprinted on the mind.
7. Close your eyes and vibrate the angel's name, in both normal and prefixed versions. In this case, OMDI and OOMDI.

8. Imagine yourself travelling through the Tablet, until you see a landscape. Here you may also communicate with the angel in question.
9. Close in the traditional manner, with the License to Depart, followed by banishing rituals relevant to the nature of the working. General banishings of a non-specific nature may also be employed.

Examples

Westcott described the landscape of OMDI, and its permutations, as follows:

> "My experience of this particular plane was a dull red crumbling earth. I first found myself in a Cave. As a symbol I was told that this Square of OMDI was like the roots of a tiger lilly; the Square MDIO to the right, representing the Life working in it. The square IOMD to the left, represented the sap flowing through the stalk and the leaves, as it were; the Square DIOM to the left of that, the orange flower with the black spots upon it, fitly representing Air, Fire and Earth—yellow, red and black."

Westcott described the appearance of various permutations of a Kerubic Angel as follows:

> "From the fiery Lesser Angle of Fire, I have seen AZODIZOD [AZIZ], the figure being fiery red with flaming wings and hair of emerald green. ZODAZODEE [ZAZI], black and white, flashing and flaming. EEZODAHZOD [IZAZ], blue and orange, with a mist of flame about him. ZODEEZODAH [ZIZA], orange, with hazy gold wings like gold gauze, and nets of gold around him."

It is worth bearing in mind, however, that these are but examples, and Westcott himself recognised that one's experience may vary.

DEE METHOD (FOR POLITICAL INFLUENCE)

Dee was heavily involved in the political machinations of his day, and he was strongly interested in the use of magic to further these aims, and the aims of the British Empire as a whole. There is, therefore, several examples of material received that has a political application, not least of all the Parts of the Earth.

Yet Dee also asked for specific instructions on how to incline the heart of the King of Spain, Philip II, "to the purpose I have in hand"[83] through the use of evocation. This was before the Parts of the Earth (the most obvious part of the system for political work) were revealed, and Hagonel responded at length, as follows:

> "First, cast thine eye unto the General prince, Governor or Angel that is principal in this world. [Δ as yet is BALIGON or Carmara.]
>
> Secondly, consider the circumstances of thy Instruction.
>
> Thirdly, place my name, which thou hast already.
>
> Fourthly, the name of him which was shewed thee yesterday, whose garments were short, and of purple.
>
> Fifthly, his power, with the rest of his six perfect Ministers."[84]

Like many of the practical instructions the angels gave, these are not particularly clear, and Dee left several notes wondering what was being referred to.

The table of the Ministers (being made of up of 42 letters) was to be placed beneath the magician's feet. Additionally, the Seal of "the first of the seven," i.e. Bagenol (the dot within a circle above a cross), is to be placed on the Table of Practice. The Ring and Lamen are also required.

It seems unlikely that placing these items alone would suffice, so an invocation, like those Dee recorded for the Heptarchic angels, would also be necessary, differing for each of the beings called.

83 Joseph H. Peterson, ed. *John Dee's Five Books of Mystery*, p. 213.

84 Ibid.

CAUTIONS

One thing I would like to point out from personal experience is that, while the Enochian angels very rarely show up to someone without having first been approached, once they have been worked with, they tend to appear more regularly uninvited. This may even result in disrupted sleep. If this does happen, and it becomes problematic, the magician should not be afraid to somewhat forcefully instruct them to go away, and to return only when called, or when it is of the utmost importance (though they may interpret the latter much differently than we would).

In some evocation traditions, such as the Goetia, some kind of pact is expected, where the spirit will only fulfil the magician's command if the spirit gets something in return. Sometimes this involves an offering, be it food, symbols, or even blood. Other times the spirit will want their seal or sigil prominently displayed, or their name advertised to other magicians (with whom they can form new pacts). Some may want a lot more in return. Suffice it to say, this is a very dangerous practice, not least of all because spirits can be very subtle in their manipulation, so the magician may not even be fully aware of what he or she is agreeing to. While such pacts are not typically part and parcel of Enochian work, the angels can still be very manipulative, and it is wise to keep one's wits about one.

XIII

CACODAEMON BINDING

Perhaps the least explored part of the Watchtower system is the Cacodaemons. They are often ignored for good reason, for there is little information on them, and those who deal with them quickly learn that this is not an area of occult work to be trifled with.

This is something we explored extensively in the OSDL, developing a particular technique for binding these forces. It is an advanced working, as will be seen by the length of the ceremony and the work and preparation that is involved, but it is also a very rewarding effort, offering a means of working on the various psychological and emotional issues the magician may have before other higher work.

THE NATURE OF CACODAEMONS

Cacodaemons are basal "entities." They have limited scope and intelligence (which is why they only have two letters to their name), and can be considered as a kind of "angelic larvae" (a term that Frater VVV, a Sentinel of the OSDL, employed). What this means is that these creatures are in an *undeveloped*, indeed primitive, form. It is only when the two letters of their name are joined with two more letters, creating a Servient Angel or Dispositor, that they come to a kind of fruition, acquiring intelligence and a broader scope of spirituality. *Caco* (from the Greek *kako*) also means "evil", and *daemon* means "spirit" (subsequently mangled to mean "evil spirit" without the *caco*), and these were named thus because they are considered to be the base, corrupt, form of our desires, and so forth. Dee was told that they could be evoked, but that they *should not be*. Instead they should be bound within the magician, who is, in essence, a Great Table of his or her own.

Dee questioned Ave on the nature of these entities and how they should be used, resulting in this interesting exchange:

> "Δ. As concerning the wicked here, Shall I call or summon them all, as I do the good ones in the name of God?
>
> *Ave.* No man calleth upon the name of God in the wicked: They are servants and vile slaves.
>
> Δ. We call upon the name of Jesus in the expulsing of devils, saying in the name of Jesus, etc.
>
> *Ave.* That *In*, is against the wicked. No just man calleth upon the name of God, to allure the devil.
>
> Δ. Then they are not to be named in the first summoning or invitation.
>
> *Ave. At no time* to be called.
>
> *E.K.* How then shall we proceed with them?
>
> *Ave.* When the Earth lieth opened unto your eyes, and when the Angels of Light, shall offer the passages of the Earth, unto the entrance of your senses (chiefly of seeing). Then shall you see the Treasures of the Earth, as you go: And the caves of the Hills shall not be unknown

unto you: Unto these, you may say, Arise, be gone, Thou art of destruction and of the places of darknesse: These are provided for the use of man. So shalt thou use the wicked, and no otherwise.

Δ. This is as concerning the natural Mines of the Earth.

Ave. Not so, for they have nothing to do with the natural Mines of the Earth, but, with that which is corrupted with man.

Δ. As concerning the coined they have power to bring it.

Ave. So they may: that they keep, and no other.

Δ. How shall we know what they keep, and what they keep not?

Ave. Read my former words; for thou dost not understand them.

Δ. I read it: beginning at the first line on this side, when the Angels of Light, etc.

Δ. I mean of coined money that they keep not; How shall we do to serve our necessities with it?

Ave. The good Angels are Ministers for that purpose. The Angels of the 4 angles shall make the Earth open unto you, and shall serve your necessities from the 4 parts of the Earth."[85]

As one can see, this is a pretty clear indication from the Angels in regards to the Cacodaemons. A few pages beforehand, in a prior working, Dee was informed that the "good Angels" (in this case the Servient Angels, being of 4 letters) of one Watchtower could find and supply metals, whereas the evil Angels (the Cacodaemons, being of 2 or 3 letters—3 with the letter from the Tablet of Union or Black Cross) could find and supply readily coined metal. Obviously this got Dee and Kelley (Kelley especially, I imagine—he was well known for counterfeit coining, and his many requests of the angels were often to

85 *A True & Faithful Relation*, p. 188.

do with wealth) a little excited. It was clearly a misreading, of course, as the angels were merely stating that these entities existed, not in the least advocating their use. Indeed, just as one group of Servient Angels may cure sickness and disease, so do the Cacodaemons of that same group *bring* death and decay, and, as one can imagine, that's not something one would want to be inviting into one's life (and the lives of one's loved ones). Dee was so preoccupied with the idea of wealth here that he totally mistook the "deep caverns" of the human mind and soul for the caves and mines of the earth, and did not truly understand the sole practice the angels would permit in regards to the Cacodaemons—that of binding ("Unto these, you may say, Arise, be gone ... So shalt thou use the wicked, and no otherwise").

Benjamin Rowe was one of the few Enochian magicians to explore the Cacodaemons and provide insight to their nature:

> "The closest one can come to directly invoking an elemental in this system is in the invocation of the so-called 'cacodemons' (Dee's appellation) or 'minimal sapient entities' (my appellation). I use this name for them because they are the least complicated beings in the system that are capable of responding to their environment and maintaining an independent existence. They are composed of two forces of opposite polarity, bound together by one additional letter from the Tablet of Union. Thus they have one force for each of the three necessary aspects, sulphur, salt, and mercury."[86]

As for how one should treat them, the angel ATAPA gave these following instructions to Rowe:

> "They seem at times to be demons, but only when their force is allowed to manifest unconstrained. Like animals in your own world, they are full of emotion, but do not have any sense. Therefore, we higher types such as myself and the other angels of the crosses must be strong gods to them, leading them both gently and firmly, as

86 Benjamin Rowe, *Enochian Temples: Invoking the Cacodemons with the Temple* (1992).

one would lead a loyal but temperamental dog."[87]

This is a vital point that must be emphasised. If the magician treats the Cacodaemons as equals, as he or she would do with higher beings in the hierarchy, it will result in the Cacodaemon running amok; if, on the other hand, the magician punishes the entity for no reason (as is sometimes done by practitioners of other arts like the Goetia so that the magician can show who is "boss," so to speak), then it will result in the same kind of aggression and resentment that a beaten dog might hold. Firm and fair is the rule here, as it is important to note that the Cacodaemons simply do not know any other way. The magician cannot sit down to chat with them, as they cannot talk. They know only the firm hand, and thus the magician must always command them, and, as ATAPA tells Rowe, "do not be afraid to treat them roughly, for it is all that they understand, until you have trained them in a new way."[88] There is no need to resort to torture and the likes (again commonly seen in the Goetia— Cacodaemons are simply not akin to Goetia entities, so such procedures are pointless and cruel), as the magician does not need that to prove their authority. Their authority is vouched by the angels of the hierarchy, which the Cacodaemon must answer to, no matter what.

I must now take some time to point out that, in the original material, Dee was only told to take the four two-letter names on the left-hand side of the cross of each sub-angle, making one Cacodaemon per Servient Angel or Dispositor. While we might limit ourselves to this arrangement, I think doing so would be a failure to understand the nature of the Watchtowers themselves. All of the Servient squares can be utilised to form Cacodaemon names, providing they read from right to left, as is custom for the Servient Angels themselves. Thus in each sub-angle there are 16 Cacodaemons, 4 per Servient Angel. Since there are also 16 possible permutations of Servient Angels (the 16 Dispositors noted in the Golden Talisman), each permutation rules over its own Cacodaemon, and may then be used in the binding ceremony for it.

Rowe was given much broader instructions for the Cacodaemons, including the possibility of using the Kerubic squares for making

87 Ibid.

88 Ibid.

such. This seems like a logical extension, but I would argue that these squares are of a spiritual nature, higher than that of the elemental nature of the Servient squares. They are not, in my experience, Cacodaemons, but more akin to the Trumpeters expressed in *Enochian Magic in Theory*. Indeed, Dee was explicitly told that they "have no participation with Devils."

There is sometimes debate over the intelligence of these beings, although I see little reason for such a debate. Any experience with the Cacodaemons, if it is a genuine one, will leave little doubt in the mind of the magician that these creatures lack any real intelligence, cannot communicate by any conventional way (being unable to speak or project visuals or symbols, like many higher entities can and do), and are, for all intents and purposes, very primitive in nature and form of expression. ATAPA confirmed this view to Rowe in the following:

> "It barely has enough intelligence to be conscious, and there is none left over for cleverness. Think of it thus, as a particularly stupid animal, which must be dealt with firmly, but without trying to change its instinctive nature.
>
> No such creature has secrets of any importance. They are merely bundles of elemental forces. If they speak, the great likelihood is that they echo the unconscious will of the magician, and speak not of their own will (of which they have none)."[89]

An example from my own experience is a Cacodaemon which manifested as a kind of fattened snake or slug-like creature. It could not speak (and I was told by the angels higher in the ranks that none of the Cacodaemons have the ability to speak or process information beyond basic instructions, and that attempting to communicate with them in such a manner was to invite illusion into the ceremony from the recesses of one's own mind, which would but feed the entity to "fatten" it all the more). It was very much a product of its landscape, for the initial letter of its name is a square that, if travelled to "in the spirit vision" (that is to say, astrally), would evoke a landscape around the magician (a process which is very useful preparation for this kind

89 Ibid.

of work). This landscape was a swamp, grey and brown, damp, dark, and murky. I got the distinct impression the entity was the only living thing in this entire swamp; whether this was because it had eaten the rest is something I still wonder about. When I advanced toward it, it flinched. Indeed, it was like an animal in the wild which had never seen a human before, and it would flee whenever I approached. This was, of course, partly because it feared me and the authority invested in me. It was then that the Kerubic Angel informed me that I had total control of the swamp, which, at my will, became so small that the creature had nowhere to run. I had to pin its tail with my foot and then physically seize it. The Kerubic Angel then, at my mental command, caged it in what appeared like white gold, and I sealed it in an orb of light. Sufficed to say, this is the kind of experience one can expect from such an entity.

THE MAGICIAN AS THE GREAT TABLE

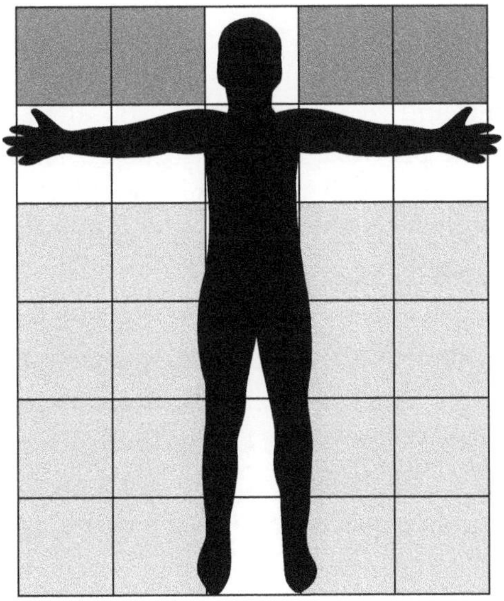

It is wise to remember that the magician is a Great Table of his or her own ("As Above, So Below"), and that they can affect their own being through the structure of the Great Table, individual Watchtowers, and then into each sub-angle, as is demonstrated in the above image.

Indeed, it is the acknowledgement that the magician is a Great Table that allows the binding of Cacodaemons of one's own nature to occur, for it relates the 2-lettered names of the Cacodaemons from each sub-angle to aspects of the human body (as personifications of their being).

As such, it can also be employed for physical healing. For example, a defect with the right leg may be exemplified in Cacodaemons on the right-hand side of the sub-angle. If the issue was inflammation of the leg, perhaps the fiery sub-angle of the Earth Tablet may be employed (Fire of Earth—Inflammation of the Body). Identifying Cacodaemons is a difficult process, and thus the elemental division of the Great Table developed by the Golden Dawn offers a key through which we may more easily find them.

The process for binding a Cacodaemon requires the usage of all ranks of angels available to the magician, starting at the top and slowly going down to the Cacodaemon itself. The Cacodaemon is awoken from its slumber through the commands of its superior angels, and it is bound through the magician's will with the aid of these same angels.

Before we continue, some may wonder why I relate the magician to the Great Table, and yet only show one sub-angle of one angle (or Watchtower) in the previous image. This is because the sub-angles are where the magician will "get things done." These are the most specialised areas of the Great Table, and the place where the "heavy lifters" of the system do their job.

However, the magician does relate to the greater aspects of each Watchtower as a whole. For example, when placing the human figure upon a Watchtower Tablet, the lines of the Father and Son would flow down through him, and the line of the Holy Spirit would flow across. This matches Christian tradition when giving the Sign of the Cross, but more than this it highlights the divine spark within each and every person.

Further still, the magician as the Great Table as a whole shows the different parts of human nature unified by the Black Cross (or Tablet of Union).

But putting these mystical associations aside, it is the sub-angles where the practical work is done—so that shall be our focus here.

IDENTIFYING CACODAEMONS

Identifying a Cacodaemon is one of the hardest parts of the work involved here, as it requires both introspection on the part of the magician, and some analysis of the elemental makeup of what was found through introspection, in an attempt to find a name in one of the Watchtowers that actually relates to the issue the magician is trying to address.

The example of an inflamed leg given above gives us our first pointer, although most work with Cacodaemons will be of a more psychological nature, as Ave's instructions were that they were the "corruptions of Man"—the neuroses, obsessions, compulsions, disorders, and so forth that plague the human mind (and, arguably, the soul). Identifying these in the first place requires meditation, reflection, initiation, and diligent magical and spiritual practice on behalf of the magician, and I can offer no shortcuts here. Often any kind of magical work, particularly when it comes to initiations, will shed light on some of the issues the individual will have to deal with (and we all have them—they may not be or seem as extreme as some of those used in examples here, but they will be there, causing their own kind of trouble).

Returning to our example of the inflamed leg, we have decided that Fire of Earth is our first step in narrowing things down. This enters us into both a Watchtower (the Earth Tablet) and a sub-angle of that Watchtower (Fire), giving us the host of angels with whom we will be working directly for this Working.

However, there are two further elemental aspects to each individual square (again, following the Golden Dawn system, as Dee's original tablets offer little aid in finding the appropriate Cacodaemon for what we would like to accomplish). To further narrow things down, we may decide to think about the cause of the inflammation. If it is inactivity, then perhaps the indolence of Earth is a good match. If if is overactivity, as in injury from exercise, then Fire sounds right. Let's assume it's the latter, which means we have Fire of Fire of Earth.

How then can we pinpoint things further? Perhaps the root cause, the most underlying issue, is poor physical shape, again suggestive of Earth. Maybe it is a blood condition, which might say Fire, but a hereditary blood condition could also indicate Water. Let's assume the latter is correct, which gives us Water of Fire of Fire of Earth.

We now know where to look on the Tablets. We go backwards, starting with the final Element, Earth. This is the Earth Tablet. Then Fire, the sub-angle of Fire of Earth (the bottom right-hand sub-angle of the Watchtower). Then Fire again, which is the file, telling us it is in the vertical line on the furthest right. Then Water, which is the rank, telling us it is in the third row from the bottom. This leads to the Square with A in it, from the Servient Angel IABA.

Of course, a Cacodaemon is made up of two letters, so we use the process of permutation to find the second. Since A is at the end, we take the next one from the beginning, I. This gives us AI. We then prefix with the applicable letter from either the Black Cross (Dee method) or Tablet of Union (Golden Dawn method), which gives us AAI for both in this example (though drawn from different names).

I have included an image on the opposite page to show how this works. I have only highlighted the elemental makeup of the Servient Squares, as these are the only Squares where Cacodaemons reside. In this case, the left-hand triangle on each Square represents the element of the Watchtower as a whole. The right-hand triangle shows the element of the sub-angle. The top triangle shows the element of the column. The bottom triangle shows the element of the row. We also see the progression from Great Table to Watchtower to sub-angle, essentially "zooming in," from general to specific, to more specific.

Of course, this method requires an understanding of the truncated pyramid system utilised by the Golden Dawn, but it is the only systematic approach for finding relevant Cacodaemons. Yet it is not the only option available. The magician may instead decide to evoke an angel and ask it directly to name a Cacodaemon. Alternatively, the magician may place the Great Table before him or her, and request (in a ritual setting) for the particular Square beginning the Cacodaemon's name to "light up." I have found the latter surprisingly effective.

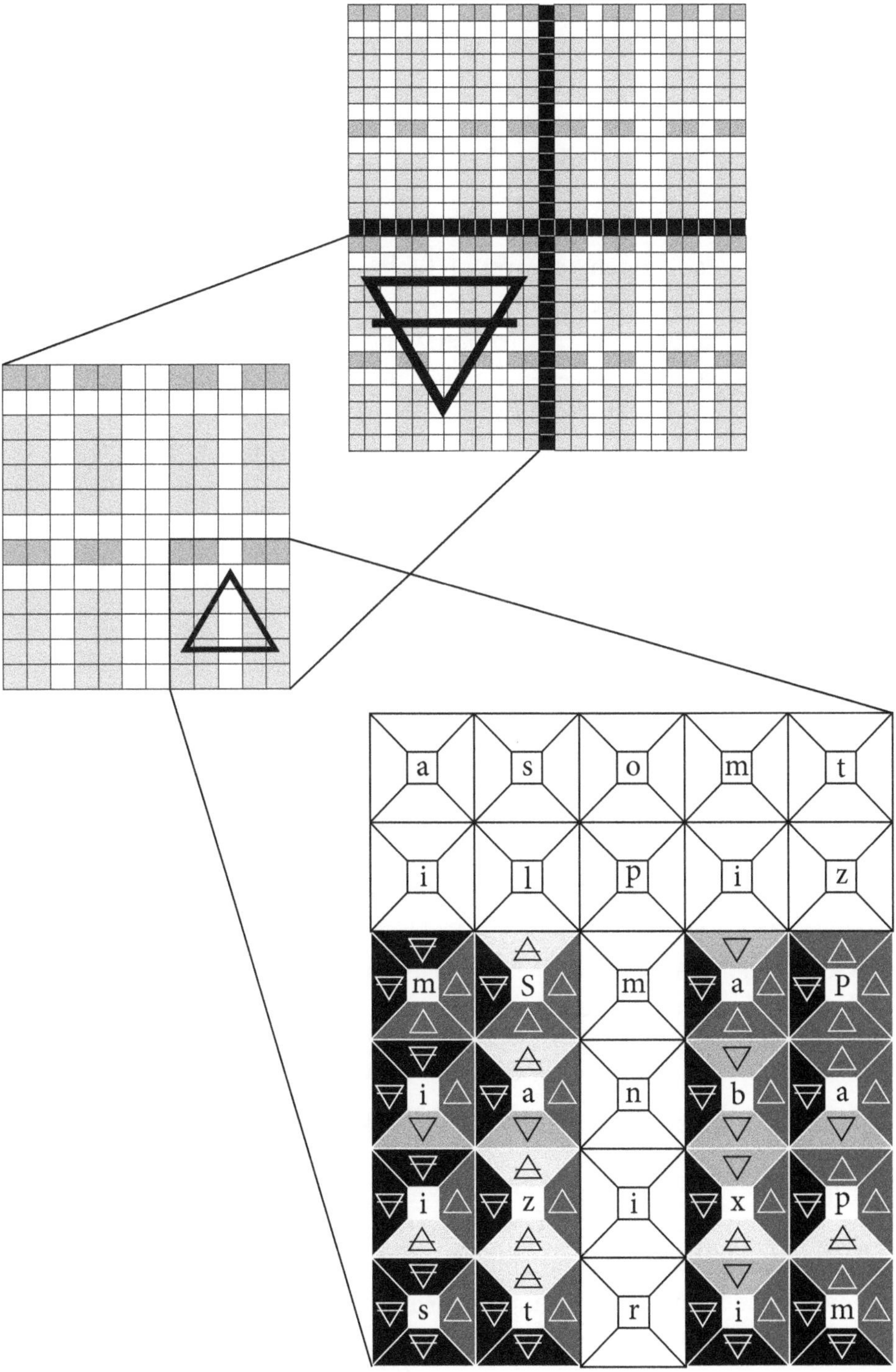
a s o m t
i l p i z
m S m a P
i a n b a
i z i x p
s t r i m

THE BASIC PROCEDURE

A simple breakdown of a typical Cacodaemon working using the OSDL procedure is as follows:

1. Opening
2. First Call – open Seal and/or Tablet of Union
3. Second Call – permutation of EHNB
4. Watchtower Call – horizontal name from Tablet of Union
5. Sub-angle Call – vertical name from Tablet of Union
6. Invocation of the Call and Command Names
7. "*Zacar Od Zamran* Archkerubic Angel" (i.e. prefixed)
8. "*Zacar Od Zamran* Kerubic Angel"
9. "*Zacar Od Zamran* Ruling Angel"
10. "*Zacar Od Zamran* Servient Angel"
11. Call of Binding – Cacodaemon
12. Closing

Initially I was taught to employ the Call of TEX to establish a temple space. This is not related to the actual Working itself, but is an approach we were employing with the Aethyrs as a temple space. This is not required for such a ceremony, however, and may actually muddy things (by bringing in Aethyric energy). The Aethyric temple relevant to the magician also depends on what Aethyr they have attained and actually "reside" in. I prefer to employ this procedure without using the Call of the Thirty Aethyrs in any form; after all, there are enough Calls used throughout.

Utilising the Seal and Tablet of Union

The First Call (as well as all others) can be found in *Enochian Magic in Theory*. It is, after an opening banishing ritual, the preliminary act employed for most Enochian work I use. Indeed, sometimes I employ the First Call without any form of previous banishings, as it tends to "clear the air" and give a "clean slate" with which to work.

I have found that the First Call has a dual purpose in opening the Sigillum Dei Aemeth and the Tablet of Union, both of which should ideally be present during the duration of this working.

The invocation given in Chapter VIII to open the Seal may be employed here if deemed necessary, not so that the Cacodaemon communicates truthfully (for it cannot communicate), but that it shows its true form, and the landscape itself does not offer illusion.

The Second Call is employed for the form of EHNB relevant to the Watchtower in question, and it will be a different permutation (EHNB for Air, HNBE for Water, NBEH for Earth, and BEHN for Fire). I find the ideal number of times to vibrate this name is four, once per letter in the name.

Let us use an example to illustrate the procedure so far: a magician is working in the Fire of Earth Watchtower, attempting to bind the Cacodaemon called AI (or AAI when prefixed), who the magician has chosen as a representation of their issue. In this case he or she would employ the First Call, then the Second Call, and vibrate NBEH four times, being the Earth variant of that ruling entity.

Entering the Watchtower

At this stage the magician should enter the Watchtower he or she is working with, and employ the relevant Call associated with it. Again, we are using the Golden Dawn system for this, which means we have a choice between Calls 3, 4, 5, and 6, being Air, Water, Earth, and Fire respectively. The Call is used to "charge" or "activate" the Watchtower in question, but first the magician must "open" and "enter" the Watchtower. This can be achieved by using the Golden Dawn's Sign of Rending the Veil.

Once the Call is finished, a formal declaration that the Watchtower is open can then be made: "I declare that the Watchtower of [Element] is duly open, and do so in the Name of [Horizontal Elemental Name]". The Elemental Names in question come from the Tablet of Union, being EXARP, HCOMA, NANTA, and BITOM—Air, Water, Earth, and Fire respectively.

Continuing our example, the magician would use a Bell to

signal the beginning of work within the Watchtower, employ the Sign of Rending the Veil, step forward, and recite Call 5 in Enochian, imagining it opening and vitalising the Watchtower of Earth (to do so I would imagine a greyscale copy of the Tablet moving forward, then turning into a Flashing Tablet of black and white as the Call is recited). Then the declaration is made, utilising the name of NANTA.

Entering the Sub-angle

The next stage is similar to the last, in that the magician must go one further level down, into the appropriate sub-angle relating to the Cacodaemon in question, using the relevant Call for the sub-angle to charge, activate, and awaken it. While the "pure" sub-angles (like Air of Air) do not require a second Call, it can be useful to repeat the relevant Call here to better symbolise that descent into the sub-angle.

A declaration can now be given: "I declare that the [Element] Sub-angle of the [Element] Watchtower is duly open, and do so in the Name of [Vertical Elemental Name]". The Elemental Names in question come from the Tablet of Union, being XCAI, AONT, RMTO, and PAAM—Air, Water, Earth, and Fire respectively.

In our example the magician would again use the Bell (ideally a different one, although the same would suffice), Sign of Rending the Veil, stepping forward again (deeper into their temple space), and would recite Call 15 in Enochian, this time imagining it opening and vitalising the Fire of Earth sub-angle (to do this I would imagine the sub-angle bursting to life in its appropriate flashing colours). Then the declaration is made, ultising the name of RMTO.

The Invocation of the Call and Command Names

Then comes the Invocation of the Call and Command Names, and this is different to the other steps, because it is literally an *invocation*, not an evocation. These names are divine forces, and one can invoke them in order to gain the necessary authority to both call (summon) and command (order) the subsequent ranks. This procedure is based on the image shown previously under the heading *The Magician as the Great Table*, where the magician stands with arms outstretched, indicative of a human calvary cross. Then the Call Name is vibrated as a beam of light is imagined descending from the heavens into the magician (and filling him or her with that light). The magician must then either make an internal note that he or she has been given the authority to call the subsequent angels of the sub-angle, or he or she can simply make another formal statement, along the lines of: "By this Name and the Power it represents I am hereby given the authority to call upon the angels of this sub-angle, and they must hearken to my call!" This procedure is repeated with the Command Name, this time imagining the beam of light passing from the right outstretched hand, through the shoulders, and out to the left hand. The following may then be said internally or externally (I prefer the latter): "By this Name and the Power it represents I am hereby given the authority to command the angels of this sub-angle, and they must fulfil those commands!"

An advanced form of the above would be to imagine the English letters of the Names descend or spread across the internal cross. The Enochian can then be employed in an even more advanced form. However, a beam of light is more than sufficient.

In our example the magician would utilise the names of OPMNIR and ILPIZ while forming a cross of light within them, followed by the statements of authority given above.

Calling the Kerubic Angels

The next step involves calling forth the relevant Kerubic Angel from above the arms of the cross. Let's assume it's the normal form, requiring no permutation: ASMT. We may choose to prefix this, which would give us PASMT or AASMT (Dee and Golden Dawn methods respectively).

In the OSDL, we would call the Kerubic Angel in the name of the Archkerubic Angel (i.e. the prefixed form), but really the prefixed form alone would suffice.

The magician would then call forth the applicable angel, saying

"Zacar Od Zamran" ("Move and Appear," a line from the Calls), followed by the angel's name. A longer invocation may be employed, requesting the aid of this angel, and asking it to command its inferiors to aid the magician also in the binding of the applicable Cacodaemon.

Additionally, the Kerubic Angel, and all that follow, may be called in the vertical name of the cross used previously, and commanded with the horizontal name.

Calling the Ruling Angel

This stage is similar to the last, except that the applicable vertical name leading down to the first letter of the Cacodaemon's name is used. Note that these angels were never mentioned in Dee's material and are an expansion of the system, based on the patterns of the other angels.

In our example, we would call TZPAPM, making sure to call this angel in the name of the Kerubic angel, who in turn is called and commanded from the names found in the calvary cross. In this manner every angel is called by order of his or her superior.

Calling the Servient Angel

As previous stages, except using the horizontal name leading across from the first letter of the Cacodaemon's name (potentially employing permutation).

In our example, the Servient Angel is IABA, but because the Cacodaemon's name starts with the last letter of this name, we would use the permutation AIAB. We can also prefix this, making it AAIAB, regardless of the preferred prefixing method. For even more potency, both prefixed and unprefixed may be used, the former ordering the latter.

Likewise, remember to call the Servient Angel in the name of the Ruling Angel, and so on.

The Call of Binding

The Call of Binding is a short Call made in Enochian. Since none was provided by the angels to Dee himself, nor indeed was such a conjuration ever indicated in his diaries, we must make do with our own creative faculties and the perusal of an Enochian dictionary (I have included my own in an appendix to *Enochian Magic in Theory*).

The following Call was written by Frater VVV of the OSDL, who initially instructed me on this particular procedure for binding Cacodaemons. I give the Enochian and English versions of this Call. The Enochian *must* be employed, but the English may also be employed (as I do) to add fervour to the ceremony, and so that the magician understands the meaning of the words.

> Zacar Od Zamran! [*name of cacodaemon*].
> Dooaip [*name or motto*] Ol Sonf Vorsg Noncf!
> [*name of cacodaemon*] Od-Ol Amgedpha!
>
> Move and appear! (*Cacodaemon*).
> In the Name of (*motto*) I reign over you!
> (*Cacodaemon*) and I begin anew!

This Call should be employed several times until the magician believes that they have been successful, or perhaps a number of some spiritual significance may be used, such as 7, 10, or 12, or if a gematria number relevant to the Cacodaemon is discovered (by finding the value of the two letters of its unprefixed name), it would be ideal to recite the Call that number of times.

Alternatively, a specific binding speech may be used here, enjoining the Cacodaemon to cause no more trouble in its particular area, encouraging it to act in its higher nature (indicated by the prefixed letter), and to serve its divine function within the Great Table of the magician.

If needed, the magician may physically or astrally bind, chain, cage, or otherwise subdue the Cacodaemon, depending on how it responds (more than likely it will try to escape). The Kerubic Angel will guide the magician in this, and will extend his or her power down through the Ruling and Servient Angels to aid in the binding. The magician should not be afraid to call upon the support of the angelic forces mustered in the previous stages.

Closing

The ceremony is closed by reversing the procedure of the opening, returning up the ranks (releasing and thanking the respective angels with a License to Depart), stepping out of the sub-angle, and then the Watchtower, using the Sign of the Closing of the Veil, and ringing the bell again where applicable.

XIV

TALISMANS

Talismans present a potent reservoir of force, a concentrated container of the will of the magician, targeted in a single direction, and sometimes even gaining power over time.

Talismans have long been part of magical tradition, going back thousands of years, and gaining particular popularity in the medieval period. The word comes from the Arabic *talsam*, which itself is derived from the Greek *telesma*, meaning "completion" or "religious rite."

The Golden Dawn described talismans, and how they work, in the following way:

> "A talisman is a magical figure charged with the force which it is intended to represent. In the construction of a talisman, care should be taken to make it so far represent the universal forces that it shall be in exact harmony with those you wish to attract, and the more exact the symbolism, the easier it is to attract the force, other things coinciding (i.e. consecration at the right

time, etc.)"[90]

In *Techniques of Solomonic Magic*, Stephen Skinner draws a distinction between talismans, amulets, and phylacteries. Talismans are active, created for specific purpose, require charging, and do not need to be worn. Amulets are passive, typically a natural item (a rabbit's foot or gemstone, for example), are employed for a general purpose, such as protection or luck, and need to worn all the time. Phylacteries typically protect the magician during a working, and are only worn in ritual (the Lamen being a good example). These distinctions have largely been lost in modern generations, but are worth considering here.

There are several examples of what are arguably talismans in Dee's journals, though the term "talisman" is not overtly used. Generally speaking, the instructions for making these are unclear, but we can extrapolate from the examples provided to create other suitable forms.

DEE PURIST TALISMANS

Heptarchic Kings

Dee was instructed to make round talismans for the Bonorum out of "sweet wood," otherwise known as laurel. They were to be held in the hand, "as thou shalt have cause to use them," and while no specific sizes were given, I have found that a diameter of around 4 inches is a good size. They should nest comfortably in the hand so that no part of the design is obscured.

The design itself consists of three parts: 1) the central circle, containing the Seal of the angel; 2) the middle ring, containing the name of the angel; and 3) the outer ring, divided into sections and containing a series of letters and numbers, some reversed.

Dee provided an example of this for King Babalel, shown on the next page.

90 D.D.C.F. (Mathers), Flying Roll XIV, *The Formation of Talismans and Flashing Tablets* (Private Collection).

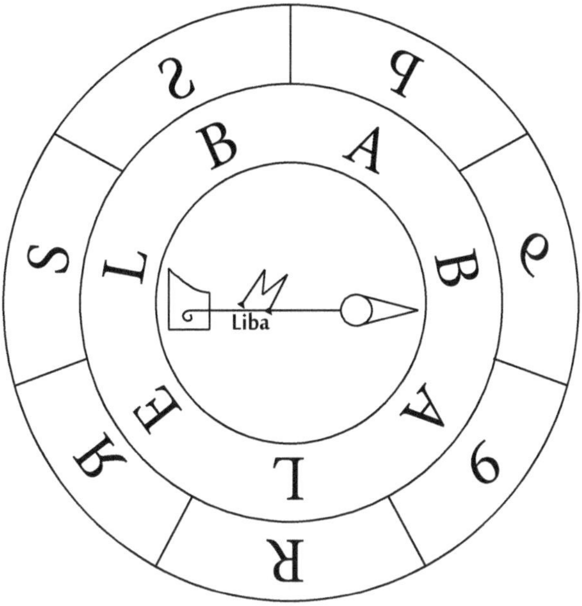

The first two stages of the design are easy to replicate for the other Kings and Princes, as we know their names and Seals. The final stage, however, has proven problematic, because there appears to be some missing table that shows us the relevant letters and numbers. It is referred to several times in Dee's diaries, but it appears it is no longer extant.

Given that we have just this one example, it is difficult to "reverse engineer" the process required for this. Aaron Leitch argues that including the letters in the outer ring on one talisman and not on the others would be imbalanced, and that if they were important, the instructions would have survived.[91] I agree with the former, but not the latter. My workings with the angels on this matter have suggested that the answer to this riddle will surface in time.

We can already learn a lot from the instructions that *have* survived, which do suggest these letters and numbers are important. Dee asks Uriel about "the great circle or globe, wherein there are capital letters under the Kings' names and Characters; and also there are other letters with numbers: of which we have received no instruction; and moreover of these letters, some are aversed, some

91 Aaron Leitch, *The Essential Enochian Grimoire*, p. 142.

reversed, etc."[92]

Clearly then, there is some kind of circular table that contains the names and seals of the Kings, underneath which are placed capital letters, numbers, and other letters, some of which are reversed in direction. This table would have had all the necessary letters and numbers for completing the talismans of the other Kings, but it appears not to have survived.

We can also extrapolate some information from Dee's example. Donald Tyson noted that the double letters and numbers match the number of letters in the angel's name: two Bs, two As, two Ls, and one E; and two Ss, two Rs, two 6s, and one P.[93] If we arrange them appropriately, we have a kind of cipher like the following:

B	A	B	A	L	E	L
6	R	6	R	S	P	S

Note that I am speculating which letter/number in the outer ring goes with which letter of the angel's name, as their positions in the talisman do not match one for one. That said, it is logical to assume that E and P go together, and that the double letters/numbers match the two instances of the same letter in the angel's name.

Assuming that the above is correct, it would seem easier to simply place them around the name of the angel in their appropriate position, but Dee was told to put multiple instances of a letter or number back to back, which makes this impossible. So the exact placement in the outer ring may be somewhat arbitrary. Indeed, when Dee drew his example, he wrote beside it: "perhaps somewhat like this,"[94] suggesting he was not entirely sure himself.

Let us look more closely at Uriel's instructions on this:

> "The letters turned back to back, (being Capital letters,) are equally to be divided, according to their numbers, with a circle cumpassing the name and Character of the king under which they are placed."[95]

92 Joseph H. Peterson, ed. *John Dee's Five Books of Mystery*, pp. 398-399.

93 Donald Tyson, *Enochian Magic for Beginners*, p. 88.

94 Joseph H. Peterson, ed. *John Dee's Five Books of Mystery*, p. 399. (footnote)

95 Ibid., p. 399.

These instructions are somewhat vague, but we know that Dee interpreted them as meaning that the cases of double letters are to be kept together, with their backs turned towards one another (resulting in one normal and one reversed). It is not clear what "according to their numbers" means, but we do have the number 6 twice, and these are turned back to back as per the preceding case in Dee's drawing (although they are also tilted at an angle, and some may instead consider them more like a 9).

While I have not yet found the answer to this riddle, I highlight these elements in case other magicians discover the process by which we may derive the other completed talismans. Until then, we may have to content ourselves with no outer ring, or ask the angels themselves to redeliver this missing piece of the puzzle. This is certainly something on the agenda for my future workings.

Heptarchic Ministers

Dee also included talisman designs for the Ministers of the Bonorum in his diaries, following a similar circular form to those of the Heptarchic Kings.

Initially, he fashioned the names of the Ministers, being six seven-letter names (making up 42 Ministers in total, one letter each), into a ring divided into six sections, placing the names clockwise around it. This design (shown on the next page) he labelled "my own fantasy,"[96] showing that this was not an instruction given to him by the angels (and also showing that there is some freedom to interpret the instructions into designs and practical applications of our own creation). It is likely that he chose this circular format to mirror the other talismans, but also because, in the prior vision, the Ministers assembled in a circle.

96 Ibid., p. 220.

Similar designs were made for other groups of Ministers, and Dee provided a full set of these in his Heptarchic "grimoire."

Initially I would have been tempted to place the Seal of the relevant Heptarchic Prince inside, so that, when combined with the previous talisman, all the Heptarchic angels are accounted for. Yet this is evidently not the intended purpose for these, because Dee later assembled another set of Ministers around the rim of a talisman-like design, but this time he included a drawing in the middle of "a little hill of clay."[97] This matches what Kelley saw, where the Ministers assembled around a hill, each holding one of the 42 letters in the positions marked upon the drawing.

97 Ibid., p. 240.

Following this, Kelley described the next 42 Ministers, being those of Prince Brorges, holding and tossing "a round Table,"[98] which was in flames. The design Dee documented is of a grim-looking head, with sharp teeth and what presumably is fiery hair.

98 Ibid., p. 241.

Indeed, this talisman is almost Goetic in design, and this depiction is likely that of King Bnapsen, who described himself during this vision as follows:

> "Lo, I govern (as I have said before) all enchanters, conjurers, witches, and wicked spirits that are hated of God and included forever in outward darkness (except a few which remain in a second pain, which gape and groan for the mercies of God, and have time of joy, whose measures I have, and keep account of) are all at my government. By me, thou shalt cast out the power of all wicked spirits. By me thou shalt know the doings and practices of evil men, and more than may be spoken or uttered to man."[99]

Clearly, then, Bnapsen is a good angel (pun not intended) for dealing with evil spirits or abusers of magic.

Dee formed the names of the other Ministers into similar "round tables," but, for whatever reason, he did not include any designs in the centre. Perhaps he did not have time, or found it difficult to translate the vision into an image. Yet the pattern and precedence is in the other two images, and is easy to replicate based on the visions Kelley described.

Number-based Talismans

There is another example of a talisman in Dee's diaries, employing a much-ignored part of the Heptarchic system: the seven tables of 49 squares (shown on pages 158-160 of *Enochian Magic in Theory*), which were arranged into an equilateral cross, and from which the names of the Bonorum were derived.

On one occasion, Dee asked for a means of spiritual healing for one Isabel Lister. The angel Murifri told him to form a series of letters and numbers on "a plate of lead."[100] The front of the talisman contains a heptagon, around which are a series of numbers. Inside the heptagon are seven letters, which Dee transcribed into the Enochian alphabet.

99 Ibid., p. 241-242.

100 *A True and Faithful Relation*, p. 5.

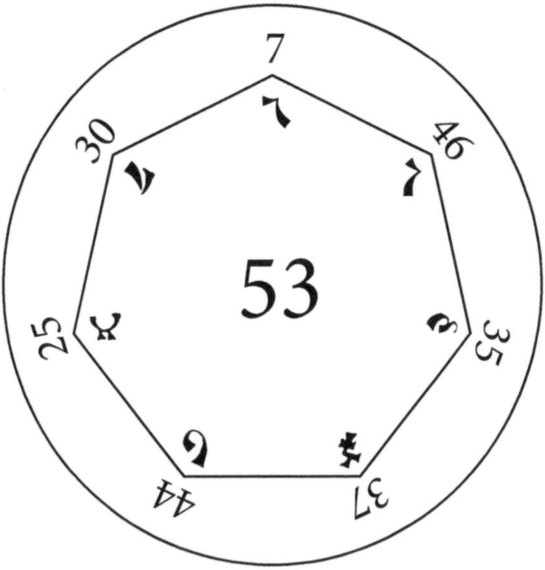

Murifri told Dee the numbers to mark down (7, 30, 25, 44, 37, 35, 46), as well as the letters, spelling SOLGARS. These seem like they were chosen at random initially, but they are actually drawn from the third table of the Bonorum. The number in the centre (53) is the first (7) and last (46) numbers added together.

6 A	**7 S**	29 A	15 B	23 I	8 B	17 Z
36 A	39 S	12 A	**30 O**	1 L	10 S	21 N
5 V	31 S	**25 L**	45 B	26 N	32 N	3 P
18 I	19 A	48 R	4 S	27 R	34 N	24 L
38 R	**44 G**	**37 A**	20 R	16 T	2 R	22 N
49 M	43 V	**35 R**	47 I	9 F	33 R	42 I
13 I	**46 S**	11 R	41 R	40 I	28 I	14 A

Why the name SOLGARS was given is unclear, but potentially this is an angel in charge of spiritual healing. Each of the seven tables of the Bonorum had a purpose assigned to them, but none of these include healing, and technically the third table is related to council, nobility and robes. Yet this was the name Dee was given.

Murifri also revealed that his own name could be found on the same table, though this one is easier to find than the latter, as it is simply read from left to right on the sixth row (noting that U and V were pretty much interchangeable in Dee's time). Knowing this gives us the numbers related to his name, so if we ever wanted a talisman linked to him (as, one might gather, an angel who teaches the secrets of numbers and tables), this is a good start.

6 A	7 S	29 A	15 B	23 I	8 B	17 Z
36 A	39 S	12 A	30 O	1 L	10 S	21 N
5 V	31 S	25 L	45 B	26 N	32 N	3 P
18 I	19 A	48 R	4 S	27 R	34 N	24 L
38 R	44 G	37 A	20 R	16 T	2 R	22 N
49 M	43 V	35 R	47 I	9 F	33 R	42 I
13 I	46 S	11 R	41 R	40 I	28 I	14 A

Murifri told Dee to write the name of the woman on the back of the talisman, not in letters, but in numbers. Dee did not know how to derive these numbers, so the angel told him to "take them out of the second Table (any Table else of the seventh will serve) so that thou take the numbers as thou findest them placed with the letters."[101]

101 Ibid.

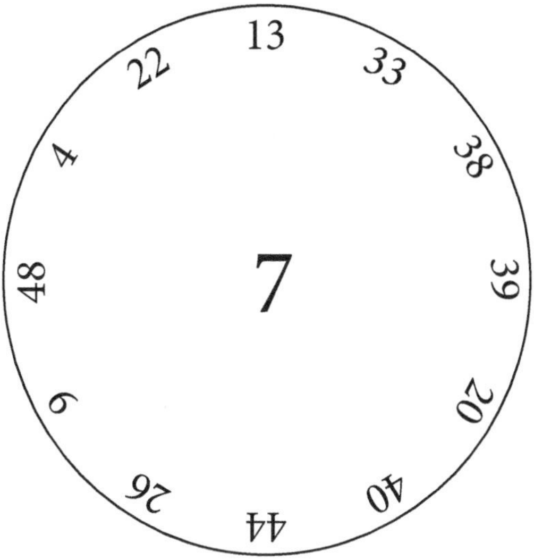

Essentially, this boils down to looking at one of the seven tables and finding the letters of the person's name. It does not matter which square is selected, even though there may be multiple squares with the applicable letter in the same table. Dee chose the seventh table, because none of the other tables had all the letters in Isabel Lister's name. The number he placed in the centre is the number of the table.

14 E	19 E	7 F	25 A	13 I	47 F	16 O
46 A	36 N	44 L	42 N	18 M	45 O	6 L
12 O	41 O	26 I	43 A	29 L	39 B	33 S
48 T	31 O	2 O	32 B	9 S	38 A	8 L
28 S	15 L	17 A	10 O	3 O	30 S	20 E
40 L	34 N	37 S	19 P	4 E	5 O	22 R
24 R	1 N	35 O	23 N	11 E	21 N	27 A

This process is easy to replicate for other talismans. One could take any seven-letter name from the table most relevant to one's goal (see the chart below), whether horizontal, vertical, diagonal, or made up entirely randomly (as in the case of SOLGARS). Prior evocation work might help find the name most suitable. It can then be inscribed, with the appropriate numbers, on the front of the talisman.

The back should contain the name of the magician (if the goal is for oneself) or the person the talisman is for, following the same procedure outlined to Dee. One may find that none of the tables have all the appropriate letters, in which case mixing and matching might work (though is less ideal). Indeed, some letters (like W) are not contained on any of the tables, which makes it impossible to find the relevant number for those. I offer no solution for those scenarios.

Table 1	Wit and wisom	Books
Table 2	Exaltation and government of princes	Kings and a crown
Table 3	Council and nobility	Nobility and robes
Table 4	Gain and trade of merchandise	Merchants, water and a multicoloured animal
Table 5	Quality of the earth and waters	Earth and herbs
Table 6	The air and all that fly in it	Air and a fan
Table 7	Fire and wisdom	Fire and a flame of fire

A note on the above chart: the second column describes the first set of attributions given to these tables, while the third column shows the second or revised set. In most of the cases the attributions match, and offer additional insight, but we can also see some variations.

As for what to do with the talisman, it is to be used on the body (at least in Isabel Lister's case), though obviously the use may differ depending on the intended purpose.

This method of talisman formation could also be extended to the formation of sigils, drawing from one letter to the next on these "magic squares." I show on the next page how the name Isabel Lister can be turned into a sigil.

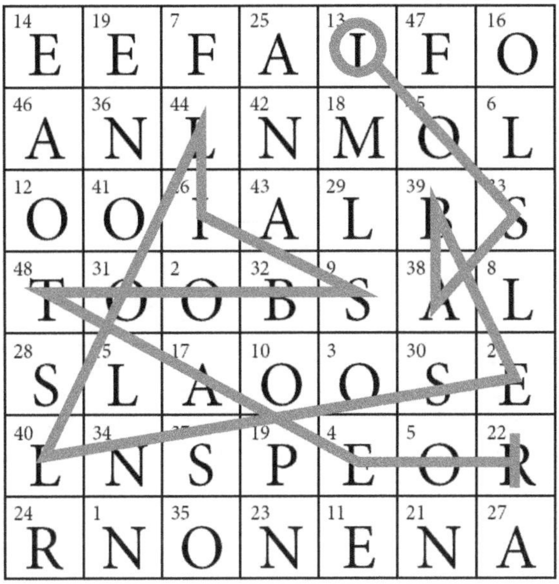

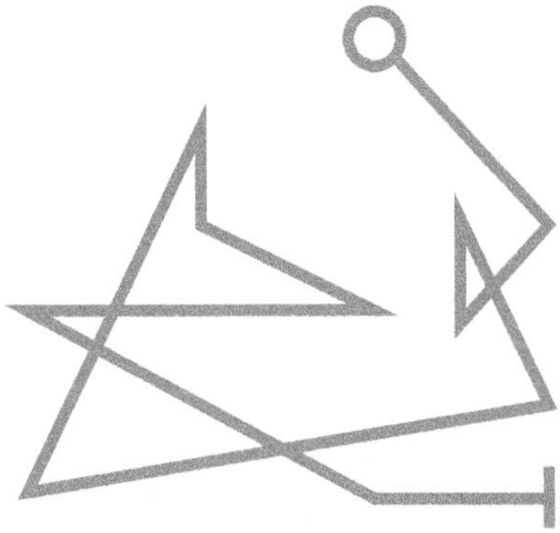

The sigil could also be split, so that there is a separate one for the first name and another for the surname. Otherwise they could potentially get out of hand (though the names combined in this example are fine).

DEE EXTRAPOLATED TALISMANS

Others parts of the Enochian system lend themselves quite readily to the creation of talismans. For example, the Governors of the Parts of the Earth have their own sigils taken from the way they are drawn upon the Tablets (see *Enochian Magic in Theory*, pp. 261-291), which can be drawn on or etched into a talisman.

These talismans are most suited for "political" work, as in influence over a region. I provide an example of such a talisman below:

Here is a talisman created for peace in Syria, employing the name (in Enochian) and sigil of PAXCOMB, the second Governor of LIL, and the second Part of the Earth in the entire system, relating to Syria and the tribe of Zebulun.

I have also included a versicle relating to the intended purpose around the rim of the talisman, and the Psalms are particularly good for this. In this case I have chosen Psalm 34:14, which says:

> "Depart from evil, and do good; seek peace, and pursue it."[102]

The magician may choose to create their own versicle, but it is often better to use an established piece, which taps into the collective consciousness and thus provides for a stronger connection to that intended purpose.

102 Psalm 34:14 (KJV)

The versicle may be in Latin, Hebrew, Greek, or a similar language associated with the Mysteries. Indeed, it can even be in Enochian, though that may limit phrases to those found within the Calls, given how little vocabulary and grammar we know about that language. It could also be in English, as in the example above.

This style of talisman, with the versicle, can be found in older grimoires like the Key of Solomon, which Dee would have been exposed to. It was also taught in the Golden Dawn.

Other Dee-inspired Talismans

Another item that may come to mind is the so-called Golden Talisman, based on Kelley's "Round House" vision. As noted in Chapter III, this item in the British Museum is based on Casaubon's drawing, not the original diaries, and so we can reliably say that it was not made or owned by Dee.

Of course, there is nothing stopping the magician from taking any image in Dee's diaries, such as the Golden Talisman or Heptagonum Stellare, and turning it into a talisman. Some of these, like the aforementioned examples, could serve good practical purposes in this form.

GOLDEN DAWN EXTRAPOLATED TALISMANS

There are many other ways to make talismans based on the Enochian material. For example, the Golden Dawn derived the names of the Overseers (called Supreme or Great Elemental Kings elsewhere) from the circular rim around the Sigillum Dei Aemeth.

Thus, if we wish to create a talisman for these, aside from their respective Seals, we can employ a rim around the talisman, divided into 40 sections, with the appropriate sections for each of the name's letters filled in. We can even combine this with the Seal, and the name of the entity in English and Enochian, for a stronger effect.

Indeed, these designs are useful in many ways, because they highlight the "makeup" of the name in question. In the above example, for Tahaoelog, the Overseer of the Watchtower of Air, we see how the entire name is located on the right-hand side of the Sigillum Dei Aemeth's outer ring. There are many mysteries to be found in these placements.

It is important to note, however, that the historical Golden Dawn did not formally instruct on these types of Enochian talismans; they are simply a natural extension of its existing teachings.

TALISMAN CONSTRUCTION

The common conception nowadays is that it is unimportant when a talisman is constructed, that the magic only really happens during consecration. While it is true that a talisman is largely an empty object until it is consecrated, the drawing or carving of sigils, letters, names, and so forth does start to set things in motion, and the most potent talismans are those where special care is afforded to the crafting as well as the consecration.

Indeed, Mathers taught that high-level adepts could impart a magnetic charge in the construction process, making this preliminary stage just as important as a formal consecration once the talisman is made.

This means that timing should be considered for those looking to get the most out of their talismans. A talisman intended for martial purposes should *ideally* be made (and later consecrated) on the day of Mars, in the hour of Mars. Tables for this can be found in Agrippa.

To understand the significance of this approach, consider the words of Israel Hibner:

> "If now the Time be exactly observed, the Sigil must be stamp'd in a Minute, because this Impression occasions the Power of the Heavenly Influences; for the Heavenly Influences of the Stars are as quick and nimble, as an Arrow out of a Bow, or a Bullet out of a Gun, so quick must this Impression be."[103]

Essentially, in order to achieve a desired end, we must put ourselves as much in sympathy with the forces governing that goal, and the more in sympathy we and our working are, the more effective the outcome will be. While it is true that effects can and do happen without following so strict a protocol, stronger effects can be observed when all procedures are followed to the letter.

This brings us onto the question of materials. Many today employ paper, and this can be effective, but for the truly dedicated, the material may also be considered to create and enhance the resonance with the desired outcome. Metals are one example, with iron being in sympathy with Mars. I include a table below showing the common pairing of these planets and metals.

Saturn	Lead
Jupiter	Tin
Mars	Iron
Sol	Gold
Venus	Copper
Mercury	Quicksilver
Luna	Silver

103 Israel Hibner, *Mysterium Sigillorum, Herbarum and Lapidum*, p. 179.

Of course, quicksilver is not exactly an ideal substance to make a talisman out of, so an alternate metal may be used (with alloys capturing the mixed nature of Mercury).

Colours may also be employed, and the Golden Dawn used these to great effect, giving detailed correspondences between the elements, planets, astrological signs, and more, and their relevant colours. A "flashing colour" (the complementary colour) is also typically employed, and it gains its name by producing a certain visual flash when properly constructed.

Once we have a talisman constructed to our specifications, we must then consider how we wish to consecrate it. Consecration means to "make sacred," and a key consideration here is not merely that we wish to charge it with a specific purpose, but that we also need to initially discharge it of any energies it might have inadvertently picked up along the way (especially if any part of it was previously touched by another person). This is why the basic first step in Golden Dawn consecration ceremonies is banishing.

The manner of consecration itself depends entirely on the magician. Those who wish to use a Golden Dawn approach can employing the invoking hexagrams of the planet(s) in question, making sure to draw a it over the talisman, and also drawing a circle around the hexagram to contain the force. An invocation may then be read, specifying the purpose, including relevant deity and angelic names, and especially including the name of the Governor, and also his/her sigil. The Saluting Sign may be used to direct energy at the talisman, followed by the Sign of Silence to end the projecting of energy.

Those looking for a more powerful and elaborate method may choose to use the Z2 Formulae, which are explained in Israel Regardie's *The Golden Dawn* and Pat Zalewski's *Talismans and Evocations of the Golden Dawn*. Essentially, Z2 breaks down the Neophyte Ceremony into its component parts and uses them as a means to achieve a similar magical goal. In the case of a talisman, it takes the place of the Candidate, and so just as a Candidate is initiated, the talisman is consecrated.

Dee purist magicians may, however, prefer a more Solomonic approach to consecration, given that this is a form that would have been known to Dee. There are numerous "exorcisms" given in that text for purifying and sanctifying a variety of items and materials.

CAUTIONS

When properly constructed and charged, talismans can house energy for a very long time—indeed, almost forever. Yet, they are easily decharged if exposed to the influence of another, or through proximity with other items that may, even inadvertently, contain a charge of their own. One should therefore consider where they are kept, and how they are stored.

It is common in some systems like the Goetia for a spirit to ask for its sigil or seal to be displayed prominently, which has led to people placing them on their mantelpiece, or, the digital equivalent, posting it on social media. In the case of Enochian talismans, I consider this unwise, as it exposes potentially vulnerable people to these potent energies, and also exposes the talisman itself to the energies of those people, which can dilute or disperse the appropriate energies, or worse. In my view, these talismans should remain unseen and be kept apart from everyday life.

While some people like to put a talisman under their pillow while sleeping, I personally think that this is unwise when it comes to Enochian magic. The often undisciplined world of dream is not a good place to experience magic for novices, and thus I would recommend that any dream-based work be kept for when sufficiently advanced to guide and control those experiences, and shut them down if needed.

XV

SKRYING THE AETHYRS

A method for "skrying" the Aethyrs was never given to Dee, but was developed later by Aleister Crowley, influenced by his training in the Golden Dawn. However, there are textual references in Dee's diaries that suggest the Aethyrs can indeed be "visited" (see *Enochian Magic in Theory*, Chapter XIII), and many magicians have found this an illuminating experience.

CROWLEY'S METHOD

Since Crowley effectively invented the concept of skrying the Aethyrs, it is only fair that we look first to his approach (at least in the case of the final 28 Aethyrs, the first two having been experienced by Crowley nine years prior).

Crowley followed in Dee and Kelley's footsteps by not working these alone, but rather having someone else (in his case Frater O.V., or Victor Neuburg) as Scribe (i.e. Dee's role), with Crowley acting as Seer (i.e. Kelley's role).

Crowley then employed a "great golden topaz (set in a Calvary

Cross of six squares, made of wood, and painted vermillion) which was engraved with a Greek Cross of five squares charged with the Rose of 49 petals,"[104] which he held in his hand. He used this somewhat unorthodox device (in the sense of the system delivered to Dee) as a shewstone, describing his visions to Neuburg.

The method of invocation was the Call of the Aethyrs, and the duo travelled throughout the desert, stopping periodically to experience one of the Aethyrs. This isolation, and the fact they were on a kind of pilgrimage, likely had a significant effect on the tone and content of the visions, while also providing fewer distractions from everyday life. It is unlikely that many modern magicians will feel inclined to follow his procedure to this extreme.

It is worth noting that Crowley worked with, on average, one Aethyr per day, sometimes two. As stated previously, I do not think this allows sufficient time to properly experience the Aethyrs. Visions might be experienced, but the energy of one will influence another. It would be like receiving several grade advances in an Order in one go. While it can (and has been) done like this before, it is far from ideal, and presents potential dangers in the sense of an overabundance of Enochian energy.

BENJAMIN ROWE'S METHOD

One of the more interesting modern magicians to work with the Enochian system was Benjamin Rowe, whose writings had a certain influence upon the OSDL.

His approach was initially quite simple, employing the Call of the Aethyrs several times, followed by the name and sigil of the Part of the Earth (or Governor). It should be noted that his intent was to experience the Parts of the Earth, not necessarily the Aethyrs themselves, but the two are so interlinked that the methodology would be essentially the same.

In time, Rowe altered his technique. Perhaps the most noteworthy aspect of these changes is the use of a magical circle created on the astral plane, with various Enochian names in the border. The name of the King (called by Rowe the Zodiacal King) was in the south,

104 Aleister Crowley, *The Vision and the Voice*, Introduction.

while the name of the Aethyr itself was in the north. The name of the Part of the Earth (or Governor), its sigil, and the number of its ministers, was written in the middle of the circle. All of this would be readable by someone facing the south.

Even more unusually, Rowe used the slate-blue wall behind his computer to skry upon (forgoing the more traditional shewstone or mirror), and typed up many of his visions as he experienced them. This is certainly practical for recording experiences, but I cannot help but think that the use of the computer is not conducive to the appropriate mood for magical experiences, being so linked with the mundane world, not to mention all the potential influences it would have on subsequent visions, especially if the computer was used for many other things.

MY METHOD

The approach I use for working with the Aethyrs is a little bit more involved, but can be done by a single person, acting both as Seer and Scribe. It can be difficult to document while skyring, but it is very possible, and the lack of presence of another means there is less risk of their personal energy and experiences influencing one's own.

Tools Required: At a minimum, I would encourage the use of the Sigillum Dei Aemeth (for accurate visions) and the Shewstone (to reduce astral strain). If possible, the full assortment of Heptarchic tools should be employed.

- Set aside at least 30 minutes for the experience. It is wise not to overextend oneself, especially in the initial workings, as this can have a tremendous toll on the body. Ensure there are no distractions, or as few as possible.
- Set up a table and chair, or an altar, or the full Table of Practice. It is best to sit for this, though kneeling is also possible. If one does the latter, it is a good idea to use a cushion, as physical discomfort will distract from the vision. Make sure to have pen and paper nearby, or use a voice recorder (this is particularly helpful). It can

be very easy to forget parts of a visionary experience.

- Set up the Sigillum Dei Aemeth upon the Table, and then the Shewstone upon this (in a special frame if possible). I usually drape red cloth over the Sigillum, so that its ornate form does not impact the vision, with a separate red cloth over the Shewstone, which is removed only when I am ready to begin.
- When relaxed and ready to begin, open the Sigillum Dei Aemeth with an appropriate prayer/invocation (see Chapter VIII). Ask especially for accuracy and truthfulness in the vision to be experienced.
- Recite the First Key. I usually use both Enochian and English, for the power of the language, and the poetry of its meaning. This Key generally gives a blank slate with which to work.
- Next, recite the 19th Key, including the name of the appropriate Aethyr. Again, I advise using both Enochian and English for extra potency.
- Call upon the Governors of the Aethyr, either in unison or separately. A sample invocation is given below:

> "I call upon you, [*name of governor*], [*first/second/third/fourth*] Governor of the Aethyr [*name*], ruler of the Part of the Earth known as [*name*], you who have [*number*] Ministers. Arise, move, and appear before me, and make me a partaker of the knowledge of this realm known as [*Aethyr name*]."

It is often a good idea to call the Governors separately, and so repeat the experience for the Aethyr three times (or four times in the case of TEX, which has four Governors), allowing the magician to experience each part of the Aethyr separately.

I would, however, caution the magician to allow some time between these visions, as the full experience is not garnered only when doing the working, but can unfold afterwards in everyday life. Allowing some rest and assimilation time is always a wise approach to magic, to avoid potential burnout. This applies doubly for Enochian.

CHANGING NAMES IN THE CALL OF THE AETHYRS

This should be common sense, but I have been asked this a number of times: what, if anything, is changed in the Call of the Aethyrs for the different forms? The answer is simple, but it is worth exploring here to avoid any potential confusion.

In the Enochian version, the name of the Aethyr is changed (LIL, the First Aethyr, is given in the original text, but this name should be substituted by the particular Aethyr one wishes to skry or visit).

In the English version, the phrase "The First Aire" (for LIL) should be changed to the number of the Aethyr in question (i.e. "The Thirtieth Aire" for TEX). Note that this phrasing is *not* a direct translation of the names of the Aethyrs (in other words, LIL does not mean literally "The First Aire"). The angels were explicit about this (though they did not offer the direct translations).

Where this becomes muddied is a suggestion by Crowley to change another name in the Call. In a footnote to the word IDOIGO in the Introduction of *The Vision and the Voice*, it says:

> "This name may be appropriately varied with the Aire."[105]

One might wonder why this was suggested, given it was not an instruction given to Dee. The reason is because this name appears in one of the Watchtowers (being the Call Name of the Air of Air sub-angle, or upper left-hand angle of the ORO Tablet, when using the Reformed Great Table), and so it is easy to understand why some may question its inclusion, and what possible links, if any, the Call of the Aethyrs has to that particular entity and Watchtower. Indeed, even Dee noted that the name was present in the Great Table.

There are many problems with this suggestion, however, not least of all the fact that Dee was explicitly told only to change the name of the Aethyr. Indeed, in Dee's collection of the Calls in Sloane MS 3191, *48 Claves Angelicae*, he underlines LIL in the text, then lists the 30 Aethyrs beside it, underlining LIL there, making it clear that this was to be changed per Aethyr. IDOIGO is capitalised (as are

105 Aleister Crowley, *The Vision and the Voice*, Introduction (footnote).

some other words), but not underlined, with no indication anywhere that it is to be altered.

A more practical problem with Crowley's suggestion is that he never gives any indication of what names might actually be appropriately employed in place of IDOIGO. One might initially think that the other Call Names could be used, but there is only one per sub-angle, or four per Tablet, or 16 in total, whereas we have 30 Aethyrs. If we also use the Command Names, we have 16 of those, adding with the Call Angels to give 32 total, yet we only have 30 Aethyrs. Essentially, no matter what way we approach this, it does not add up.

Of course, if one does choose to alter IDOIGO, it is important to also alter the translation (which, in this case, is "Him That Sitteth On the Holy Throne"). Another problem that surfaces here is that we do not have translations for many of the other names within the Tablets, so exactly what would we put here?

While it might seem strange to have a name from the Tablets in this Call, this is not the only place we see a name from one area show up in another. The name BORNOGO (one of the Heptarchic Princes) can be found in Liber Loagaeth. To me, this shows the interlinked nature of the various facets of the wider Enochian system. Further, it is not necessarily the case that the entities in question are identical. There may be two forms that share the same name, but a different purpose.

However, there *is* a name that can be changed in one of the Calls, but it is not the Call of the Aethyrs—it is the First Call. Dee noted the following:

> "Vooan is spoken with them that fall, but Vaoan with them that are, and are glorified. The devils have lost the dignity of their sounds."[106]

Given that most people will not want to work with the infernal entities of this system—which is wise—the latter name can generally always be adopted, as it has in most renditions of this call.

---

106 *A True and Faithful Relation*, p. 80.

BARRIERS TO PROGRESS

It is interesting to note some common experiences many magicians have had with the concept of barriers in the Aethyrs, particularly the 28th (or third experienced when starting with the last), BAG, and the 10th (or twentieth experienced), ZAX. The latter is perhaps the most iconical, being the place where Crowley confronted Choronzon (or Coronzom), the Angelic name for Satan. Less well-known is a lesser form of barrier demon in BAG.

Crowley skried the first two Aethyrs in November 1900, just three days apart (not long enough, in my opinion, to get a full experience of either, given that the energies of the first would still be around when the second was approached). He then found it impossible to progress any further, blaming this block on his grade. Essentially, he had to receive further initiation before he could advance.

Of course, the Aethyrs themselves can act as initiations, and it was Crowley's experience of ZAX that made him claim he had crossed the Abyss and was therefore a Magister Templi, or Master of the Temple, holding the 8=3 grade attributed to the Sephirah of Binah in the Qabalistic grade system employed by the Golden Dawn (a grade which, out of interest, none of the Golden Dawn's founders claimed). So, if we go by Crowley's accounts, the Aethyrs can block progress and can also be the very means through which barriers to progress can be overcome.

XVI

THE 19-DAY WORKING

While much of magical work is populated by one-off workings, there are also numerous examples of operations conducted over a longer period of time, be it days, weeks, or—in the case of something like Abramelin—upwards of 18 months.

Dee was instructed to conduct one of these operations for gaining the attention and obedience of the angels of the Great Table, after which time they could be summoned at ease. This was to be conducted over a period of 19 days, and so has become known as the 19-day working.

This working is relatively simple in nature, with the primary requirement being a book, prepared in advance, which would be used to call forth all ranks of angels from the Watchtowers, acting as a kind of initiation into this part of the wider Enochian system.

The Book of Supplications

Dee was instructed to create a "book of supplications" (or conjurations or invocations), which, in the words of Ave, "consisteth (1) of Invocations of the names of God, and (2) of the Angels, by the names of God."[107] This book would then be read from over the course of the working, invoking first God, and then the angels in turn, and charging the latter to appear when called and fulfil the petitions of the magician.

This concept can be found in other grimoire-style magic, such as the Key of Solomon, which reads:

> "Thou shouldest further make a Book of virgin paper, and therein write the foregoing conjurations, and constrain the Demons to swear upon the same Book that they will come whenever they are called, and present themselves before thee, wherever thou shalt wish to consult them. Afterwards thou canst cover this Book with sacred Sigils on a plate of silver, and therein write or engrave the Holy Pentacles."[108]

Indeed, this is such a common practice that when Ave told Dee the manner of it, Kelley said, "This is somewhat like the old fashion of Magick."[109] Ave dismissed Kelley's comment by suggesting that the magicians of the past merely "played at this."

Dee wondered what form the invocations should take, as shown in this exchange with Ave:

> "Δ. As for the form of our Petition or Invitation of the good Angels, what sort should it be of?
> Ave. A short and brief speech.
> Δ. We beseech you to give us an example: we would have confidence, it should be of more effect.
> Ave. I may not do so.
> E.K. And why?
> Ave. Invocation proceedeth of the good will of man, and of the heat and fervency of the spirit: And therefore is prayer of such effect with God.
> Δ. We beseech you, shall we use one form to all?
> Ave. Every one, after a divers form.

107 *A True & Faithful Relation*, p. 189.

108 S. Liddell MacGregor Mathers, trans. *The Key of Solomon the King*, p. 43.

109 *A True & Faithful Relation*, p. 184.

Δ. If the mind do dictate or prompt a divers form, you mean.
Ave. I know not: for I dwell not in the soul of man."[110]

From this we can take that the invocations are to be written by the magician him or herself, unlike, for example, the Calls. They are to be short, with each form unique to the spirits in question. There will naturally be some overlap, and clearly Ave is allowing maximum freedom here, seeing as it is by the fervent summoning of the magician that the spirits are called.

As to the language employed in these invocations, Ave agreed with Dee's observation that they were to be written "in *verbis conceptis*, in formal words." Indeed, one might treat it like one would write a letter of supplication or petition to a dignitary, being quite cordial, solemn, and dignified. Of course, this does not mean that the magician cannot be firm. Indeed, Dee alternated between "humbly beseech[ing]" and "demand[ing]" the angels to appear and fulfil their appointed offices.

Interestingly, however, when Dee asked Ave to read over his invocations, the angel told him that he "may not use the word *Obedientes*." Dee thought he had selected an appropriate word, based on the idea that, in the sub-angles of the Watchtowers, the horizontal name in the cross is used to "constrain" the angels (this was elsewhere given as "command"). Ave explained that by this was meant "urgeth them more in God." Therefore asking the angels to be "obedient" would be inappropriate. This is, to my knowledge, the only correction made to Dee's invocations.

Dee's surviving book, being part of Sloane MS 3191, includes invocations for the Watchtower angels and diagrams of the Watchtowers, among other things. This was, for the most part, all in Latin, but an English translation, with additional material, can be found in *The Enochian Evocation of John Dee* by Geoffrey James.

A point of curiosity: Dee ended his various invocations with a stylised calvary cross made up of seven triangles—likely meant to signify the Greek letter Delta (Δ), which he used to represent himself throughout his diaries. Dee initially filled in the triangles, but then left them blank for the vast majority. This emblem was rendered as a

110 Ibid., p. 188.

simple equilateral cross in Geoffrey James' transcription.

I point this out, because the idea of stamping one's name, motto, seal or sigil upon a magical tool or text has great importance, linking the latter strongly with the magician. Those attempting to create their own book of conjurations should therefore consider adopting a different mark, of a more personal nature, at the end of these invocations.

Indeed, while Dee's invocations can be used as a template, I would not consider them sacrosanct. Ideally the magician would create his or her own invocations, using Dee as an inspiration, not a limitation.

THE MAKING OF THE BOOK

Dee wondered about the "fashion, paper, and binding" of the book, to which Ave answered: "Thou mayest use thy discretion."[111]

Elsewhere he was given these, somewhat scant, instructions:

> "One book of perfect paper. One labour of a few days. The calling them together, and the yielding of their promise, the repetition of the names of God, are sufficient."[112]

One might wonder what is meant by "perfect paper." Indeed, Dee

111 Ibid., p. 184.
112 Ibid., p. 182.

wondered the same, but Ave evaded his question. In other grimoires this is described as "virgin paper." This is what the Key of Solomon says about this material:

> "Virgin paper, or card, is that which is new, pure, clean, and exorcised, never having served for any other purpose."[113]

I simply used a brand new journal, bought specifically for this task. To "exorcise" it I performed the Lesser Ritual of the Pentagram and the Lesser Ritual of the Hexagram, and drew the banishing figures over the journal, but within a circle, so as to contain and direct the force. This technique is obviously from the Golden Dawn, but it proved very effective.

Dee really wanted firmer instructions on this, asking even how many pages were to be employed in the book (a question that was likely inspired by there being a specific number of pages in another book Dee was instructed to make for the Gebofal working. Ave evaded the question, and it seems the number of pages was of little importance.

If a specific volume of pages *is* chosen, then it is a good idea to ensure that the invocations will fit. Writing these on separate pages, and then binding them afterwards, is one way of solving this potential issue. At least then if an extra page is needed, it can be added at leisure.

It is also wise to prepare the invocations beforehand, so that no mistakes are made in the book itself. The inscribing should be done in a slow and careful manner. This is as much a magical act as the recitation of the conjurations later on, and the book will serve as a kind of talisman in the operation—indeed, a beacon to the angels.

Different coloured pens may be employed for this task, so that, for example, the main text is in black, and the names of angels, etc. are in blue, green, or otherwise. Dee used different colour inks in his Book of Invocations, and a similar approach, essentially treating the book as a calligraphic project, or even an illuminated manuscript, was taken by many who assembled grimoires and important magical texts. In fact, Dee annotated many texts in his library, including lots

113 S.L. MacGregor Mathers, trans. *The Key of Solomon the King*, p. 111.

of his own illustrations in the margins.

Just as the paper should be clean and unused, the pen/s should be too. It is a good idea to buy special pens just for this purpose, either calligraphy pens or fountain pens. Failing that, an ordinary ballpoint pen will do, but the more effort put into the writing of the book, the better the results later on will be. Indeed, if the angels were to put the same effort into manifesting, or answering one's questions, then perhaps skipping corners is unwise.

THE WORKING

As to the working itself, Dee was given the following instructions:

> "Thou hast three names of God, out of the line of the holy Ghost, in the principal Cross of the first Angle, so hast thou three in the second, etc. Four days (after your book is made, that is to say, written) must you only call upon those names of God, or on the God of Hosts, in those names:
>
> And 14 days after you shall (in this, or in some convenient place) Call the Angels by Petition, and by the name of God, unto the which they are obedient.
>
> The 15 day you shall clothe your selves, in vestures made of linen, white: and so have the apparition, use, and practice of the Creatures. For, it is not a labour of years, nor many days."[114]

The first four days are therefore spent invoking the Three Holy Names of God from each of the Watchtowers. This can be interpreted in two ways: 1) that each day should be devoted to a separate set of three names from the four quarters; or 2) that each day should include all twelve names, with the same invocation repeated. The latter approach is what Dee took in his book.

It is interesting to note that the angels can be called in the name of the "God of Hosts," a matter Dee took quite literally, employing the Hebrew name Ieovah Zebaoth (Yehovah Tzabaoth) in his conjurations. I do not see this quite so literally, and think that any sacred

114 *A True & Faithful Relation*, p. 184.

name of God may be employed for this purpose. In Donald Tyson's rendition, he included several different Hebrew Divine Names.

Once the first four days are over, and the magician has secured the authority of God, the actual conjurations of the angels take place. The angels are called in the appropriate Name of God. Dee interpreted this to mean that the Seniors are called forth by the King, which he labelled "Dei Nomen" or "Name of God," that the Dispositors were called forth by the "Names of God" that are the vertical Call and horizontal Command names, and that the Kerubic Angels (to use the Golden Dawn name, in the absence of any better) are to be called by the prefixed Kerubic Angels.

I do not see all of these as actually being Names of God, per se (the central names formed in a spiral are, after all, referred to as "Kings" in Dee's diaries), so I would initially call them in the Three Holy Names of God, and then work down to the Call and Command angels, and so on. This chain of command ensures that the highest names are always called first, a Golden Dawn principle (indeed, part of the Adeptus Minor Obligation), and one that is wise to follow in magic in general.

Dee wondered if he "should summon the wicked here recorded (out of the black cross, having their offspring) likewise 14 days,"[115] to which Ave later answered by explicitly prohibiting this. Yet Dee did include the names of the Cacodaemons in his Book of Spirits, along with the reversed Call and Command names.

On the final day, the fifteenth after the conjurations of the angels are begun, or the nineteenth after the initial invocations to God are begun, the Magician and Seer (if used) don white robes, often symbolic of purity, and are thenceforth entitled to see the angels, and employ them.

It is worth pointing out that, while the invocations spoken on the preceding days ask for the spirits to appear visibly, etc., they are not expected to actually do so until the final day of the working (and any time of the magician's choosing thereafter). At no time should results, in terms of manifestation, be expected until the nineteenth day.

What then on the nineteenth day, or any day thereafter? The garment and book are no longer to be used. This is the exchange

115 Ibid., p. 185.

between Ave, Kelley and Dee:

> "Ave. You must never use the Garment after, but that once only, neither the book.
> E.K. To what end is the book made then, if it be not to be used after?
> Dee. It is made for to be used that day only."[116]

Clearly Dee was not in one of his more questioning moods, as one might imagine hearing that all this work results in a book that is no longer to be used might irk someone, as it did Kelley. This approach does seem counter-intuitive, in that the book may be seen as the link forged between the magician and the angels, but the angels are thereby bidden to show up at the magician's call, by whatever means necessary, so that the book really is not needed after this initial operation.

The white robe is typically worn in all workings in grimoire tradition, but here only for a single day, which is very unusual. There are no instructions on what to wear at any other time, suggesting normal attire (which for Dee was perhaps more well-dressed than magicians nowadays) may be sufficient. For me, robes are part and parcel of most of my magical work.

It is important to note that Ave does not tell Dee to destroy the robe and book, though, of course, if they are not to be used thereafter, one might question why they should be kept. It could be argued that destroying the book might destroy the connection, though evidently the book was only ever intended as a means to an end, so I would argue that the book's existence thereafter should have little bearing on one's relationship with the angels. A book of Dee's conjurations has survived in Sloane MS 3191, though this is likely just a copy, and not the one Dee used in his working, if indeed he ever actually performed it.

THE CONJURATIONS

The pattern for the invocations in Dee's book is as follows:

116 Ibid., p. 183.

- Fundamental Obeisance
- Six Seniors of the East
- Six Seniors of the South
- Six Seniors of the West
- Six Seniors of the North
- Four Good Angels of the East - Natural Substances
- Four Good Angels of the South - Natural Substances
- Four Good Angels of the West - Natural Substances
- Four Good Angels of the North - Natural Substances
- Four Good Angels of the East - Transportation
- Four Good Angels of the South - Transportation
- Four Good Angels of the West - Transportation
- Four Good Angels of the North - Transportation
- Four Good Angels of the East - Mechanical Arts
- Four Good Angels of the South - Mechanical Arts
- Four Good Angels of the West - Mechanical Arts
- Four Good Angels of the North - Mechanical Arts
- Four Good Angels of the East - Delivery of Secrets
- Four Good Angels of the South - Delivery of Secrets
- Four Good Angels of the West - Delivery of Secrets
- Four Good Angels of the North - Delivery of Secrets
- Four Dispositors of the East - Medicine
- Four Dispositors of the South - Medicine
- Four Dispositors of the West - Medicine
- Four Dispositors of the North - Medicine
- Four Dispositors of the East - Metals and Jewels
- Four Dispositors of the South - Metals and Jewels
- Four Dispositors of the West - Metals and Jewels
- Four Dispositors of the North - Metals and Jewels
- Four Dispositors of the East - Transformation
- Four Dispositors of the South - Transformation
- Four Dispositors of the West - Transformation
- Four Dispositors of the North - Transformation
- Four Dispositors of the East - Elements
- Four Dispositors of the South - Elements
- Four Dispositors of the West - Elements
- Four Dispositors of the North - Elements

The first invocation, called by Dee the *Fundamental Obeisance* (though this name is Dee's own wording), is repeated over the first four days. Dee compiled a single invocation for all twelve Names of God, rather than devoting a separate invocation to each set of three. I think the latter is a more accurate interpretation of Ave's instructions, and more accurate to the natural divisions in the Great Table itself. This is, therefore, the manner I have adopted in my own Book of Invocations, but either approach has merit.

This leaves 36 invocations for the various angels, to be split up over the next 14-day period. As one can see, this number of invocations does not match up mathematically with the number of days for the invocations. Even if we grouped four invocations together in one day, as in all the Dispositors of the East, or all the Dispositors of a particular office, it just does not add up.

It may be that Dee intended to recite all 36 invocations on each of the 14 days, perhaps even repeating the Fundamental Obeisance before this process began. This would certainly solve the problem of dividing up the invocations. It does, however, make for a much more tiring and time-consuming operation, which is possibly why Ave advocated that the invocations should be "a short and brief speech." There is some merit to such an approach, in that it requires greater dedication to the operation, but by the time the magician gets to the later invocations, he or she will likely merely be speaking the words, not making them heart-felt.

An alternative method is to include invocations that Dee did not choose for his own book. After all, the angels did not explicitly say which angels were to be included, or in what manner, and clearly left this to the imagination and inspiration of the magician. Dee calls on the Seniors in the names of the Kings (treating them as Names of God), but two separate invocations could be employed for them directly, one for the severe and one for the merciful form. This would result in a layout as follows:

Day 1	ORO, IBAH, AOZPI
Day 2	MOR, DIAL, HCTGA
Day 3	MPH, ARSL, GAIOL
Day 4	OIP, TEAA, PDOCE

Day 5	Kings, Severe
Day 6	Kings, Merciful
Day 7	Seniors of the East
Day 8	Seniors of the South
Day 9	Seniors of the West
Day 10	Seniors of the North
Day 11	(Kerubic) Angels of the East
Day 12	(Kerubic) Angels of the South
Day 13	(Kerubic) Angels of the West
Day 14	(Kerubic) Angels of the North
Day 15	Dispositors of the East
Day 16	Dispositors of the South
Day 17	Dispositors of the West
Day 18	Dispositors of the North
Day 19	Manifestation

This does, of course, mean that the Kings of all four quarters are being called all at once, which does not match up with the form used for all of the other names. Yet there is no way to employ a four-fold division to another group of angels, because once we put in the Seniors, Kerubic Angels (or simply "good angels"), and Dispositors, we only have two days left in the main 14-day section of the working. So, the dual nature of the Kings makes them, to me, the most likely candidate to fill those positions, if the magician is adamant on splitting up the invocations over separate days. This is the solution I adopted in my own work.

Donald Tyson includes his own "Book of Spirits" in his *Enochian Magic for Beginners*, with his own invocations (adopting wording selected from the Calls) and a different approach to the days of the operation:

Day 1	ORO, IBAH, AOZPI
Day 2	MOR, DIAL, HCTGA
Day 3	MPH, ARSL, GAIOL
Day 4	OIP, TEAA, PDOCE
Day 5	Seniors of Spirit, Left
Day 6	Seniors of the Son, Above
Day 7	Seniors of the Father, Above

Day 8	Seniors of the Spirit, Right
Day 9	Seniors of the Father, Below
Day 10	Seniors of the Son, Below
Day 11	Dispositors of Joining
Day 12	Dispositors of Transporting
Day 13	Dispositors of the Sciences
Day 14	Dispositors of Secrets
Day 15	Angels of Medicine
Day 16	Angels of Metals and Stones
Day 17	Angels of Transformation
Day 18	Angels of the Elements
Day 19	Orison

Tyson attempted to address the mathematical problem by dividing up the Seniors into six groupings, based not only on their presence in the *Linea Patri et Filii* and *Linea Spiritus Sancti*, but on their positions right and left. Suffice it to say, this is a somewhat inelegant solution, and I personally prefer Dee's more straightforward inclusion of all six Seniors from one Watchtower in a single invocation.

I include below the "Fundamental Obeisance," the initial prayer or invocation Dee wrote for the Watchtower work. The original is in Latin, and this English translation comes from Geoffrey James:

> This is the fundamental obeisance to God, and the conjuration for obtaining the benign ministry of the good angels.
>
> O IEOVAH ZEBAOTH, I, John Dee (your unworthy servant) most earnestly invoke and call upon your divine power, wisdom, and goodness. I humbly and faithfully seek your favour and assistance to me in all my deeds, words, and thoughts, and in the promoting, procuring, and mingling of your praise, honour, and glory. Through these, your twelve mystical Names: ORO, IBAH, AOZPI, MOR, DIAL, HCTGA, OIP, TEAA, PDOCE, MPH, ARSL, GAIOL, I conjure and pray most zealously to your divine and omnipotent majesty, that all your angelic spirits (whose mystical names are contained in this book, and whose offices are herein briefly noted) might

be called from any and all parts of the universe, or at any time in my life, through the special domination and controlling power of your holy Names (which are also in this book). Let them come most quickly to me. Let them appear visibly, friendly, and peacefully to me. Let them remain visible according to my will. Let them vanish from me and from my sight when I so request. Let them give reverence and obedience before you and your 12 mystical Names. I command that they happily satisfy me in all things and at all times in my life, by accomplishing each and every one of my petitions—if not by one means, then by another—goodly, virtuously, and perfectly, with an excellent and thorough completeness, according to their virtues and powers, both general and unique, and by Your united ministry and office.

O God. Amen.
Through you, Jesu Christi,
Amen.

This invocation covers all the necessary things, from ensuring the spirits appear at will, anywhere, and at any time, to ensuring they also leave when asked. The power of the Names of God drawn from the Watchtowers is employed to give the magician authority over the angels.

One thing I object to, as noted in the chapter on prayer, is the "your unworthy servant" phrasing. If Dee thought he was so unworthy, then why even attempt this work? Surely someone truly unworthy could never obtain the ministry of the good angels. This is largely a product of the times he lived in, and the manner in which a faithful Christian was expected to behave. While humility is important, this phrase is something I would not include in my own invocations.

I provide an alternative to the above conjuration, employed in my own wording, in Chapter XVIII, where I have largely followed the same structure as Dee, but opted for several different clauses.

It is worth noting that, while Dee included the names of the

Cacodaemons with the Dispositors, and even included the reversed names of God to call them by, he was explicitly told by Ave that they were "*at not time* to be called"[117] (Dee's italics). It seems likely that Dee included their names in his book of invocations more for completeness than anything else, especially considering that they are not mentioned in the actual text of his invocations, but rather in preceding charts of names. See Chapter XIII for more details on the Cacodaemons.

OTHER LONG-TERM WORKINGS

While the long-term workings that Dee was instructed to perform are limited to the 19-day Working and Gebofal (see the next chapter), we can easily apply a similar approach to other parts of the system.

For example, the Bonorum of the Heptarchic system could be called in much the same way, employing a 49-day working, the number of days having a strong resonance with the important number 7 in that part of the Enochian corpus.

An approach taught in the OSDL by one of my mentors, VVV, allowed for a gradual progress through the ranks of the Watchtower angels, essentially gaining their favour and support, before going on to bind a Cacodaemon. A whole week would be spent at each stage, first with the Three Holy Names of God, then the next with the King, the next with the Seniors, the next with the Call Name, the next with the Command Name, the next with the Kerubic Angel, the next with the Servient Angel or Dispositor, and finally the Cacodaemon itself. This included a gradual opening of the Watchtower itself, descending deeper into it. By the time of the binding ceremony, the operation would have lasted several months, and this involved daily practice.

This approach is extremely powerful, and something that is useful when that extra "oomph" is required. It is not to be approached lightly, however, and, once begun, the operation should be finished. Indeed, the latter rule of thumb applies for all magical work.

117 *A True and Faithful Relation*, p. 188.

XVII

GEBOFAL

Dee received instructions for another long-term working featuring a far more difficult to produce book, the mysterious Liber Loagaeth, in an operation "which is called in the Holy Art Gebofal."[118] The meaning of this word was never given.

It is expected that the magician will have constructed all of the Heptarchic tools, and I do not recommend the Gebofal operation be started without them. Their inclusion will likely make the process much smoother and safer, as they do in other aspects of Enochian work.

Yet it is Liber Loagaeth itself that is the centrepiece of this art, and this is a more elaborate construction than the book of invocations required for the 19-day working. Indeed, it is considered so holy that even the angel Uriel questioned why it was to be given to mere mortals:

> "This book, and holy key, which unlocketh the secrets of god his determination, as concerning the beginning, present being, and end of the world, is so reverent and

118 *A True and Faithful Relation*, p. 373.

> holy, that I wonder (I speak in your sense) why it is delivered to those, that shall decay: So excellent and great are the Mysteries therein contained, above the capacity of man."[119]

The book is to contain all 48 double-sided tables (the 49th being hidden) of Liber Loagaeth, each of them (barring the first) forming a table of 49x49 squares, which will result in a finished product that is very large. Even if just 1cm is allowed for each square, this will be an unwieldy tome. Of course, the magician may choose to draw up each page as a loose sheet, and then bind them later, which may make it easier to complete.

The book should be covered in "a blue silk sendal,"[120] this being a fine silk fabric commonly used in the Middle Ages. On this the words "Amzes naghézes Hardeh" should be painted in gold (presumably in Enochian lettering). Of this title, Kelley said "it signifieth the universal name of him that created universally be praised and extoled forever."[121]

The angel Galvah told Dee that "the first leaf (as you call it) is the last of the Book," instructing him to "write the Book (after your order) backward, but alter not the form of the letters, I speak in respect of the places."[122] Thus, it is read, like Hebrew texts, from what native English-speakers would consider the back cover. This makes sense, given that Enochian, also like Hebrew, is written from right to left. While surviving examples of the tables are given in English, the finished product is expected to be in Enochian lettering. It has been suggested by others that this would mean the tables should be written backwards as well, but I think Galvah's words indicate otherwise.

Dee was hesitant to begin working on the book until he knew if it "were to be written in paper or parchment; in what colour the lines were to be ruled, green or blue, etc."[123] Uriel told him to "form and write the book after thine own Judgement," to which Dee added the footnote: "The form of the book committed to my discretion." Much

119 Jeffrey H. Peterson, ed., *John Dee's Five Books of Mystery*, p. 395.

120 Ibid., p. 324.

121 Ibid., p. 325.

122 *A True and Faithful Relation*, p. 19.

123 Jeffrey H. Peterson, ed., *John Dee's Five Books of Mystery*, p. 406.

later, Dee wondered of the letters of the 49th leaf if he should "write them in Letters of Gold," to which Galvah replied, "The writing hath been referred to thy discretion with colours, and such things as appertain to the writing thereof."[124] The magician may then write them all in monochrome, or do as Dee did in his book of spirits for the Great Table, and employ different colours for specific words, or the lines of the tables, etc.

Aaron Leitch gives a stylised example of how the outer form of this book might look in *The Essential Enochian Grimoire*,[125] with the "Galethog" seals from the Sigillum Dei Aemeth employed to bind the book, harking to a reference in Revelations 5:1. However, the inclusion of these seals is artistic license.

I should point out at this stage that I have not conducted this operation, and am not aware of anyone who has (though there are several people currently in the process of constructing the book), given a number of problems in producing a "perfect" copy of Liber Loagaeth, as we shall see below.

When I inquired about Liber Loagaeth, I was told it was "not ready," which befuddled me for years. I think there are two likely explanations for this answer the angels gave: 1) that the "end of days" (which the completion of the operation is, among other things, supposed to herald) is not yet upon us; and 2) that there are no complete and perfect copies of Liber Loagaeth currently in existence, and so the operation cannot currently be proceeded with.

The first scenario is supported by numerous comments made by the angels, such as these words of Uriel:

> "God shall make clear when it pleaseth him, and open all the secrets of wisdom when he unlocketh. Therefore seek not to know the mysteries of this book, till the very hour that he shall call thee."[126]

Part of the problem of replicating the Gebofal procedure is that some of the extant pages of the required book (most of them in Kelley's handwriting) are no longer legible, at least in the case of Sloane

124 Ibid., p. 20.

125 Aaron Leitch, *The Essential Enochian Grimoire*, p. 13.

126 Jeffrey H. Peterson, ed., *John Dee's Five Books of Mystery*, p. 351.

3189. For example, in the page below, we see how the letters along the edges are obscured, faded, or blackened, not to mention issues with interpretation of handwriting, making it extremely difficult to reproduce.

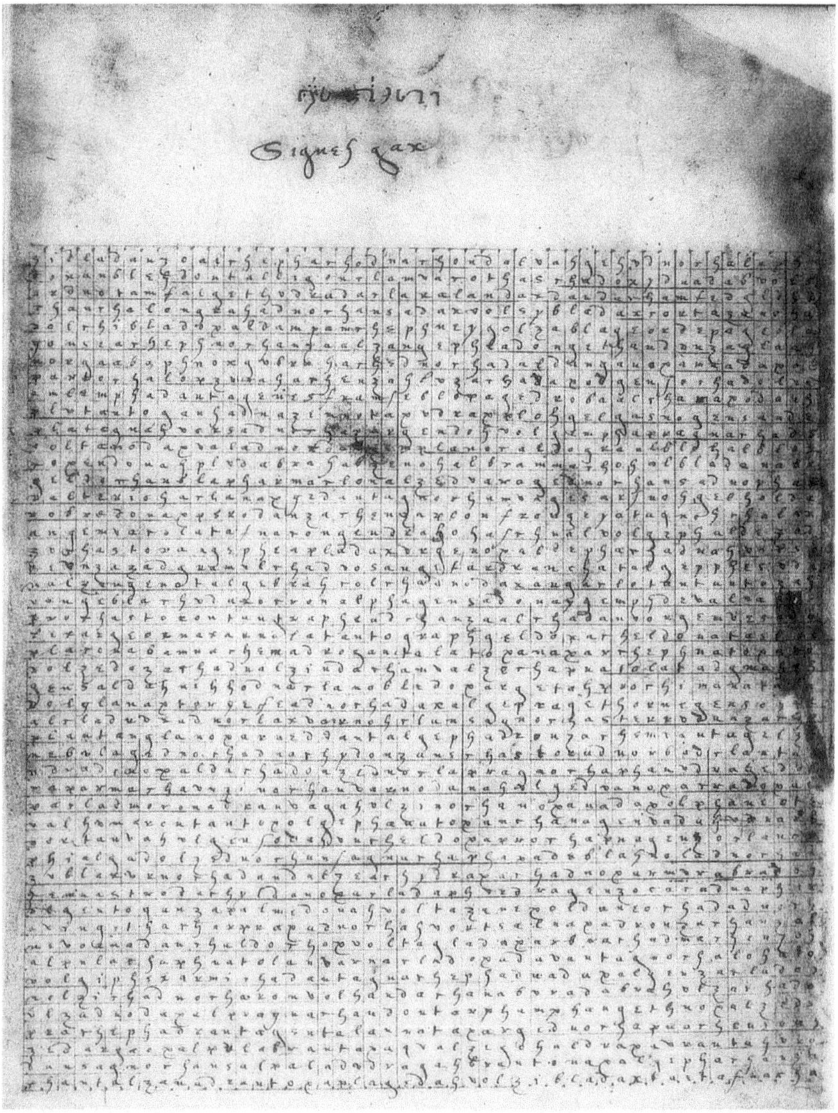

The above issue is partly solved by the existence of a (unfortunately only partial) transcription of the tables in Sloane 2599, which may have been made by Elias Ashmole. Some parts of this version are also difficult to read, but cross-referencing the two would help.

There are other problems, however, such as there being too many letters in some instances to actually make up the right number of single-letter squares. A variety of potential solutions have been proposed for these issues, such as dropping select letters or rendering particular combinations of letters (ch, for example) as a single Enochian letter, and converting cases where the word "zed" is used into the single letter 'z' (or Ceph in Enochian), which Leitch has argued.[127]

We could, of course, go through Dee's diaries and write up the letters, etc. from what was there transmitted, but even Dee had doubts about some of the reception, marking multiple letters as possibilities.

This says nothing of the first table, which is not really a table at all, but several pages of text, followed by a 9x49 table, followed by more text. No matter what way this is worked, it will never make a 49x49 table, and rather than being a single leaf, it is inevitable that it will span multiple pages in the finished book.

The creation of this book is, therefore, a monumental task, perhaps moreso than that faced by Dee himself, and even he initially failed to produce it within the timeframe asked of by the angels: a mere 40 days, which did not even allow a page per day.

For those looking for a complete set of the 49 tables of Liber Loagaeth for use in the Gebofal operation, check out *Decoding the Enochian Secrets* by John DeSalvo.[128] These images, in larger form, can also be found online, so they can be zoomed in on for working out specific letters, etc. Alternatively, one could wait for Aaron Leitch's future publication of Liber Loagaeth.[129]

As for the preparation for this operation, Uriel said:

> "Humble yourselves nine days before: yea, unrip (I say) the cankers of your infected souls: that you may be apt and meet to understand the Secrets, that shall be delivered."[130]

127 Aaron Leitch, *The Angelical Language*, pp. 89-91.

128 John DeSalvo, *Decoding the Enochian Secrets*, pp. 92-216.

129 Aaron Leitch, *The Essential Enochian Grimoire*, p. 151.

130 Joseph H. Peterson, ed. *John Dee's Five Books of Mystery*, p. 394.

Dee added "our nine days contrition preparative" in a footnote to the above, but beyond this there is no clarification on the manner of this humbling. There are, however, similar nine-day preparations in other magical traditions, such as the Key of Solomon, to which we can look for inspiration:

> "It is absolutely necessary to ordain and to prescribe care and observation, to abstain from all things unlawful, and from every kind of impiety, impurity, wickedness, or immodesty, as well of body as of soul; as, for example, eating and drinking superabundantly, and all sorts of vain words, buffooneries, slanders, calumnies, and other useless discourse; but instead to do good deeds, speak honestly, keep a strict decency in all things, never lose sight of modesty in walking, in conversation, in eating and drinking, and in all things; the which should be principally done and observed for nine days, before the commencement of the Operation."[131]

Fasting and ritual washing are a key part of that preparation, and while the angels did not clarify the preparation for the Gebofal operation, it is likely they intended something similar to the above. At the very least, prayer—and a lot of it—can be pretty much taken for granted as an important part of this nine-day period of contrition.

The operation itself would consist of 49 days, relating to the 49 Tables of Liber Loagaeth, the mysteries of which would be unlocked through the use of the 49 Calls. A final day may be appended, bringing the total to 50, which is important, as we shall see later.

The angel Gabriel told Dee that when the Calls that he looked for were delivered, by them he would "enter the knowledge and perfect understanding of the 49 Gates and Tables if you will."[132] These Calls are the 49 Keys, only 48 of which were given, the first being unvoiced. There is strong supporting evidence then for a direct link between the Calls and Liber Loagaeth, though the Calls also appear to have other uses (such as the Call of the Aethyrs linked with the Parts

131 S.L. MacGregor Mathers, trans. *The Key of Solomon the King*, p. 88.

132 *A True and Faithful Relation*, p. 198.

of the Earth), which I would argue means that the Golden Dawn's assignments to the Great Table (given in Chapter X) still have merit.

If we are to use these Keys as a means to unlock the Gates of Liber Loagaeth, then we must consider the words of Ilemese:

> "But you must understand that in speaking of the first Table, I speak of the second. So that the second, with you is the first."[133]

So, the real first Table is not revealed, and what Dee received as his first Table is actually the second in the grand scheme of things. We also know that the first Table "can have no call," for it is spoken by God. What this means in practical application is that the first day of the Gebofal working would have an Unwritten Table and an Unvoiced Call. The magician should not, therefore, start immediately into what we commonly call the First Call, saving that instead for the second day.

Days 2 to 49 would be taken up by recitations of the 48 documented Calls (18 and the Call of the Aethyrs, the latter repeated 30 times, alternating the name of the Aethyr in question). But what of Day 50? Ave told Dee that Enoch made the tables, as Dee had done, and that "Enoch laboured 50 days," praying thrice a day in the following words:

> Lord God the Fountain of true wisdom, thou that openest the secrets of thy own self unto man, thou knowest mine imperfection, and my inward darkness: How can I (therefore) speak unto them that speak not after the voice of man; or worthily call on thy name, considering that my imagination is variable and fruitless, and unknown to myself? Shall the sands seem to invite the Mountains: or can the small rivers entertain the wonderful and unknown waves?
>
> Can the vessel of fear, fragility, or that is of a determined proportion, lift up himself, heave up his hands, or gather the Sun into his bosom? Lord it cannot be: Lord, my imperfection is great: Lord I am less than

133 Ibid., p. 199.

sand: Lord, thy good Angels and Creatures excel me far: our proportion is not alike; our sense agreeth not: Notwithstanding I am comforted; For that we have all one God, all one beginning from thee, that we respect thee a Creator: Therefore will I call upon thy name, and in thee, I will become mighty. Thou shalt light me, and I will become a seer; I will see thy creatures and will magnify thy name among them. Those that come unto thee have the same gate, and through the same gate, descend, such as thou sendest. Behold, I offer my house, my labour, my heart and soul, If it will please thy Angels to dwell with me, and I with them; to rejoice with me, that I may rejoice with them; to minister unto me, that I may magnify thy name. Then, lo, the Tables (which I have provided and, according to thy will, prepared) I offer unto thee, and unto thy holy Angels, desiring them, in and through thy holy names: That as thou art their light, and comforted them, so they, in thee will be my light and comfort. Lord, they prescribe not laws unto thee, so it is not meet that I prescribe laws unto them: What it pleaseth thee to offer, they receive; so what it pleaseth them to offer unto me, will I also receive. Behold, I say (O Lord) If I shall call upon them in thy name, be it unto me in mercy, as unto the servant of the Highest. Let them also manifest unto me, how, by what words, and at what time, I shall call them. O Lord, is there any that measure the heavens, that is mortal? How, therefore, can the heavens enter into mans imagination? Thy creatures are the glory of thy countenance: Hereby thou glorifiest all things, which Glory excelleth and (O Lord) is far above my understanding. Is it great wisdom, to speak and talk according to understanding with Kings: But to command kings by a subtle commandment, is not wisdom, unless it come from thee. Behold, Lord, how shall I therefore ascend into the heavens? The air will not carry me, but resisteth my folly; I fall down, for I am of the earth. Therefore, O thou very Light and true

> Comfort, that canst, and mayst, and dost command the heavens; behold I offer these Tables unto thee, Command them as it pleaseth thee: and O you Ministers, and true lights of understanding, Governing this earthly frame, and the elements wherein we live, Do for me as for the servant of the Lord: and unto whom it hath pleased the Lord to talk of you.
>
> Behold, Lord, thou hast appointed me 50 times; Thrice 50 times will I lift my hands unto thee. Be it unto me as it pleaseth thee, and thy holy Ministers. I require nothing but thee, and through thee, and thy honour and glory; but I hope I shall be satisfied, and shall not die, (as thou hast promised) until thou gather the clouds together, and judge all things, when in a moment I shall be changed and dwell with thee forever.[134]

The magician may then choose to mimic Enoch by giving that same prayer three times daily during a 50-day operation, treating the final day as, as it were, a day of manifestation, in much the same way the final day of the 19-day Working is.

At the end of his 50 days praying, Enoch "enjoyed the fruit of God his promise, and received the benefit of his faith."[135] By this, and by the end of Enoch's prayer, we can probably take this to mean that "Enoch walked with God: and he was not; for God took him."[136] Apocryphal tradition tells us that Enoch was transformed into the angel Metatron, whom some considered to be so powerful that he was, in essence, "the lesser Yahweh." Whether or not the magician following this process can expect something similar is a matter for debate.

134 Ibid., pp. 196-197.

135 Ibid., p. 197.

136 Genesis 5:24 (KJV).

THE 49TH TABLE

In a later working, the angel Galvah told Dee to write the 49th table, for he only had 48 so far. She transmitted a short piece, beginning with the word "Loagaeth," which may be a title or brief description of the book. These words were to be turned into five tables of 21 letters, a matter that has presented a puzzle to Enochian magicians, as there are more than 105 letters in the words given by Galvah. John DeSalvo has proposed a solution to this by omitting the word "Loagaeth," treating it instead as the title of the leaf.[137]

Dee wondered how many of the tables should be on the front of the page and how many on the back, to which Galvah gave two conflicting answers, initially telling him "as thou seest cause," and then telling him to put three on the front and two on the back. Dee agonised over the manner in which to make these tables, eventually settling on "five little Triangles," which Galvah recognised as being "sufficient."

A simpler method would have been to put three rows of seven, which would have linked up with the division of the Enochian alphabet, but since Dee used the triangle to represent himself, this particular approach obviously had much resonance with him. Since Galvah afford some discretion on this layout, the magician may adopt a different format, while still keeping the same number of tables on each side of the page.

This smaller set of tables is a far cry from what was originally seen by Kelley in his vision of Liber Loagaeth, which resulted in Sloane MS 3189 having a blank 49x49 table at the end.

137 John DeSalvo, *Decoding the Enochian Secrets*, p. 46.

XVIII

BOOK OF INVOCATIONS

This is my own personal Book of Invocations, modelled after Dee's, and written in my own words. I have omitted a few elements of a more personal nature, replacing my personal seal with a simple Hebrew Yod, emblematic of my magical motto.

This text is offered as an *example*, not as something to reproduce wholesale. While the latter will work, to some degree, it is far wiser to make the creative act of writing one's own Book of Invocations, and so forge a deeper, personal connection with the angels of this system.

Additionally, while it is easier nowadays to just print off invocations like this, I think there is something to be said for writing it all by hand. The added effort, and the use of one's personal handwriting, helps with the links to the spirits, and makes for a more aesthetically appealing Book of Invocations, which in turn aids the "magical mindset" necessary for the work.

It should be noted that for this project I employed the original Dee instructions on things like the prefixing of names (which Dee himself seems to have misinterpreted, for he took letters from the cross in the sub-angle, not the Black Cross). However, these can easily be substituted for those wishing to employ this set of invocations in a Golden Dawn context.

Likewise, I have adopted the Reformed Great Table and the appropriate directions, which places ORO in the East, MPH in the South, MOR in the West, and OIP in the North. Those using the Original Great Table will have ORO in the East, MOR in the South, OIP in the West, and MPH in the North. These two attributions are based on a simple clockwise rotation around the Great Table.

Those using the Golden Dawn assignments of the Tablets to the Elements will have another layout entirely: ORO in the East, MPH in the West, OIP in the South, and MOR in the North.

Any changes in system will require changing the text of the invocations, for there are references to the directions in them.

Dee opted to use the various names only once in his invocations, while I felt it was better to repeat them several times. Neither approach is inherently right or wrong on this.

These invocations naturally include significant repetition, as did Dee's originals, but this goes with the territory. Each set of spirits needs to be called in the same manner, and enjoined to fulfil their office by the appropriate divine names. There is only so much this can be shortened.

Note also that I have used the common pronoun "he" in reference to God, but this may be changed if felt appropriate. I do not personally see God as being either male or female (and yet the divine must paradoxically be both, simultaneously separate and combined, and yet still neither), and though language fails us, and will always fail us in capturing the totality of the divine, it may allude to that which is indefinable. In this sense, all mystical texts are allusion.

INVOCATION OF GOD

EAST

ORO, IBAH, AOZPI

Face East

O Lord God Almighty, Lord of Hosts, Tetragrammaton Tzabaoth, you who are called IAIDA, I, [*name*], being a servant of the Highest, call upon your most holy name. I invoke you with both humility and fervour, seeking your divine grace and aid, that I may more truly come to know you, and so in time come into the knowledge of Truth.

Through these, your Three Secret Holy Names, ORO, IBAH, AOZPI, I call upon you to make your divine majesty known in my life, and by those names, and by all names considered most holy unto you, I request the ministry, communication, and confidence of your good angels, who did minister to the prophets of old, and whose names and offices are contained within this book.

Move them, O Lord, and let them appear before me, that they may manifest visibly unto my eyes, audibly unto my ears, and sentiently unto my thoughts. By your holy names, let them come peacefully, with friendly counsel, no matter what their office or rank, or task or duty, knowing me as one who works with you, O Lord God, the Highest.

Let them come when called, and depart when licensed to do so, and inbetween their coming and their going, let them remain with me, visibly, audibly, and sentiently, until my will shall be complete.

O Lord, by your supreme majesty, and by your glorious and most powerful names, ORO, IBAH, AOZPI, let your good angels fulfil my requests, doing so in a timely fashion (within the timeframe asked of them), and with completeness and good will, knowing fully the intent of my summoning, neither evading nor misinterpreting those

requests, and never failing in these their duties. And should one of my requests not fall within the remit of their office, let them guide me to another more fitting, or make move and appear the same, that my will shall ultimately be complete.

O Lord, let only your good angels come before me, and come in truth, neither misleading nor evading me. Lock up the devils, that they may not interfere with my work, and guide me towards true discernment, and protect me from lies and illusion.

In your holy names, ORO, IBAH, AOZPI, I ask this of you. In your holy names, ORO, IBAH, AOZPI, I request your aid. In your holy names, ORO, IBAH, AOZPI, I call upon your ministers.

Through you,
O Lord God the Father,
Jesus Christ the Son,
and the Holy Spirit,
Amen.

י

INVOCATION OF GOD

SOUTH

MPH, ARSL, GAIOL

Face South

O Lord God Almighty, Lord of Hosts, Tetragrammaton Tzabaoth, you who are called IAIDA, I, [*name*], being a servant of the Highest, call upon your most holy name. I invoke you with both humility and fervour, seeking your divine grace and aid, that I may more truly come to know you, and so in time come into the knowledge of Truth.

Through these, your Three Secret Holy Names, MPH, ARSL, GAIOL, I call upon you to make your divine majesty known in my life, and by those names, and by all names considered most holy unto you, I request the ministry, communication, and confidence of your good angels, who did minister to the prophets of old, and whose names and offices are contained within this book.

Move them, O Lord, and let them appear before me, that they may manifest visibly unto my eyes, audibly unto my ears, and sentiently unto my thoughts. By your holy names, let them come peacefully, with friendly counsel, no matter what their office or rank, or task or duty, knowing me as one who works with you, O Lord God, the Highest.

Let them come when called, and depart when licensed to do so, and inbetween their coming and their going, let them remain with me, visibly, audibly, and sentiently, until my will shall be complete.

O Lord, by your supreme majesty, and by your glorious and most powerful names, MPH, ARSL, GAIOL, let your good angels fulfil my requests, doing so in a timely fashion (within the timeframe asked of them), and with completeness and good will, knowing fully the intent of my summoning, neither evading nor misinterpreting those

requests, and never failing in these their duties. And should one of my requests not fall within the remit of their office, let them guide me to another more fitting, or make move and appear the same, that my will shall ultimately be complete.

O Lord, let only your good angels come before me, and come in truth, neither misleading nor evading me. Lock up the devils, that they may not interfere with my work, and guide me towards true discernment, and protect me from lies and illusion.

In your holy names, MPH, ARSL, GAIOL, I ask this of you. In your holy names, MPH, ARSL, GAIOL, I request your aid. In your holy names, MPH, ARSL, GAIOL, I call upon your ministers.

Through you,
O Lord God the Father,
Jesus Christ the Son,
and the Holy Spirit,
Amen.

י

INVOCATION OF GOD

WEST

OIP, TEAA, PDOCE

Face West

O Lord God Almighty, Lord of Hosts, Tetragrammaton Tzabaoth, you who are called IAIDA, I, [*name*], being a servant of the Highest, call upon your most holy name. I invoke you with both humility and fervour, seeking your divine grace and aid, that I may more truly come to know you, and so in time come into the knowledge of Truth.

Through these, your Three Secret Holy Names, OIP, TEAA, PDOCE, I call upon you to make your divine majesty known in my life, and by those names, and by all names considered most holy unto you, I request the ministry, communication, and confidence of your good angels, who did minister to the prophets of old, and whose names and offices are contained within this book.

Move them, O Lord, and let them appear before me, that they may manifest visibly unto my eyes, audibly unto my ears, and sentiently unto my thoughts. By your holy names, let them come peacefully, with friendly counsel, no matter what their office or rank, or task or duty, knowing me as one who works with you, O Lord God, the Highest.

Let them come when called, and depart when licensed to do so, and inbetween their coming and their going, let them remain with me, visibly, audibly, and sentiently, until my will shall be complete.

O Lord, by your supreme majesty, and by your glorious and most powerful names, OIP, TEAA, PDOCE, let your good angels fulfil my requests, doing so in a timely fashion (within the timeframe asked of them), and with completeness and good will, knowing fully the intent of my summoning, neither evading nor misinterpreting those

requests, and never failing in these their duties. And should one of my requests not fall within the remit of their office, let them guide me to another more fitting, or make move and appear the same, that my will shall ultimately be complete.

O Lord, let only your good angels come before me, and come in truth, neither misleading nor evading me. Lock up the devils, that they may not interfere with my work, and guide me towards true discernment, and protect me from lies and illusion.

In your holy names, OIP, TEAA, PDOCE, I ask this of you. In your holy names, OIP, TEAA, PDOCE, I request your aid. In your holy names, OIP, TEAA, PDOCE, I call upon your ministers.

Through you,
O Lord God the Father,
Jesus Christ the Son,
and the Holy Spirit,
Amen.

י

INVOCATION OF GOD

NORTH

MOR, DIAL, HCTGA

Face North

O Lord God Almighty, Lord of Hosts, Tetragrammaton Tzabaoth, you who are called IAIDA, I, [*name*], being a servant of the Highest, call upon your most holy name. I invoke you with both humility and fervour, seeking your divine grace and aid, that I may more truly come to know you, and so in time come into the knowledge of Truth.

Through these, your Three Secret Holy Names, MOR, DIAL, HCTGA, I call upon you to make your divine majesty known in my life, and by those names, and by all names considered most holy unto you, I request the ministry, communication, and confidence of your good angels, who did minister to the prophets of old, and whose names and offices are contained within this book.

Move them, O Lord, and let them appear before me, that they may manifest visibly unto my eyes, audibly unto my ears, and sentiently unto my thoughts. By your holy names, let them come peacefully, with friendly counsel, no matter what their office or rank, or task or duty, knowing me as one who works with you, O Lord God, the Highest.

Let them come when called, and depart when licensed to do so, and inbetween their coming and their going, let them remain with me, visibly, audibly, and sentiently, until my will shall be complete.

O Lord, by your supreme majesty, and by your glorious and most powerful names, MOR, DIAL, HCTGA, let your good angels fulfil my requests, doing so in a timely fashion (within the timeframe asked of them), and with completeness and good will, knowing fully the intent of my summoning, neither evading nor misinterpreting those requests, and never failing in these their duties. And should one of my requests not fall within the remit of their office, let them guide me to another more fitting, or make move and appear the same, that my will shall ultimately be complete.

O Lord, let only your good angels come before me, and come in truth, neither misleading nor evading me. Lock up the devils, that they may not interfere with my work, and guide me towards true discernment, and protect me from lies and illusion.

In your holy names, MOR, DIAL, HCTGA, I ask this of you. In your holy names, MOR, DIAL, HCTGA, I request your aid. In your holy names, MOR, DIAL, HCTGA, I call upon your ministers.

Through you,
O Lord God the Father,
Jesus Christ the Son,
and the Holy Spirit,
Amen.

י

INVOCATION OF THE KINGS

SEVERE

BATAIVA, RAAGIOS, EDLPRNA, ICZHIHA

Face East

In the name of the Lord God Almighty, Lord of Hosts, Tetragrammaton Tzabaoth, he who is called IAIDA, I, [*name*], being a servant of the Highest, call upon you, great and severe Kings of the Watchtowers, you whom the good angels follow, and who act by your royal authority and decree, which is granted unto you by God alone, in whose names I call you now.

By the names ORO, IBAH, AOZPI, I call to you, BATAIVA, great and severe King of the East. Move and appear, and hearken to my call.

Face South

By the names MPH, ARSL, GAIOL, I call to you, RAAGIOS, great and severe King of the South. Move and appear, and hearken to my call.

Face West

By the names OIP, TEAA, PDOCE, I call to you, EDLPRNA, great and severe King of the West. Move and appear, and hearken to my call.

Face North

By the names MOR, DIAL, HCTGA, I call to you, ICZHIHA, great and severe King of the North. Move and appear, and hearken to my call.

Face East again

By these holy names by which the Lord God is known, I beseech your aid, BATAIVA, RAAGIOS, EDLPRNA, and ICZHIHA. Move and appear unto me, at any time I request, in any manner I deem fit. Manifest visibly unto my eyes, audibly unto my ears, and sentiently unto my thoughts. Come peacefully, with friendly counsel, no matter your office or rank, or task or duty, knowing me as one who works with him, the Lord God, the Highest.

Come when you are called, and depart when licensed to do so, and inbetween your coming and your going, remain with me, visibly, audibly, and sentiently, until my will shall be complete.

Come together or separately, in any combination I request, and by your royal authority and decree, move those who work under you to come and fulfil their offices and duties in the same manner, as if they had come to serve their king.

O great and severe kings, BATAIVA, RAAGIOS, EDLPRNA, and ICZHIHA, by the divine names ORO, IBAH, AOZPI, MPH, ARSL, GAIOL, OIP, TEAA, PDOCE, MOR, DIAL HCTGA, I beseech you to fulfil my requests, and to do so in a timely fashion (within the timeframe asked of you), and with completeness and good will, knowing fully the intent of my summoning, neither evading nor misinterpreting those requests, and never failing in these your duties. And should one of my requests not fall within the remit of your office, guide me to another more fitting, or make move and appear the same, that my will shall ultimately be complete.

Allow me, O great and severe Kings, into your kingly court, that I may have your good counsel, severe though it may be. Guide me in all things where severity is needed, where judgement is called for, and unite with your merciful form to help me balance my own nature, that I go to neither extreme.

In the holy names, ORO, IBAH, AOZPI, MPH, ARSL, GAIOL, OIP, TEAA, PDOCE, MOR, DIAL HCTGA, I ask this of you. In the holy names, ORO, IBAH, AOZPI, MPH, ARSL, GAIOL, OIP, TEAA, PDOCE, MOR, DIAL HCTGA, I request your aid. In the holy names, ORO, IBAH, AOZPI, MPH, ARSL, GAIOL, OIP, TEAA, PDOCE, MOR, DIAL HCTGA, I call upon you, O great and severe Kings of the Watchtowers.

Through him,
O Lord God the Father,
Jesus Christ the Son,
and the Holy Spirit,
Amen.

י

INVOCATION OF THE KINGS

MERCIFUL

BATAIVH, RAAGIOL, EDLPRNA, ICZHIHL

Face East

In the name of the Lord God Almighty, Lord of Hosts, Tetragrammaton Tzabaoth, he who is called IAIDA, I, [*name*], being a servant of the Highest, call upon you, great and merciful Kings of the Watchtowers, you whom the good angels follow, and who act by your royal authority and decree, which is granted unto you by God alone, in whose names I call you now.

By the names ORO, IBAH, AOZPI, I call to you, BATAIVH, great and merciful king of the East. Move and appear, and hearken to my call.

Face South

By the names MPH, ARSL, GAIOL, I call to you, RAAGIOL, great and merciful king of the South. Move and appear, and hearken to my call.

Face West

By the names OIP, TEAA, PDOCE, I call to you, EDLPRNA, great and merciful king of the West. Move and appear, and hearken to my call.

Face North

By the names MOR, DIAL, HCTGA, I call to you, ICZHIHL, great and merciful king of the North. Move and appear, and hearken to my call.

Face East again

By these holy names by which the Lord God is known, I beseech your aid, BATAIVH, RAAGIOL, EDLPRNA, and ICZHIHL. Move and appear unto me, at any time I request, in any manner I deem fit. Manifest visibly unto my eyes, audibly unto my ears, and sentiently unto my thoughts. Come peacefully, with friendly counsel, no matter your office or rank, or task or duty, knowing me as one who works with him, the Lord God, the Highest.

Come when you are called, and depart when licensed to do so, and inbetween your coming and your going, remain with me, visibly, audibly, and sentiently, until my will shall be complete.

Come together or separately, in any combination I request, now and forever. And by your royal authority and decree, move those who work under you to come and fulfil their offices and duties in the same manner, as if they had come to serve their king.

O great and merciful Kings, BATAIVH, RAAGIOL, EDLPRNA, and ICZHIHL, by the divine names ORO, IBAH, AOZPI, MPH, ARSL, GAIOL, OIP, TEAA, PDOCE, MOR, DIAL HCTGA, I beseech you to fulfil my requests, and to do so in a timely fashion (within the timeframe asked of you), and with completeness and good will, knowing fully the intent of my summoning, neither evading nor misinterpreting those requests, and never failing in these your duties. And should one of my requests not fall within the remit of your office, guide me to another more fitting, or make move and appear the same, that my will shall ultimately be complete.

Allow me, O great and merciful Kings, into your kingly court, that I may have your good counsel, merciful though it may be. Guide me in all things where mercy is needed, where forgiveness is called for, and unite with your severe form to help me balance my own nature, that I go to neither extreme.

In the holy names, ORO, IBAH, AOZPI, MPH, ARSL, GAIOL, OIP, TEAA, PDOCE, MOR, DIAL HCTGA, I ask this of you. In the holy names, ORO, IBAH, AOZPI, MPH, ARSL, GAIOL, OIP, TEAA, PDOCE, MOR, DIAL HCTGA, I request your aid. In the holy names, ORO, IBAH, AOZPI, MPH, ARSL, GAIOL, OIP, TEAA, PDOCE, MOR, DIAL HCTGA, I call upon you, O great and merciful Kings of the Watchtowers.

Through him,
O Lord God the Father,
Jesus Christ the Son,
and the Holy Spirit,
Amen.

ו

INVOCATION OF THE SENIORS

EAST

HABIORO, AAOZAIF, HTMORDA, AHAOZPI, HIPOTGA, AVTOTAR

Face East

In the name of the Lord God Almighty, Lord of Hosts, Tetragrammaton Tzabaoth, he who is called IAIDA, I, [*name*], being a servant of the Highest, call upon you, Seniors of the East, you who have especial jurisdiction in the knowledge and judgement of human affairs, an office granted unto you by God alone, in whose names I call you now.

By the divine names ORO, IBAH, AOZPI, and by the names of your King, BATAIVA and BATAIVH, I call to you, HABIORO, AAOZAIF, HTMORDA, AHAOZPI, HIPOTGA, and AVTOTAR, Seniors of the East. Move and appear, and hearken to my call.

By these holy names by which the Lord God is known, I beseech your aid. Move and appear unto me, at any time I request, in any manner I deem fit. Manifest visibly unto my eyes, audibly unto my ears, and sentiently unto my thoughts. Come peacefully, with friendly counsel, no matter your office or rank, or task or duty, knowing me as one who works with him, the Lord God, the Highest.

Come when you are called, and depart when licensed to do so, and inbetween your coming and your going, remain with me, visibly, audibly, and sentiently, until my will shall be complete.

Come together or separately, in any combination I request, now and forever. And by your wisdom and knowledge, make me a partaker thereof, according to the nature of your parts, that I may gradually come to know more of God, myself, and the universe at large.

O Seniors of the East, HABIORO, AAOZAIF, HTMORDA,

AHAOZPI, HIPOTGA, and AVTOTAR, by the divine names ORO, IBAH, AOZPI, I beseech you to fulfil my requests, and to do so in a timely fashion (within the timeframe asked of you), and with completeness and good will, knowing fully the intent of my summoning, neither evading nor misinterpreting those requests, and never failing in these your duties. And should one of my requests not fall within the remit of your office, guide me to another more fitting, or make move and appear the same, that my will shall ultimately be complete.

Allow me, O Seniors of the East, into your estate, and offer me your wise counsel, that I may be made the wiser for it. Grant me your ear, and I shall grant you mine, and together we shall learn of things unknown.

In the holy names, ORO, IBAH, AOZPI, I ask this of you. In the holy names, ORO, IBAH, AOZPI, I request your aid. In the holy names, ORO, IBAH, AOZPI, I call upon you, O Seniors of the East.

Through him,
O Lord God the Father,
Jesus Christ the Son,
and the Holy Spirit,
Amen.

י

INVOCATION OF THE SENIORS

SOUTH

LSRAHPM, SAIINOU, LAOAXRP, SLGAIOL, LIGDISA, SONIZNT

Face South

In the name of the Lord God Almighty, Lord of Hosts, Tetragrammaton Tzabaoth, he who is called IAIDA, I, [*name*], being a servant of the Highest, call upon you, Seniors of the South, you who have especial jurisdiction in the knowledge and judgement of human affairs, an office granted unto you by God alone, in whose names I call you now.

By the divine names MPH, ARSL, GAIOL, and by the names of your King, RAAGIOS and RAAGIOL, I call to you, LSRAHPM, SAIINOU, LAOAXRP, SLGAIOL, LIGDISA, and SONIZNT, Seniors of the South. Move and appear, and hearken to my call.

By these holy names by which the Lord God is known, I beseech your aid. Move and appear unto me, at any time I request, in any manner I deem fit. Manifest visibly unto my eyes, audibly unto my ears, and sentiently unto my thoughts. Come peacefully, with friendly counsel, no matter your office or rank, or task or duty, knowing me as one who works with him, the Lord God, the Highest.

Come when you are called, and depart when licensed to do so, and inbetween your coming and your going, remain with me, visibly, audibly, and sentiently, until my will shall be complete.

Come together or separately, in any combination I request, now and forever. And by your wisdom and knowledge, make me a partaker thereof, according to the nature of your parts, that I may gradually come to know more of God, myself, and the universe at large.

O Seniors of the South, LSRAHPM, SAIINOU, LAOAXRP,

SLGAIOL, LIGDISA, and SONIZNT, by the divine names MPH, ARSL, GAIOL, I beseech you to fulfil my requests, and to do so in a timely fashion (within the timeframe asked of you), and with completeness and good will, knowing fully the intent of my summoning, neither evading nor misinterpreting those requests, and never failing in these your duties. And should one of my requests not fall within the remit of your office, guide me to another more fitting, or make move and appear the same, that my will shall ultimately be complete.

Allow me, O Seniors of the South, into your estate, and offer me your wise counsel, that I may be made the wiser for it. Grant me your ear, and I shall grant you mine, and together we shall learn of things unknown.

In the holy names, MPH, ARSL, GAIOL, I ask this of you. In the holy names, MPH, ARSL, GAIOL, I request your aid. In the holy names, MPH, ARSL, GAIOL, I call upon you, O Seniors of the South.

Through him,
O Lord God the Father,
Jesus Christ the Son,
and the Holy Spirit,
Amen.

י

INVOCATION OF THE SENIORS

WEST

LAIDROM, ACZINOR, LZINOPO, ALHCTGA, LIIANSA, AHMLICV

Face West

In the name of the Lord God Almighty, Lord of Hosts, Tetragrammaton Tzabaoth, he who is called IAIDA, I, [*name*], being a servant of the Highest, call upon you, Seniors of the West, you who have especial jurisdiction in the knowledge and judgement of human affairs, an office granted unto you by God alone, in whose names I call you now.

By the divine names OIP, TEAA, PDOCE, and by the names of your King, EDLPRNA and EDLPRNA, I call to you, LAIDROM, ACZINOR, LZINOPO, ALHCTGA, LIIANSA, and AHMLICV, Seniors of the West. Move and appear, and hearken to my call.

By these holy names by which the Lord God is known, I beseech your aid. Move and appear unto me, at any time I request, in any manner I deem fit. Manifest visibly unto my eyes, audibly unto my ears, and sentiently unto my thoughts. Come peacefully, with friendly counsel, no matter your office or rank, or task or duty, knowing me as one who works with him, the Lord God, the Highest.

Come when you are called, and depart when licensed to do so, and inbetween your coming and your going, remain with me, visibly, audibly, and sentiently, until my will shall be complete.

Come together or separately, in any combination I request, now and forever. And by your wisdom and knowledge, make me a partaker thereof, according to the nature of your parts, that I may gradually come to know more of God, myself, and the universe at large.

O Seniors of the West, LAIDROM, ACZINOR, LZINOPO,

ALHCTGA, LIIANSA, and AHMLICV, by the divine names OIP, TEAA, PDOCE, I beseech you to fulfil my requests, and to do so in a timely fashion (within the timeframe asked of you), and with completeness and good will, knowing fully the intent of my summoning, neither evading nor misinterpreting those requests, and never failing in these your duties. And should one of my requests not fall within the remit of your office, guide me to another more fitting, or make move and appear the same, that my will shall ultimately be complete.

Allow me, O Seniors of the West, into your estate, and offer me your wise counsel, that I may be made the wiser for it. Grant me your ear, and I shall grant you mine, and together we shall learn of things unknown.

In the holy names, OIP, TEAA, PDOCE, I ask this of you. In the holy names, OIP, TEAA, PDOCE, I request your aid. In the holy names, OIP, TEAA, PDOCE, I call upon you, O Seniors of the West.

Through him,
O Lord God the Father,
Jesus Christ the Son,
and the Holy Spirit,
Amen.

י

INVOCATION OF THE SENIORS

NORTH

AAETPIO, ADOEOET, ALNDVOD, AAPDOCE, ARINNAP, ANODOIN

Face North

In the name of the Lord God Almighty, Lord of Hosts, Tetragrammaton Tzabaoth, he who is called IAIDA, I, [*name*], being a servant of the Highest, call upon you, Seniors of the North, you who have especial jurisdiction in the knowledge and judgement of human affairs, an office granted unto you by God alone, in whose names I call you now.

By the divine names MOR, DIAL, HCTGA, and by the names of your King, ICZHIHA and ICZHIHL, I call to you, AAETPIO, ADOEOET, ALNDVOD, AAPDOCE, ARINNAP, and ANODOIN, Seniors of the North. Move and appear, and hearken to my call.

By these holy names by which the Lord God is known, I beseech your aid. Move and appear unto me, at any time I request, in any manner I deem fit. Manifest visibly unto my eyes, audibly unto my ears, and sentiently unto my thoughts. Come peacefully, with friendly counsel, no matter your office or rank, or task or duty, knowing me as one who works with him, the Lord God, the Highest.

Come when you are called, and depart when licensed to do so, and inbetween your coming and your going, remain with me, visibly, audibly, and sentiently, until my will shall be complete.

Come together or separately, in any combination I request, now and forever. And by your wisdom and knowledge, make me a partaker thereof, according to the nature of your parts, that I may gradually come to know more of God, myself, and the universe at large.

O Seniors of the North, AAETPIO, ADOEOET, ALNDVOD,

AAPDOCE, ARINNAP, and ANODOIN, by the divine names MOR, DIAL, HCTGA, I beseech you to fulfil my requests, and to do so in a timely fashion (within the timeframe asked of you), and with completeness and good will, knowing fully the intent of my summoning, neither evading nor misinterpreting those requests, and never failing in these your duties. And should one of my requests not fall within the remit of your office, guide me to another more fitting, or make move and appear the same, that my will shall ultimately be complete.

Allow me, O Seniors of the North, into your estate, and offer me your wise counsel, that I may be made the wiser for it. Grant me your ear, and I shall grant you mine, and together we shall learn of things unknown.

In the holy names, MOR, DIAL, HCTGA, I ask this of you. In the holy names, MOR, DIAL, HCTGA, I request your aid. In the holy names, MOR, DIAL, HCTGA, I call upon you, O Seniors of the North.

Through him,
O Lord God the Father,
Jesus Christ the Son,
and the Holy Spirit,
Amen.

י

GOOD ANGELS ABOVE CROSS

NATURAL SUBSTANCES – EAST

RZLA, ZLAR, LARZ, ARZL

Face East

In the name of the Lord God Almighty, Lord of Hosts, Tetragrammaton Tzabaoth, he who is called IAIDA, I, [*name*], being a servant of the Highest, call upon you, good angels of the East, you who have especial jurisdiction in the mixing together of natural substances, an office granted unto you by God alone, in whose names I call you now.

By the divine name IDOIGO, I call you forth, and by the divine name ARDZA, I command you, O good angels of the East in charge of natural substances, RZLA, ZLAR, LARZ, and ARZL, and even you in your greater forms, ERZLA, EZLAR, ELARZ, and EARZL. Move and appear, and hearken to my call.

By these holy names by which the Lord God is known, I beseech your aid, RZLA, ZLAR, LARZ, and ARZL. Move and appear unto me, at any time I request, in any manner I deem fit. Manifest visibly unto my eyes, audibly unto my ears, and sentiently unto my thoughts. Come peacefully, with friendly counsel, no matter your office or rank, or task or duty, knowing me as one who works with him, the Lord God, the Highest.

Come when you are called, and depart when licensed to do so, and inbetween your coming and your going, remain with me, visibly, audibly, and sentiently, until my will shall be complete.

Come together or separately, in any combination I request, whether prefixed or unprefixed, now and forever. Grant me the knowledge of natural substances, and the mixing thereof, and reveal unto me the secrets of nature, that I might come to a perfect

knowledge of the world.

O good angels of the East, RZLA, ZLAR, LARZ, and ARZL, by the divine names IDOIGO and ARDZA, I call and command you to fulfil my requests, and to do so in a timely fashion (within the timeframe asked of you), and with completeness and good will, knowing fully the intent of my summoning, neither evading nor misinterpreting those requests, and never failing in these your duties. And should one of my requests not fall within the remit of your office, guide me to another more fitting, or make move and appear the same, that my will shall ultimately be complete.

In the divine name IDOIGO, I call you forth, and by the divine name ARDZA do I command you, O good angels of the East.

Through him,
O Lord God the Father,
Jesus Christ the Son,
and the Holy Spirit,
Amen.

י

GOOD ANGELS ABOVE CROSS

NATURAL SUBSTANCES – SOUTH

TAAD, AADT, ADTA, DTAA

Face South

In the name of the Lord God Almighty, Lord of Hosts, Tetragrammaton Tzabaoth, he who is called IAIDA, I, [*name*], being a servant of the Highest, call upon you, good angels of the South, you who have especial jurisdiction in the mixing together of natural substances, an office granted unto you by God alone, in whose names I call you now.

By the divine name OBGOTA, I call you forth, and by the divine name AABCO, I command you, O good angels of the South in charge of natural substances, TAAD, AADT, ADTA, and DTAA, and even you in your greater forms, ETAAD, EAADT, EADTA, and EDTAA. Move and appear, and hearken to my call.

By these holy names by which the Lord God is known, I beseech your aid, TAAD, AADT, ADTA, and DTAA. Move and appear unto me, at any time I request, in any manner I deem fit. Manifest visibly unto my eyes, audibly unto my ears, and sentiently unto my thoughts. Come peacefully, with friendly counsel, no matter your office or rank, or task or duty, knowing me as one who works with him, the Lord God, the Highest.

Come when you are called, and depart when licensed to do so, and inbetween your coming and your going, remain with me, visibly, audibly, and sentiently, until my will shall be complete.

Come together or separately, in any combination I request, whether prefixed or unprefixed, now and forever. Grant me the knowledge of natural substances, and the mixing thereof, and reveal unto me the secrets of nature, that I might come to a perfect

knowledge of the world.

O good angels of the South, TAAD, AADT, ADTA, and DTAA, by the divine names OBGOTA and AABCO, I call and command you to fulfil my requests, and to do so in a timely fashion (within the timeframe asked of you), and with completeness and good will, knowing fully the intent of my summoning, neither evading nor misinterpreting those requests, and never failing in these your duties. And should one of my requests not fall within the remit of your office, guide me to another more fitting, or make move and appear the same, that my will shall ultimately be complete.

In the divine name OBGOTA, I call you forth, and by the divine name AABCO do I command you, O good angels of the South.

Through him,
O Lord God the Father,
Jesus Christ the Son,
and the Holy Spirit,
Amen.

י

GOOD ANGELS ABOVE CROSS

NATURAL SUBSTANCES – WEST

DOPA, OPAD, PADO, ADOP

Face West

In the name of the Lord God Almighty, Lord of Hosts, Tetragrammaton Tzabaoth, he who is called IAIDA, I, [*name*], being a servant of the Highest, call upon you, good angels of the West, you who have especial jurisdiction in the mixing together of natural substances, an office granted unto you by God alone, in whose names I call you now.

By the divine name NOALMR, I call you forth, and by the divine name OLOAG, I command you, O good angels of the West in charge of natural substances, DOPA, OPAD, PADO, and ADOP, and even you in your greater forms, ADOPA, AOPAD, APADO, and AADOP. Move and appear, and hearken to my call.

By these holy names by which the Lord God is known, I beseech your aid, DOPA, OPAD, PADO, and ADOP. Move and appear unto me, at any time I request, in any manner I deem fit. Manifest visibly unto my eyes, audibly unto my ears, and sentiently unto my thoughts. Come peacefully, with friendly counsel, no matter your office or rank, or task or duty, knowing me as one who works with him, the Lord God, the Highest.

Come when you are called, and depart when licensed to do so, and inbetween your coming and your going, remain with me, visibly, audibly, and sentiently, until my will shall be complete.

Come together or separately, in any combination I request, whether prefixed or unprefixed, now and forever. Grant me the knowledge of natural substances, and the mixing thereof, and reveal unto me the secrets of nature, that I might come to a perfect

knowledge of the world.

O good angels of the West, DOPA, OPAD, PADO, and ADOP, by the divine names NOALMR and OLOAG, I call and command you to fulfil my requests, and to do so in a timely fashion (within the timeframe asked of you), and with completeness and good will, knowing fully the intent of my summoning, neither evading nor misinterpreting those requests, and never failing in these your duties. And should one of my requests not fall within the remit of your office, guide me to another more fitting, or make move and appear the same, that my will shall ultimately be complete.

In the divine name NOALMR, I call you forth, and by the divine name OLOAG do I command you, O good angels of the West.

Through him,
O Lord God the Father,
Jesus Christ the Son,
and the Holy Spirit,
Amen.

י

GOOD ANGELS ABOVE CROSS

NATURAL SUBSTANCES – NORTH

BOZA, OZAB, ZABO, ABOZ

Face North

In the name of the Lord God Almighty, Lord of Hosts, Tetragrammaton Tzabaoth, he who is called IAIDA, I, [*name*], being a servant of the Highest, call upon you, good angels of the North, you who have especial jurisdiction in the mixing together of natural substances, an office granted unto you by God alone, in whose names I call you now.

By the divine name ANGPOI, I call you forth, and by the divine name UNNAX, I command you, O good angels of the North in charge of natural substances, BOZA, OZAB, ZABO, and ABOZ, and even you in your greater forms, ABOZA, AOZAB, AZABO, and AABOZ. Move and appear, and hearken to my call.

By these holy names by which the Lord God is known, I beseech your aid, BOZA, OZAB, ZABO, and ABOZ. Move and appear unto me, at any time I request, in any manner I deem fit. Manifest visibly unto my eyes, audibly unto my ears, and sentiently unto my thoughts. Come peacefully, with friendly counsel, no matter your office or rank, or task or duty, knowing me as one who works with him, the Lord God, the Highest.

Come when you are called, and depart when licensed to do so, and inbetween your coming and your going, remain with me, visibly, audibly, and sentiently, until my will shall be complete.

Come together or separately, in any combination I request, whether prefixed or unprefixed, now and forever. Grant me the knowledge of natural substances, and the mixing thereof, and reveal unto me the secrets of nature, that I might come to a perfect

knowledge of the world.

O good angels of the North, BOZA, OZAB, ZABO, and ABOZ, by the divine names ANGPOI and UNNAX, I call and command you to fulfil my requests, and to do so in a timely fashion (within the timeframe asked of you), and with completeness and good will, knowing fully the intent of my summoning, neither evading nor misinterpreting those requests, and never failing in these your duties. And should one of my requests not fall within the remit of your office, guide me to another more fitting, or make move and appear the same, that my will shall ultimately be complete.

In the divine name ANGPOI, I call you forth, and by the divine name UNNAX do I command you, O good angels of the North.

Through him,
O Lord God the Father,
Jesus Christ the Son,
and the Holy Spirit,
Amen.

י

GOOD ANGELS ABOVE CROSS

TRANSPORTATION – EAST

YTPA, TPAY, PAYT, AYTP

Face East

In the name of the Lord God Almighty, Lord of Hosts, Tetragrammaton Tzabaoth, he who is called IAIDA, I, [*name*], being a servant of the Highest, call upon you, good angels of the East, you who have especial jurisdiction in transporting from place to place, an office granted unto you by God alone, in whose names I call you now.

By the divine name LLACZA, I call you forth, and by the divine name PALAM, I command you, O good angels of the East in charge of transportation, YTPA, TPAY, PAYT, and AYTP, and even you in your greater forms, EYTPA, ETPAY, EPAYT, and EAYTP. Move and appear, and hearken to my call.

By these holy names by which the Lord God is known, I beseech your aid, YTPA, TPAY, PAYT, and AYTP. Move and appear unto me, at any time I request, in any manner I deem fit. Manifest visibly unto my eyes, audibly unto my ears, and sentiently unto my thoughts. Come peacefully, with friendly counsel, no matter your office or rank, or task or duty, knowing me as one who works with him, the Lord God, the Highest.

Come when you are called, and depart when licensed to do so, and inbetween your coming and your going, remain with me, visibly, audibly, and sentiently, until my will shall be complete.

Come together or separately, in any combination I request, whether prefixed or unprefixed, now and forever. Grant me the knowledge of transportation, in all its forms and modes, and reveal unto me the secrets of movement, that I may at length come to know the divine motion in all things.

O good angels of the East, YTPA, TPAY, PAYT, and AYTP, by the divine names LLACZA and PALAM, I call and command you to fulfil my requests, and to do so in a timely fashion (within the timeframe asked of you), and with completeness and good will, knowing fully the intent of my summoning, neither evading nor misinterpreting those requests, and never failing in these your duties. And should one of my requests not fall within the remit of your office, guide me to another more fitting, or make move and appear the same, that my will shall ultimately be complete.

In the divine name LLACZA, I call you forth, and by the divine name PALAM do I command you, O good angels of the East.

Through him,
O Lord God the Father,
Jesus Christ the Son,
and the Holy Spirit,
Amen.

י

GOOD ANGELS ABOVE CROSS

TRANSPORTATION - SOUTH

TDIM, DIMT, IMTD, MTDI

Face South

In the name of the Lord God Almighty, Lord of Hosts, Tetragrammaton Tzabaoth, he who is called IAIDA, I, [*name*], being a servant of the Highest, call upon you, good angels of the South, you who have especial jurisdiction in transporting from place to place, an office granted unto you by God alone, in whose names I call you now.

By the divine name NELAPR, I call you forth, and by the divine name OMEBB, I command you, O good angels of the South in charge of transportation, TDIM, DIMT, IMTD, and MTDI, and even you in your greater forms, ETDIM, EDIMT, EIMTD, and EMTDI. Move and appear, and hearken to my call.

By these holy names by which the Lord God is known, I beseech your aid, TDIM, DIMT, IMTD, and MTDI. Move and appear unto me, at any time I request, in any manner I deem fit. Manifest visibly unto my eyes, audibly unto my ears, and sentiently unto my thoughts. Come peacefully, with friendly counsel, no matter your office or rank, or task or duty, knowing me as one who works with him, the Lord God, the Highest.

Come when you are called, and depart when licensed to do so, and inbetween your coming and your going, remain with me, visibly, audibly, and sentiently, until my will shall be complete.

Come together or separately, in any combination I request, whether prefixed or unprefixed, now and forever. Grant me the knowledge of transportation, in all its forms and modes, and reveal unto me the secrets of movement, that I may at length come to know the divine motion in all things.

O good angels of the South, TDIM, DIMT, IMTD, and MTDI, by the divine names NELAPR and OMEBB, I call and command you to fulfil my requests, and to do so in a timely fashion (within the timeframe asked of you), and with completeness and good will, knowing fully the intent of my summoning, neither evading nor misinterpreting those requests, and never failing in these your duties. And should one of my requests not fall within the remit of your office, guide me to another more fitting, or make move and appear the same, that my will shall ultimately be complete.

In the divine name NELAPR, I call you forth, and by the divine name OMEBB do I command you, O good angels of the South.

Through him,
O Lord God the Father,
Jesus Christ the Son,
and the Holy Spirit,
Amen.

י

GOOD ANGELS ABOVE CROSS

TRANSPORTATION – WEST

ANAA, NAAA, AAAN, AANA

Face West

In the name of the Lord God Almighty, Lord of Hosts, Tetragrammaton Tzabaoth, he who is called IAIDA, I, [*name*], being a servant of the Highest, call upon you, good angels of the West, you who have especial jurisdiction in transporting from place to place, an office granted unto you by God alone, in whose names I call you now.

By the divine name VADALI, I call you forth, and by the divine name OBAUA, I command you, O good angels of the West in charge of transportation, ANAA, NAAA, AAAN, and AANA, and even you in your greater forms, AANAA, ANAAA, AAAAN, and AAANA. Move and appear, and hearken to my call.

By these holy names by which the Lord God is known, I beseech your aid, ANAA, NAAA, AAAN, and AANA. Move and appear unto me, at any time I request, in any manner I deem fit. Manifest visibly unto my eyes, audibly unto my ears, and sentiently unto my thoughts. Come peacefully, with friendly counsel, no matter your office or rank, or task or duty, knowing me as one who works with him, the Lord God, the Highest.

Come when you are called, and depart when licensed to do so, and inbetween your coming and your going, remain with me, visibly, audibly, and sentiently, until my will shall be complete.

Come together or separately, in any combination I request, whether prefixed or unprefixed, now and forever. Grant me the knowledge of transportation, in all its forms and modes, and reveal unto me the secrets of movement, that I may at length come to know the divine motion in all things.

O good angels of the West, ANAA, NAAA, AAAN, and AANA, by the divine names VADALI and OBAUA, I call and command you to fulfil my requests, and to do so in a timely fashion (within the timeframe asked of you), and with completeness and good will, knowing fully the intent of my summoning, neither evading nor misinterpreting those requests, and never failing in these your duties. And should one of my requests not fall within the remit of your office, guide me to another more fitting, or make move and appear the same, that my will shall ultimately be complete.

In the divine name VADALI, I call you forth, and by the divine name OBAUA do I command you, O good angels of the West.

Through him,
O Lord God the Father,
Jesus Christ the Son,
and the Holy Spirit,
Amen.

י

GOOD ANGELS ABOVE CROSS

TRANSPORTATION – NORTH

PHRA, HRAP, RAPH, APHR

Face North

In the name of the Lord God Almighty, Lord of Hosts, Tetragrammaton Tzabaoth, he who is called IAIDA, I, [*name*], being a servant of the Highest, call upon you, good angels of the North, you who have especial jurisdiction in transporting from place to place, an office granted unto you by God alone, in whose names I call you now.

By the divine name ANAEEM, I call you forth, and by the divine name SONDN, I command you, O good angels of the North in charge of transportation, PHRA, HRAP, RAPH, and APHR, and even you in your greater forms, APHRA, AHRAP, ARAPH, and AAPHR. Move and appear, and hearken to my call.

By these holy names by which the Lord God is known, I beseech your aid, PHRA, HRAP, RAPH, and APHR. Move and appear unto me, at any time I request, in any manner I deem fit. Manifest visibly unto my eyes, audibly unto my ears, and sentiently unto my thoughts. Come peacefully, with friendly counsel, no matter your office or rank, or task or duty, knowing me as one who works with him, the Lord God, the Highest.

Come when you are called, and depart when licensed to do so, and inbetween your coming and your going, remain with me, visibly, audibly, and sentiently, until my will shall be complete.

Come together or separately, in any combination I request, whether prefixed or unprefixed, now and forever. Grant me the knowledge of transportation, in all its forms and modes, and reveal unto me the secrets of movement, that I may at length come to know the divine motion in all things.

O good angels of the North, PHRA, HRAP, RAPH, and APHR, by the divine names ANAEEM and SONDN, I call and command you to fulfil my requests, and to do so in a timely fashion (within the timeframe asked of you), and with completeness and good will, knowing fully the intent of my summoning, neither evading nor misinterpreting those requests, and never failing in these your duties. And should one of my requests not fall within the remit of your office, guide me to another more fitting, or make move and appear the same, that my will shall ultimately be complete.

In the divine name ANAEEM, I call you forth, and by the divine name SONDN do I command you, O good angels of the North.

Through him,
O Lord God the Father,
Jesus Christ the Son,
and the Holy Spirit,
Amen.

י

GOOD ANGELS ABOVE CROSS

MECHANICAL ARTS – EAST

TNBR, NBRT, BRTN, RTNB

Face East

In the name of the Lord God Almighty, Lord of Hosts, Tetragrammaton Tzabaoth, he who is called IAIDA, I, [*name*], being a servant of the Highest, call upon you, good angels of the East, you who have especial jurisdiction in mechanical arts, an office granted unto you by God alone, in whose names I call you now.

By the divine name AIAOAI, I call you forth, and by the divine name OIIIT, I command you, O good angels of the East in charge of mechanical arts, TNBR, NBRT, BRTN, and RTNB, and even you in your greater forms, HTNBR, HNBRT, HBRTN, and HRTNB. Move and appear, and hearken to my call.

By these holy names by which the Lord God is known, I beseech your aid, TNBR, NBRT, BRTN, and RTNB. Move and appear unto me, at any time I request, in any manner I deem fit. Manifest visibly unto my eyes, audibly unto my ears, and sentiently unto my thoughts. Come peacefully, with friendly counsel, no matter your office or rank, or task or duty, knowing me as one who works with him, the Lord God, the Highest.

Come when you are called, and depart when licensed to do so, and inbetween your coming and your going, remain with me, visibly, audibly, and sentiently, until my will shall be complete.

Come together or separately, in any combination I request, whether prefixed or unprefixed, now and forever. Grant me the knowledge of mechanical things, in all their forms, and reveal unto me the secrets of mechanics, tried or untested, that I and the world at large may benefit from this knowledge.

O good angels of the East, TNBR, NBRT, BRTN, and RTNB, by the divine names AIAOAI and OIIIT, I call and command you to fulfil my requests, and to do so in a timely fashion (within the timeframe asked of you), and with completeness and good will, knowing fully the intent of my summoning, neither evading nor misinterpreting those requests, and never failing in these your duties. And should one of my requests not fall within the remit of your office, guide me to another more fitting, or make move and appear the same, that my will shall ultimately be complete.

In the divine name AIAOAI, I call you forth, and by the divine name OIIIT do I command you, O good angels of the East.

Through him,
O Lord God the Father,
Jesus Christ the Son,
and the Holy Spirit,
Amen.

י

GOOD ANGELS ABOVE CROSS

MECHANICAL ARTS – SOUTH

MAGL, AGLM, GLMA, LMAG

Face South

In the name of the Lord God Almighty, Lord of Hosts, Tetragrammaton Tzabaoth, he who is called IAIDA, I, [*name*], being a servant of the Highest, call upon you, good angels of the South, you who have especial jurisdiction in mechanical arts, an office granted unto you by God alone, in whose names I call you now.

By the divine name MALADI, I call you forth, and by the divine name OPAAD, I command you, O good angels of the South in charge of mechanical arts, MAGL, AGLM, GLMA, and LMAG, and even you in your greater forms, HMAGL, HAGLM, HGLMA, and HLMAG. Move and appear, and hearken to my call.

By these holy names by which the Lord God is known, I beseech your aid, MAGL, AGLM, GLMA, and LMAG. Move and appear unto me, at any time I request, in any manner I deem fit. Manifest visibly unto my eyes, audibly unto my ears, and sentiently unto my thoughts. Come peacefully, with friendly counsel, no matter your office or rank, or task or duty, knowing me as one who works with him, the Lord God, the Highest.

Come when you are called, and depart when licensed to do so, and inbetween your coming and your going, remain with me, visibly, audibly, and sentiently, until my will shall be complete.

Come together or separately, in any combination I request, whether prefixed or unprefixed, now and forever. Grant me the knowledge of mechanical things, in all their forms, and reveal unto me the secrets of mechanics, tried or untested, that I and the world at large may benefit from this knowledge.

O good angels of the South, MAGL, AGLM, GLMA, and LMAG, by the divine names MALADI and OPAAD, I call and command you to fulfil my requests, and to do so in a timely fashion (within the timeframe asked of you), and with completeness and good will, knowing fully the intent of my summoning, neither evading nor misinterpreting those requests, and never failing in these your duties. And should one of my requests not fall within the remit of your office, guide me to another more fitting, or make move and appear the same, that my will shall ultimately be complete.

In the divine name MALADI, I call you forth, and by the divine name OPAAD do I command you, O good angels of the South.

Through him,
O Lord God the Father,
Jesus Christ the Son,
and the Holy Spirit,
Amen.

י

GOOD ANGELS ABOVE CROSS

MECHANICAL ARTS – WEST

PSAC, SACP, ACPS, CPSA

Face West

In the name of the Lord God Almighty, Lord of Hosts, Tetragrammaton Tzabaoth, he who is called IAIDA, I, [*name*], being a servant of the Highest, call upon you, good angels of the West, you who have especial jurisdiction in mechanical arts, an office granted unto you by God alone, in whose names I call you now.

By the divine name UOLXDO, I call you forth, and by the divine name SIODA, I command you, O good angels of the West in charge of mechanical arts, PSAC, SACP, ACPS, and CPSA, and even you in your greater forms, PPSAC, PSACP, PACPS, and PCPSA. Move and appear, and hearken to my call.

By these holy names by which the Lord God is known, I beseech your aid, PSAC, SACP, ACPS, and CPSA. Move and appear unto me, at any time I request, in any manner I deem fit. Manifest visibly unto my eyes, audibly unto my ears, and sentiently unto my thoughts. Come peacefully, with friendly counsel, no matter your office or rank, or task or duty, knowing me as one who works with him, the Lord God, the Highest.

Come when you are called, and depart when licensed to do so, and inbetween your coming and your going, remain with me, visibly, audibly, and sentiently, until my will shall be complete.

Come together or separately, in any combination I request, whether prefixed or unprefixed, now and forever. Grant me the knowledge of mechanical things, in all their forms, and reveal unto me the secrets of mechanics, tried or untested, that I and the world at large may benefit from this knowledge.

O good angels of the West, PSAC, SACP, ACPS, and CPSA, by the divine names UOLXDO and SIODA, I call and command you to fulfil my requests, and to do so in a timely fashion (within the timeframe asked of you), and with completeness and good will, knowing fully the intent of my summoning, neither evading nor misinterpreting those requests, and never failing in these your duties. And should one of my requests not fall within the remit of your office, guide me to another more fitting, or make move and appear the same, that my will shall ultimately be complete.

In the divine name UOLXDO, I call you forth, and by the divine name SIODA do I command you, O good angels of the West.

Through him,
O Lord God the Father,
Jesus Christ the Son,
and the Holy Spirit,
Amen.

GOOD ANGELS ABOVE CROSS

MECHANICAL ARTS – NORTH

OCNC, CNCO, NCOC, COCN

Face North

In the name of the Lord God Almighty, Lord of Hosts, Tetragrammaton Tzabaoth, he who is called IAIDA, I, [*name*], being a servant of the Highest, call upon you, good angels of the North, you who have especial jurisdiction in mechanical arts, an office granted unto you by God alone, in whose names I call you now.

By the divine name ABALPT, I call you forth, and by the divine name ARBIZ, I command you, O good angels of the North in charge of mechanical arts, OCNC, CNCO, NCOC, and COCN, and even you in your greater forms, POCNC, PCNCO, PNCOC, and PCOCN. Move and appear, and hearken to my call.

By these holy names by which the Lord God is known, I beseech your aid, OCNC, CNCO, NCOC, and COCN. Move and appear unto me, at any time I request, in any manner I deem fit. Manifest visibly unto my eyes, audibly unto my ears, and sentiently unto my thoughts. Come peacefully, with friendly counsel, no matter your office or rank, or task or duty, knowing me as one who works with him, the Lord God, the Highest.

Come when you are called, and depart when licensed to do so, and inbetween your coming and your going, remain with me, visibly, audibly, and sentiently, until my will shall be complete.

Come together or separately, in any combination I request, whether prefixed or unprefixed, now and forever. Grant me the knowledge of mechanical things, in all their forms, and reveal unto me the secrets of mechanics, tried or untested, that I and the world at large may benefit from this knowledge.

O good angels of the North, OCNC, CNCO, NCOC, and COCN, by the divine names ABALPT and ARBIZ, I call and command you to fulfil my requests, and to do so in a timely fashion (within the timeframe asked of you), and with completeness and good will, knowing fully the intent of my summoning, neither evading nor misinterpreting those requests, and never failing in these your duties. And should one of my requests not fall within the remit of your office, guide me to another more fitting, or make move and appear the same, that my will shall ultimately be complete.

In the divine name ABALPT, I call you forth, and by the divine name ARBIZ do I command you, O good angels of the North.

Through him,
O Lord God the Father,
Jesus Christ the Son,
and the Holy Spirit,
Amen.

י

GOOD ANGELS ABOVE CROSS

DISCOVERY OF SECRETS – EAST

XGSD, GSDX, SDXG, DXGS

Face East

In the name of the Lord God Almighty, Lord of Hosts, Tetragrammaton Tzabaoth, he who is called IAIDA, I, [*name*], being a servant of the Highest, call upon you, good angels of the East, you who have especial jurisdiction in the discovery of secrets, an office granted unto you by God alone, in whose names I call you now.

By the divine name AOURRZ, I call you forth, and by the divine name ALOAI, I command you, O good angels of the East in charge of the discovery of secrets, XGSD, GSDX, SDXG, and DXGS, and even you in your greater forms, HXGSD, HGSDX, HSDXG, and HDXGS. Move and appear, and hearken to my call.

By these holy names by which the Lord God is known, I beseech your aid, XGSD, GSDX, SDXG, and DXGS. Move and appear unto me, at any time I request, in any manner I deem fit. Manifest visibly unto my eyes, audibly unto my ears, and sentiently unto my thoughts. Come peacefully, with friendly counsel, no matter your office or rank, or task or duty, knowing me as one who works with him, the Lord God, the Highest.

Come when you are called, and depart when licensed to do so, and inbetween your coming and your going, remain with me, visibly, audibly, and sentiently, until my will shall be complete.

Come together or separately, in any combination I request, whether prefixed or unprefixed, now and forever. Grant me the knowledge of secret things, and reveal unto me the secrets of men, regardless of position or rank, that none may deceive me.

O good angels of the East, XGSD, GSDX, SDXG, and DXGS,

by the divine names AOURRZ and ALOAI, I call and command you to fulfil my requests, and to do so in a timely fashion (within the timeframe asked of you), and with completeness and good will, knowing fully the intent of my summoning, neither evading nor misinterpreting those requests, and never failing in these your duties. And should one of my requests not fall within the remit of your office, guide me to another more fitting, or make move and appear the same, that my will shall ultimately be complete.

In the divine name AOURRZ, I call you forth, and by the divine name ALOAI do I command you, O good angels of the East.

Through him,
O Lord God the Father,
Jesus Christ the Son,
and the Holy Spirit,
Amen.

י

GOOD ANGELS ABOVE CROSS

DISCOVERY OF SECRETS – SOUTH

NLRX, LRXN, RXNL, XNLR

Face South

In the name of the Lord God Almighty, Lord of Hosts, Tetragrammaton Tzabaoth, he who is called IAIDA, I, [*name*], being a servant of the Highest, call upon you, good angels of the South, you who have especial jurisdiction in the discovery of secrets, an office granted unto you by God alone, in whose names I call you now.

By the divine name IAAASD, I call you forth, and by the divine name ATAPA, I command you, O good angels of the South in charge of the discovery of secrets, NLRX, LRXN, RXNL, and XNLR, and even you in your greater forms, HLRX, HLRXN, HRXNL, and HXNLR. Move and appear, and hearken to my call.

By these holy names by which the Lord God is known, I beseech your aid, NLRX, LRXN, RXNL, and XNLR. Move and appear unto me, at any time I request, in any manner I deem fit. Manifest visibly unto my eyes, audibly unto my ears, and sentiently unto my thoughts. Come peacefully, with friendly counsel, no matter your office or rank, or task or duty, knowing me as one who works with him, the Lord God, the Highest.

Come when you are called, and depart when licensed to do so, and inbetween your coming and your going, remain with me, visibly, audibly, and sentiently, until my will shall be complete.

Come together or separately, in any combination I request, whether prefixed or unprefixed, now and forever. Grant me the knowledge of secret things, and reveal unto me the secrets of men, regardless of position or rank, that none may deceive me.

O good angels of the South, NLRX, LRXN, RXNL, and XNLR,

by the divine names IAAASD and ATAPA, I call and command you to fulfil my requests, and to do so in a timely fashion (within the timeframe asked of you), and with completeness and good will, knowing fully the intent of my summoning, neither evading nor misinterpreting those requests, and never failing in these your duties. And should one of my requests not fall within the remit of your office, guide me to another more fitting, or make move and appear the same, that my will shall ultimately be complete.

In the divine name IAAASD, I call you forth, and by the divine name ATAPA do I command you, O good angels of the South.

Through him,
O Lord God the Father,
Jesus Christ the Son,
and the Holy Spirit,
Amen.

י

GOOD ANGELS ABOVE CROSS

DISCOVERY OF SECRETS – WEST

ZIZA, IZAZ, ZAZI, AZIZ

Face West

In the name of the Lord God Almighty, Lord of Hosts, Tetragrammaton Tzabaoth, he who is called IAIDA, I, [*name*], being a servant of the Highest, call upon you, good angels of the West, you who have especial jurisdiction in the discovery of secrets, an office granted unto you by God alone, in whose names I call you now.

By the divine name RZIONR, I call you forth, and by the divine name NRZFM, I command you, O good angels of the West in charge of the discovery of secrets, ZIZA, IZAZ, ZAZI, and AZIZ, and even you in your greater forms, PZIZA, PIZAZ, PZAZI, and PAZIZ. Move and appear, and hearken to my call.

By these holy names by which the Lord God is known, I beseech your aid, ZIZA, IZAZ, ZAZI, and AZIZ. Move and appear unto me, at any time I request, in any manner I deem fit. Manifest visibly unto my eyes, audibly unto my ears, and sentiently unto my thoughts. Come peacefully, with friendly counsel, no matter your office or rank, or task or duty, knowing me as one who works with him, the Lord God, the Highest.

Come when you are called, and depart when licensed to do so, and inbetween your coming and your going, remain with me, visibly, audibly, and sentiently, until my will shall be complete.

Come together or separately, in any combination I request, whether prefixed or unprefixed, now and forever. Grant me the knowledge of secret things, and reveal unto me the secrets of men, regardless of position or rank, that none may deceive me.

O good angels of the West, ZIZA, IZAZ, ZAZI, and AZIZ, by the divine names RZIONR and NRZFM, I call and command you to fulfil my requests, and to do so in a timely fashion (within the timeframe asked of you), and with completeness and good will, knowing fully the intent of my summoning, neither evading nor misinterpreting those requests, and never failing in these your duties. And should one of my requests not fall within the remit of your office, guide me to another more fitting, or make move and appear the same, that my will shall ultimately be complete.

In the divine name RZIONR, I call you forth, and by the divine name NRZFM do I command you, O good angels of the West.

Through him,
O Lord God the Father,
Jesus Christ the Son,
and the Holy Spirit,
Amen.

י

GOOD ANGELS ABOVE CROSS

DISCOVERY OF SECRETS – NORTH

ASMT, SMTA, MTAS, TASM

Face North

In the name of the Lord God Almighty, Lord of Hosts, Tetragrammaton Tzabaoth, he who is called IAIDA, I, [*name*], being a servant of the Highest, call upon you, good angels of the North, you who have especial jurisdiction in the discovery of secrets, an office granted unto you by God alone, in whose names I call you now.

By the divine name OPMNIR, I call you forth, and by the divine name ILPIZ, I command you, O good angels of the North in charge of the discovery of secrets, ASMT, SMTA, MTAS, and TASM, and even you in your greater forms, PASMT, PSMTA, PMTAS, and PTASM. Move and appear, and hearken to my call.

By these holy names by which the Lord God is known, I beseech your aid, ASMT, SMTA, MTAS, and TASM. Move and appear unto me, at any time I request, in any manner I deem fit. Manifest visibly unto my eyes, audibly unto my ears, and sentiently unto my thoughts. Come peacefully, with friendly counsel, no matter your office or rank, or task or duty, knowing me as one who works with him, the Lord God, the Highest.

Come when you are called, and depart when licensed to do so, and inbetween your coming and your going, remain with me, visibly, audibly, and sentiently, until my will shall be complete.

Come together or separately, in any combination I request, whether prefixed or unprefixed, now and forever. Grant me the knowledge of secret things, and reveal unto me the secrets of men, regardless of position or rank, that none may deceive me.

O good angels of the North, ASMT, SMTA, MTAS, and TASM,

by the divine names OPMNIR and ILPIZ, I call and command you to fulfil my requests, and to do so in a timely fashion (within the timeframe asked of you), and with completeness and good will, knowing fully the intent of my summoning, neither evading nor misinterpreting those requests, and never failing in these your duties. And should one of my requests not fall within the remit of your office, guide me to another more fitting, or make move and appear the same, that my will shall ultimately be complete.

In the divine name OPMNIR, I call you forth, and by the divine name ILPIZ do I command you, O good angels of the North.

Through him,
O Lord God the Father,
Jesus Christ the Son,
and the Holy Spirit,
Amen.

י

DISPOSITORS BELOW CROSS

MEDICINE – EAST

CZNS, TOTT, SIAS, FMND

Face East

In the name of the Lord God Almighty, Lord of Hosts, Tetragrammaton Tzabaoth, he who is called IAIDA, I, [*name*], being a servant of the Highest, call upon you, dispositors of the East, you who have especial jurisdiction in medicine and cures, an office granted unto you by God alone, in whose names I call you now.

By the divine name IDOIGO, I call you forth, and by the divine name ARDZA, I command you, O dispositors of the East in charge of medicine, CZNS, TOTT, SIAS, and FMND, and all your variations and permutations, and even you in your greater forms, XCZNS, ATOTT, RSIAS, and PFMND, and all variations and permutations thereof. Move and appear, and hearken to my call.

By these holy names by which the Lord God is known, I beseech your aid, CZNS, TOTT, SIAS, and FMND. Move and appear unto me, at any time I request, in any manner I deem fit. Manifest visibly unto my eyes, audibly unto my ears, and sentiently unto my thoughts. Come peacefully, with friendly counsel, no matter your office or rank, or task or duty, knowing me as one who works with him, the Lord God, the Highest.

Come when you are called, and depart when licensed to do so, and inbetween your coming and your going, remain with me, visibly, audibly, and sentiently, until my will shall be complete.

Come together or separately, in any combination I request, whether prefixed or unprefixed, now and forever. Grant me the power of healing, physical and spiritual, and reveal unto me the secrets of medicine and the discovery of cures, that I and the world

at large may be mended.

O dispositors of the East, CZNS, TOTT, SIAS, and FMND, by the divine names IDOIGO and ARDZA, I call and command you to fulfil my requests, and to do so in a timely fashion (within the timeframe asked of you), and with completeness and good will, knowing fully the intent of my summoning, neither evading nor misinterpreting those requests, and never failing in these your duties. And should one of my requests not fall within the remit of your office, guide me to another more fitting, or make move and appear the same, that my will shall ultimately be complete.

In the divine name IDOIGO, I call you forth, and by the divine name ARDZA do I command you, O dispositors of the East.

Through him,
O Lord God the Father,
Jesus Christ the Son,
and the Holy Spirit,
Amen.

DISPOSITORS BELOW CROSS

MEDICINE – SOUTH

TOCO, NHDD, PAAX, SAIX

Face South

In the name of the Lord God Almighty, Lord of Hosts, Tetragrammaton Tzabaoth, he who is called IAIDA, I, [*name*], being a servant of the Highest, call upon you, dispositors of the South, you who have especial jurisdiction in medicine and cures, an office granted unto you by God alone, in whose names I call you now.

By the divine name OBGOTA, I call you forth, and by the divine name AABCO, I command you, O dispositors of the South in charge of medicine, TOCO, NHDD, PAAX, and SAIX, and all your variations and permutations, and even you in your greater forms, XTOCO, ANHDD, RPAAX, and PSAIX, and all variations and permutations thereof. Move and appear, and hearken to my call.

By these holy names by which the Lord God is known, I beseech your aid, TOCO, NHDD, PAAX, and SAIX. Move and appear unto me, at any time I request, in any manner I deem fit. Manifest visibly unto my eyes, audibly unto my ears, and sentiently unto my thoughts. Come peacefully, with friendly counsel, no matter your office or rank, or task or duty, knowing me as one who works with him, the Lord God, the Highest.

Come when you are called, and depart when licensed to do so, and inbetween your coming and your going, remain with me, visibly, audibly, and sentiently, until my will shall be complete.

Come together or separately, in any combination I request, whether prefixed or unprefixed, now and forever. Grant me the power of healing, physical and spiritual, and reveal unto me the secrets of medicine and the discovery of cures, that I and the world

at large may be mended.

O dispositors of the South, TOCO, NHDD, PAAX, and SAIX, by the divine names OBGOTA and AABCO, I call and command you to fulfil my requests, and to do so in a timely fashion (within the timeframe asked of you), and with completeness and good will, knowing fully the intent of my summoning, neither evading nor misinterpreting those requests, and never failing in these your duties. And should one of my requests not fall within the remit of your office, guide me to another more fitting, or make move and appear the same, that my will shall ultimately be complete.

In the divine name OBGOTA, I call you forth, and by the divine name AABCO do I command you, O dispositors of the South.

Through him,
O Lord God the Father,
Jesus Christ the Son,
and the Holy Spirit,
Amen.

י

DISPOSITORS BELOW CROSS

MEDICINE – WEST

OPMN, APST, SCIO, VASG

Face West

In the name of the Lord God Almighty, Lord of Hosts, Tetragrammaton Tzabaoth, he who is called IAIDA, I, [*name*], being a servant of the Highest, call upon you, dispositors of the West, you who have especial jurisdiction in medicine and cures, an office granted unto you by God alone, in whose names I call you now.

By the divine name NOALMR, I call you forth, and by the divine name OLOAG, I command you, O dispositors of the West in charge of medicine, OPMN, APST, SCIO, and VASG, and all your variations and permutations, and even you in your greater forms, MOPMN, OAPST, CSCIO, and HVASG, and all variations and permutations thereof. Move and appear, and hearken to my call.

By these holy names by which the Lord God is known, I beseech your aid, OPMN, APST, SCIO, and VASG. Move and appear unto me, at any time I request, in any manner I deem fit. Manifest visibly unto my eyes, audibly unto my ears, and sentiently unto my thoughts. Come peacefully, with friendly counsel, no matter your office or rank, or task or duty, knowing me as one who works with him, the Lord God, the Highest.

Come when you are called, and depart when licensed to do so, and inbetween your coming and your going, remain with me, visibly, audibly, and sentiently, until my will shall be complete.

Come together or separately, in any combination I request, whether prefixed or unprefixed, now and forever. Grant me the power of healing, physical and spiritual, and reveal unto me the secrets of medicine and the discovery of cures, that I and the world

at large may be mended.

O dispositors of the West, OPMN, APST, SCIO, and VASG, by the divine names NOALMR and OLOAG, I call and command you to fulfil my requests, and to do so in a timely fashion (within the timeframe asked of you), and with completeness and good will, knowing fully the intent of my summoning, neither evading nor misinterpreting those requests, and never failing in these your duties. And should one of my requests not fall within the remit of your office, guide me to another more fitting, or make move and appear the same, that my will shall ultimately be complete.

In the divine name NOALMR, I call you forth, and by the divine name OLOAG do I command you, O dispositors of the West.

Through him,
O Lord God the Father,
Jesus Christ the Son,
and the Holy Spirit,
Amen.

י

DISPOSITORS BELOW CROSS

MEDICINE – NORTH

AIRA, ORMN, RSNI, IZNR

Face North

In the name of the Lord God Almighty, Lord of Hosts, Tetragrammaton Tzabaoth, he who is called IAIDA, I, [*name*], being a servant of the Highest, call upon you, dispositors of the North, you who have especial jurisdiction in medicine and cures, an office granted unto you by God alone, in whose names I call you now.

By the divine name ANGPOI, I call you forth, and by the divine name UNNAX, I command you, O dispositors of the North in charge of medicine, AIRA, ORMN, RSNI, and IZNR, and all your variations and permutations, and even you in your greater forms, MAIRA, OORMN, CRSNI, and HIZNR, and all variations and permutations thereof. Move and appear, and hearken to my call.

By these holy names by which the Lord God is known, I beseech your aid, AIRA, ORMN, RSNI, and IZNR. Move and appear unto me, at any time I request, in any manner I deem fit. Manifest visibly unto my eyes, audibly unto my ears, and sentiently unto my thoughts. Come peacefully, with friendly counsel, no matter your office or rank, or task or duty, knowing me as one who works with him, the Lord God, the Highest.

Come when you are called, and depart when licensed to do so, and inbetween your coming and your going, remain with me, visibly, audibly, and sentiently, until my will shall be complete.

Come together or separately, in any combination I request, whether prefixed or unprefixed, now and forever. Grant me the power of healing, physical and spiritual, and reveal unto me the secrets of medicine and the discovery of cures, that I and the world

at large may be mended.

O dispositors of the North, AIRA, ORMN, RSNI, and IZNR, by the divine names ANGPOI and UNNAX, I call and command you to fulfil my requests, and to do so in a timely fashion (within the timeframe asked of you), and with completeness and good will, knowing fully the intent of my summoning, neither evading nor misinterpreting those requests, and never failing in these your duties. And should one of my requests not fall within the remit of your office, guide me to another more fitting, or make move and appear the same, that my will shall ultimately be complete.

In the divine name ANGPOI, I call you forth, and by the divine name UNNAX do I command you, O dispositors of the North.

Through him,
O Lord God the Father,
Jesus Christ the Son,
and the Holy Spirit,
Amen.

י

DISPOSITORS BELOW CROSS

METALS AND JEWELS – EAST

OYUB, PAOC, RBNH, DIRI

Face East

In the name of the Lord God Almighty, Lord of Hosts, Tetragrammaton Tzabaoth, he who is called IAIDA, I, [*name*], being a servant of the Highest, call upon you, dispositors of the East, you who have especial jurisdiction over metals and jewels, an office granted unto you by God alone, in whose names I call you now.

By the divine name LLCAZA, I call you forth, and by the divine name PALAM, I command you, O dispositors of the East in charge of metals and jewels, OYUB, PAOC, RBNH, and DIRI, and all your variations and permutations, and even you in your greater forms, XOYUB, APAOC, RRBNH, and PDIRI, and all variations and permutations thereof. Move and appear, and hearken to my call.

By these holy names by which the Lord God is known, I beseech your aid, OYUB, PAOC, RBNH, and DIRI. Move and appear unto me, at any time I request, in any manner I deem fit. Manifest visibly unto my eyes, audibly unto my ears, and sentiently unto my thoughts. Come peacefully, with friendly counsel, no matter your office or rank, or task or duty, knowing me as one who works with him, the Lord God, the Highest.

Come when you are called, and depart when licensed to do so, and inbetween your coming and your going, remain with me, visibly, audibly, and sentiently, until my will shall be complete.

Come together or separately, in any combination I request, whether prefixed or unprefixed, now and forever. Grant me the knowledge of metals and jewels, their formation and properties, and show me where they may be found and gathered, that my life may be

prosperous and wanting of nothing.

O dispositors of the East, OYUB, PAOC, RBNH, and DIRI, by the divine names LLCAZA and PALAM, I call and command you to fulfil my requests, and to do so in a timely fashion (within the timeframe asked of you), and with completeness and good will, knowing fully the intent of my summoning, neither evading nor misinterpreting those requests, and never failing in these your duties. And should one of my requests not fall within the remit of your office, guide me to another more fitting, or make move and appear the same, that my will shall ultimately be complete.

In the divine name LLCAZA, I call you forth, and by the divine name PALAM do I command you, O dispositors of the East.

Through him,
O Lord God the Father,
Jesus Christ the Son,
and the Holy Spirit,
Amen.

י

DISPOSITORS BELOW CROSS

METALS AND JEWELS – SOUTH

MAGM, LEOC, VSSN, RVOI

Face South

In the name of the Lord God Almighty, Lord of Hosts, Tetragrammaton Tzabaoth, he who is called IAIDA, I, [*name*], being a servant of the Highest, call upon you, dispositors of the South, you who have especial jurisdiction over metals and jewels, an office granted unto you by God alone, in whose names I call you now.

By the divine name NELAPR, I call you forth, and by the divine name OMEBB, I command you, O dispositors of the South in charge of metals and jewels, MAGM, LEOC, VSSN, and RVOI, and all your variations and permutations, and even you in your greater forms, XMAGM, ALEOC, RVSSN, and PRVOI, and all variations and permutations thereof. Move and appear, and hearken to my call.

By these holy names by which the Lord God is known, I beseech your aid, MAGM, LEOC, VSSN, and RVOI. Move and appear unto me, at any time I request, in any manner I deem fit. Manifest visibly unto my eyes, audibly unto my ears, and sentiently unto my thoughts. Come peacefully, with friendly counsel, no matter your office or rank, or task or duty, knowing me as one who works with him, the Lord God, the Highest.

Come when you are called, and depart when licensed to do so, and inbetween your coming and your going, remain with me, visibly, audibly, and sentiently, until my will shall be complete.

Come together or separately, in any combination I request, whether prefixed or unprefixed, now and forever. Grant me the knowledge of metals and jewels, their formation and properties, and show me where they may be found and gathered, that my life may be

prosperous and wanting of nothing.

O dispositors of the South, MAGM, LEOC, VSSN, and RVOI, by the divine names NELAPR and OMEBB, I call and command you to fulfil my requests, and to do so in a timely fashion (within the timeframe asked of you), and with completeness and good will, knowing fully the intent of my summoning, neither evading nor misinterpreting those requests, and never failing in these your duties. And should one of my requests not fall within the remit of your office, guide me to another more fitting, or make move and appear the same, that my will shall ultimately be complete.

In the divine name NELAPR, I call you forth, and by the divine name OMEBB do I command you, O dispositors of the South.

Through him,
O Lord God the Father,
Jesus Christ the Son,
and the Holy Spirit,
Amen.

י

DISPOSITORS BELOW CROSS

METALS AND JEWELS – WEST

GMNM, ECOP, AMOX, BRAP

Face West

In the name of the Lord God Almighty, Lord of Hosts, Tetragrammaton Tzabaoth, he who is called IAIDA, I, [*name*], being a servant of the Highest, call upon you, dispositors of the West, you who have especial jurisdiction over metals and jewels, an office granted unto you by God alone, in whose names I call you now.

By the divine name VADALI, I call you forth, and by the divine name OBAUA, I command you, O dispositors of the West in charge of metals and jewels, GMNM, ECOP, AMOX, and BRAP, and all your variations and permutations, and even you in your greater forms, MGMNM, OECOP, CAMOX, and HBRAP, and all variations and permutations thereof. Move and appear, and hearken to my call.

By these holy names by which the Lord God is known, I beseech your aid, GMNM, ECOP, AMOX, and BRAP. Move and appear unto me, at any time I request, in any manner I deem fit. Manifest visibly unto my eyes, audibly unto my ears, and sentiently unto my thoughts. Come peacefully, with friendly counsel, no matter your office or rank, or task or duty, knowing me as one who works with him, the Lord God, the Highest.

Come when you are called, and depart when licensed to do so, and inbetween your coming and your going, remain with me, visibly, audibly, and sentiently, until my will shall be complete.

Come together or separately, in any combination I request, whether prefixed or unprefixed, now and forever. Grant me the knowledge of metals and jewels, their formation and properties, and show me where they may be found and gathered, that my life may be

prosperous and wanting of nothing.

O dispositors of the West, GMNM, ECOP, AMOX, and BRAP, by the divine names VADALI and OBAUA, I call and command you to fulfil my requests, and to do so in a timely fashion (within the timeframe asked of you), and with completeness and good will, knowing fully the intent of my summoning, neither evading nor misinterpreting those requests, and never failing in these your duties. And should one of my requests not fall within the remit of your office, guide me to another more fitting, or make move and appear the same, that my will shall ultimately be complete.

In the divine name VADALI, I call you forth, and by the divine name OBAUA do I command you, O dispositors of the West.

Through him,
O Lord God the Father,
Jesus Christ the Son,
and the Holy Spirit,
Amen.

DISPOSITORS BELOW CROSS

METALS AND JEWELS – NORTH

OMGG, GBAL, RLMU, IAHL

Face North

In the name of the Lord God Almighty, Lord of Hosts, Tetragrammaton Tzabaoth, he who is called IAIDA, I, [*name*], being a servant of the Highest, call upon you, dispositors of the North, you who have especial jurisdiction over metals and jewels, an office granted unto you by God alone, in whose names I call you now.

By the divine name ANAEEM, I call you forth, and by the divine name SONDN, I command you, O dispositors of the North in charge of metals and jewels, OMGG, GBAL, RLMU, and IAHL, and all your variations and permutations, and even you in your greater forms, MOMGG, OGBAL, CRLMU, and HIAHL, and all variations and permutations thereof. Move and appear, and hearken to my call.

By these holy names by which the Lord God is known, I beseech your aid, OMGG, GBAL, RLMU, and IAHL. Move and appear unto me, at any time I request, in any manner I deem fit. Manifest visibly unto my eyes, audibly unto my ears, and sentiently unto my thoughts. Come peacefully, with friendly counsel, no matter your office or rank, or task or duty, knowing me as one who works with him, the Lord God, the Highest.

Come when you are called, and depart when licensed to do so, and inbetween your coming and your going, remain with me, visibly, audibly, and sentiently, until my will shall be complete.

Come together or separately, in any combination I request, whether prefixed or unprefixed, now and forever. Grant me the knowledge of metals and jewels, their formation and properties, and show me where they may be found and gathered, that my life may be

prosperous and wanting of nothing.

O dispositors of the North, OMGG, GBAL, RLMU, and IAHL, by the divine names ANAEEM and SONDN, I call and command you to fulfil my requests, and to do so in a timely fashion (within the timeframe asked of you), and with completeness and good will, knowing fully the intent of my summoning, neither evading nor misinterpreting those requests, and never failing in these your duties. And should one of my requests not fall within the remit of your office, guide me to another more fitting, or make move and appear the same, that my will shall ultimately be complete.

In the divine name ANAEEM, I call you forth, and by the divine name SONDN do I command you, O dispositors of the North.

Through him,
O Lord God the Father,
Jesus Christ the Son,
and the Holy Spirit,
Amen.

DISPOSITORS BELOW CROSS

TRANSFORMATION – EAST

ABMO, NACO, OCNM, SHAL

Face East

In the name of the Lord God Almighty, Lord of Hosts, Tetragrammaton Tzabaoth, he who is called IAIDA, I, [*name*], being a servant of the Highest, call upon you, dispositors of the East, you who have especial jurisdiction over transformation, an office granted unto you by God alone, in whose names I call you now.

By the divine name AIAOAI, I call you forth, and by the divine name OIIIT, I command you, O dispositors of the East in charge of transformation, ABMO, NACO, OCNM, and SHAL, and all your variations and permutations, and even you in your greater forms, CABMO, ONACO, MOCNM, and ASHAL, and all variations and permutations thereof. Move and appear, and hearken to my call.

By these holy names by which the Lord God is known, I beseech your aid, ABMO, NACO, OCNM, and SHAL. Move and appear unto me, at any time I request, in any manner I deem fit. Manifest visibly unto my eyes, audibly unto my ears, and sentiently unto my thoughts. Come peacefully, with friendly counsel, no matter your office or rank, or task or duty, knowing me as one who works with him, the Lord God, the Highest.

Come when you are called, and depart when licensed to do so, and inbetween your coming and your going, remain with me, visibly, audibly, and sentiently, until my will shall be complete.

Come together or separately, in any combination I request, whether prefixed or unprefixed, now and forever. Grant me the knowledge of transformation, whether of things or people, or anything else whatsoever, and teach me the secrets of alchemy,

whereby I may transform myself, my surroundings, and the world at large.

O dispositors of the East, ABMO, NACO, OCNM, and SHAL, by the divine names AIAOAI and OIIIT, I call and command you to fulfil my requests, and to do so in a timely fashion (within the timeframe asked of you), and with completeness and good will, knowing fully the intent of my summoning, neither evading nor misinterpreting those requests, and never failing in these your duties. And should one of my requests not fall within the remit of your office, guide me to another more fitting, or make move and appear the same, that my will shall ultimately be complete.

In the divine name AIAOAI, I call you forth, and by the divine name OIIIT do I command you, O dispositors of the East.

Through him,
O Lord God the Father,
Jesus Christ the Son,
and the Holy Spirit,
Amen.

י

DISPOSITORS BELOW CROSS

TRANSFORMATION – SOUTH

PACO, NDZN, IIPO, XRNH

Face South

In the name of the Lord God Almighty, Lord of Hosts, Tetragrammaton Tzabaoth, he who is called IAIDA, I, [*name*], being a servant of the Highest, call upon you, dispositors of the South, you who have especial jurisdiction over transformation, an office granted unto you by God alone, in whose names I call you now.

By the divine name MALADI, I call you forth, and by the divine name OPAAD, I command you, O dispositors of the South in charge of transformation, PACO, NDZN, IIPO, and XRNH, and all your variations and permutations, and even you in your greater forms, CPACO, ONDZN, MIIPO, and AXRNH, and all variations and permutations thereof. Move and appear, and hearken to my call.

By these holy names by which the Lord God is known, I beseech your aid, PACO, NDZN, IIPO, and XRNH. Move and appear unto me, at any time I request, in any manner I deem fit. Manifest visibly unto my eyes, audibly unto my ears, and sentiently unto my thoughts. Come peacefully, with friendly counsel, no matter your office or rank, or task or duty, knowing me as one who works with him, the Lord God, the Highest.

Come when you are called, and depart when licensed to do so, and inbetween your coming and your going, remain with me, visibly, audibly, and sentiently, until my will shall be complete.

Come together or separately, in any combination I request, whether prefixed or unprefixed, now and forever. Grant me the knowledge of transformation, whether of things or people, or anything else whatsoever, and teach me the secrets of alchemy,

whereby I may transform myself, my surroundings, and the world at large.

O dispositors of the South, PACO, NDZN, IIPO, and XRNH, by the divine names MALADI and OPAAD, I call and command you to fulfil my requests, and to do so in a timely fashion (within the timeframe asked of you), and with completeness and good will, knowing fully the intent of my summoning, neither evading nor misinterpreting those requests, and never failing in these your duties. And should one of my requests not fall within the remit of your office, guide me to another more fitting, or make move and appear the same, that my will shall ultimately be complete.

In the divine name MALADI, I call you forth, and by the divine name OPAAD do I command you, O dispositors of the South.

Through him,
O Lord God the Father,
Jesus Christ the Son,
and the Holy Spirit,
Amen.

י

DISPOSITORS BELOW CROSS

TRANSFORMATION – WEST

DATT, DIOM, OOPZ, RGAN

Face West

In the name of the Lord God Almighty, Lord of Hosts, Tetragrammaton Tzabaoth, he who is called IAIDA, I, [*name*], being a servant of the Highest, call upon you, dispositors of the West, you who have especial jurisdiction over transformation, an office granted unto you by God alone, in whose names I call you now.

By the divine name UOLXDO, I call you forth, and by the divine name SIODA, I command you, O dispositors of the West in charge of transformation, DATT, DIOM, OOPZ, and RGAN, and all your variations and permutations, and even you in your greater forms, RDATT, ADIOM, XOOPZ, and ERGAN, and all variations and permutations thereof. Move and appear, and hearken to my call.

By these holy names by which the Lord God is known, I beseech your aid, DATT, DIOM, OOPZ, and RGAN. Move and appear unto me, at any time I request, in any manner I deem fit. Manifest visibly unto my eyes, audibly unto my ears, and sentiently unto my thoughts. Come peacefully, with friendly counsel, no matter your office or rank, or task or duty, knowing me as one who works with him, the Lord God, the Highest.

Come when you are called, and depart when licensed to do so, and inbetween your coming and your going, remain with me, visibly, audibly, and sentiently, until my will shall be complete.

Come together or separately, in any combination I request, whether prefixed or unprefixed, now and forever. Grant me the knowledge of transformation, whether of things or people, or anything else whatsoever, and teach me the secrets of alchemy,

whereby I may transform myself, my surroundings, and the world at large.

O dispositors of the West, DATT, DIOM, OOPZ, and RGAN, by the divine names UOLXDO and SIODA, I call and command you to fulfil my requests, and to do so in a timely fashion (within the timeframe asked of you), and with completeness and good will, knowing fully the intent of my summoning, neither evading nor misinterpreting those requests, and never failing in these your duties. And should one of my requests not fall within the remit of your office, guide me to another more fitting, or make move and appear the same, that my will shall ultimately be complete.

In the divine name UOLXDO, I call you forth, and by the divine name SIODA do I command you, O dispositors of the West.

Through him,
O Lord God the Father,
Jesus Christ the Son,
and the Holy Spirit,
Amen.

י

DISPOSITORS BELOW CROSS

TRANSFORMATION – NORTH

OPNA, DOOP, RXAO, AXIR

Face North

In the name of the Lord God Almighty, Lord of Hosts, Tetragrammaton Tzabaoth, he who is called IAIDA, I, [*name*], being a servant of the Highest, call upon you, dispositors of the North, you who have especial jurisdiction over transformation, an office granted unto you by God alone, in whose names I call you now.

By the divine name ABALPT, I call you forth, and by the divine name ARBIZ, I command you, O dispositors of the North in charge of transformation, OPNA, DOOP, RXAO, and AXIR, and all your variations and permutations, and even you in your greater forms, ROPNA, ADOOP, XRXAO, and EAXIR, and all variations and permutations thereof. Move and appear, and hearken to my call.

By these holy names by which the Lord God is known, I beseech your aid, OPNA, DOOP, RXAO, and AXIR. Move and appear unto me, at any time I request, in any manner I deem fit. Manifest visibly unto my eyes, audibly unto my ears, and sentiently unto my thoughts. Come peacefully, with friendly counsel, no matter your office or rank, or task or duty, knowing me as one who works with him, the Lord God, the Highest.

Come when you are called, and depart when licensed to do so, and inbetween your coming and your going, remain with me, visibly, audibly, and sentiently, until my will shall be complete.

Come together or separately, in any combination I request, whether prefixed or unprefixed, now and forever. Grant me the knowledge of transformation, whether of things or people, or anything else whatsoever, and teach me the secrets of alchemy,

whereby I may transform myself, my surroundings, and the world at large.

O dispositors of the North, OPNA, DOOP, RXAO, and AXIR, by the divine names ABALPT and ARBIZ, I call and command you to fulfil my requests, and to do so in a timely fashion (within the timeframe asked of you), and with completeness and good will, knowing fully the intent of my summoning, neither evading nor misinterpreting those requests, and never failing in these your duties. And should one of my requests not fall within the remit of your office, guide me to another more fitting, or make move and appear the same, that my will shall ultimately be complete.

In the divine name ABALPT, I call you forth, and by the divine name ARBIZ do I command you, O dispositors of the North.

Through him,
O Lord God the Father,
Jesus Christ the Son,
and the Holy Spirit,
Amen.

י

DISPOSITORS BELOW CROSS

ELEMENTS – EAST

ACCA, NPNT, OTOI, PMOX

Face East

In the name of the Lord God Almighty, Lord of Hosts, Tetragrammaton Tzabaoth, he who is called IAIDA, I, [*name*], being a servant of the Highest, call upon you, dispositors of the East, you who have especial jurisdiction over the elements, an office granted unto you by God alone, in whose names I call you now.

By the divine name AOURRZ, I call you forth, and by the divine name ALOAI, I command you, O dispositors of the East in charge of the elements, ACCA, NPNT, OTOI, and PMOX, and all your variations and permutations, and even you in your greater forms, CACCA, ONPNT, MOTOI, and APMOX, and all variations and permutations thereof. Move and appear, and hearken to my call.

By these holy names by which the Lord God is known, I beseech your aid, ACCA, NPNT, OTOI, and PMOX. Move and appear unto me, at any time I request, in any manner I deem fit. Manifest visibly unto my eyes, audibly unto my ears, and sentiently unto my thoughts. Come peacefully, with friendly counsel, no matter your office or rank, or task or duty, knowing me as one who works with him, the Lord God, the Highest.

Come when you are called, and depart when licensed to do so, and inbetween your coming and your going, remain with me, visibly, audibly, and sentiently, until my will shall be complete.

Come together or separately, in any combination I request, whether prefixed or unprefixed, now and forever. Grant me the knowledge of the elements, revealing their qualities, mixed and unmixed, and teach me the secrets of those creatures unique to the

elements, and all other matters connected therewith.

O dispositors of the East, ACCA, NPNT, OTOI, and PMOX, by the divine names AOURRZ and ALOAI, I call and command you to fulfil my requests, and to do so in a timely fashion (within the timeframe asked of you), and with completeness and good will, knowing fully the intent of my summoning, neither evading nor misinterpreting those requests, and never failing in these your duties. And should one of my requests not fall within the remit of your office, guide me to another more fitting, or make move and appear the same, that my will shall ultimately be complete.

In the divine name AOURRZ, I call you forth, and by the divine name ALOAI do I command you, O dispositors of the East.

Through him,
O Lord God the Father,
Jesus Christ the Son,
and the Holy Spirit,
Amen.

DISPOSITORS BELOW CROSS

ELEMENTS – SOUTH

XPCN, VASA, DAPI, RNIL

Face South

In the name of the Lord God Almighty, Lord of Hosts, Tetragrammaton Tzabaoth, he who is called IAIDA, I, [*name*], being a servant of the Highest, call upon you, dispositors of the South, you who have especial jurisdiction over the elements, an office granted unto you by God alone, in whose names I call you now.

By the divine name IAAASD, I call you forth, and by the divine name ATAPA, I command you, O dispositors of the South in charge of the elements, XPCN, VASA, DAPI, and RNIL, and all your variations and permutations, and even you in your greater forms, CXPCN, OVASA, MDAPI, and ARNIL, and all variations and permutations thereof. Move and appear, and hearken to my call.

By these holy names by which the Lord God is known, I beseech your aid, XPCN, VASA, DAPI, and RNIL. Move and appear unto me, at any time I request, in any manner I deem fit. Manifest visibly unto my eyes, audibly unto my ears, and sentiently unto my thoughts. Come peacefully, with friendly counsel, no matter your office or rank, or task or duty, knowing me as one who works with him, the Lord God, the Highest.

Come when you are called, and depart when licensed to do so, and inbetween your coming and your going, remain with me, visibly, audibly, and sentiently, until my will shall be complete.

Come together or separately, in any combination I request, whether prefixed or unprefixed, now and forever. Grant me the knowledge of the elements, revealing their qualities, mixed and unmixed, and teach me the secrets of those creatures unique to the

elements, and all other matters connected therewith.

O dispositors of the South, XPCN, VASA, DAPI, and RNIL, by the divine names IAAASD and ATAPA, I call and command you to fulfil my requests, and to do so in a timely fashion (within the timeframe asked of you), and with completeness and good will, knowing fully the intent of my summoning, neither evading nor misinterpreting those requests, and never failing in these your duties. And should one of my requests not fall within the remit of your office, guide me to another more fitting, or make move and appear the same, that my will shall ultimately be complete.

In the divine name IAAASD, I call you forth, and by the divine name ATAPA do I command you, O dispositors of the South.

Through him,
O Lord God the Father,
Jesus Christ the Son,
and the Holy Spirit,
Amen.

י

DISPOSITORS BELOW CROSS

ELEMENTS – WEST

ADRE, SISP, PALI, ACAR

Face West

In the name of the Lord God Almighty, Lord of Hosts, Tetragrammaton Tzabaoth, he who is called IAIDA, I, [*name*], being a servant of the Highest, call upon you, dispositors of the West, you who have especial jurisdiction over the elements, an office granted unto you by God alone, in whose names I call you now.

By the divine name RZIONR, I call you forth, and by the divine name NRZFM, I command you, O dispositors of the West in charge of the elements, ADRE, SISP, PALI, and ACAR, and all your variations and permutations, and even you in your greater forms, RADRE, ASISP, XPALI, and EACAR, and all variations and permutations thereof. Move and appear, and hearken to my call.

By these holy names by which the Lord God is known, I beseech your aid, ADRE, SISP, PALI, and ACAR. Move and appear unto me, at any time I request, in any manner I deem fit. Manifest visibly unto my eyes, audibly unto my ears, and sentiently unto my thoughts. Come peacefully, with friendly counsel, no matter your office or rank, or task or duty, knowing me as one who works with him, the Lord God, the Highest.

Come when you are called, and depart when licensed to do so, and inbetween your coming and your going, remain with me, visibly, audibly, and sentiently, until my will shall be complete.

Come together or separately, in any combination I request, whether prefixed or unprefixed, now and forever. Grant me the knowledge of the elements, revealing their qualities, mixed and unmixed, and teach me the secrets of those creatures unique to the

elements, and all other matters connected therewith.

O dispositors of the West, ADRE, SISP, PALI, and ACAR, by the divine names RZIONR and NRZFM, I call and command you to fulfil my requests, and to do so in a timely fashion (within the timeframe asked of you), and with completeness and good will, knowing fully the intent of my summoning, neither evading nor misinterpreting those requests, and never failing in these your duties. And should one of my requests not fall within the remit of your office, guide me to another more fitting, or make move and appear the same, that my will shall ultimately be complete.

In the divine name RZIONR, I call you forth, and by the divine name NRZFM do I command you, O dispositors of the West.

Through him,
O Lord God the Father,
Jesus Christ the Son,
and the Holy Spirit,
Amen.

י

DISPOSITORS BELOW CROSS

ELEMENTS – NORTH

MSAP, IABA, IZXP, STIM

Face North

In the name of the Lord God Almighty, Lord of Hosts, Tetragrammaton Tzabaoth, he who is called IAIDA, I, [*name*], being a servant of the Highest, call upon you, dispositors of the North, you who have especial jurisdiction over the elements, an office granted unto you by God alone, in whose names I call you now.

By the divine name OPMNIR, I call you forth, and by the divine name ILPIZ, I command you, O dispositors of the North in charge of the elements, MSAP, IABA, IZXP, and STIM, and all your variations and permutations, and even you in your greater forms, RMSAP, AIABA, XIZXP, and ESTIM, and all variations and permutations thereof. Move and appear, and hearken to my call.

By these holy names by which the Lord God is known, I beseech your aid, MSAP, IABA, IZXP, and STIM. Move and appear unto me, at any time I request, in any manner I deem fit. Manifest visibly unto my eyes, audibly unto my ears, and sentiently unto my thoughts. Come peacefully, with friendly counsel, no matter your office or rank, or task or duty, knowing me as one who works with him, the Lord God, the Highest.

Come when you are called, and depart when licensed to do so, and inbetween your coming and your going, remain with me, visibly, audibly, and sentiently, until my will shall be complete.

Come together or separately, in any combination I request, whether prefixed or unprefixed, now and forever. Grant me the knowledge of the elements, revealing their qualities, mixed and unmixed, and teach me the secrets of those creatures unique to the

elements, and all other matters connected therewith.

O dispositors of the North, MSAP, IABA, IZXP, and STIM, by the divine names OPMNIR and ILPIZ, I call and command you to fulfil my requests, and to do so in a timely fashion (within the timeframe asked of you), and with completeness and good will, knowing fully the intent of my summoning, neither evading nor misinterpreting those requests, and never failing in these your duties. And should one of my requests not fall within the remit of your office, guide me to another more fitting, or make move and appear the same, that my will shall ultimately be complete.

In the divine name OPMNIR, I call you forth, and by the divine name ILPIZ do I command you, O dispositors of the North.

Through him,
O Lord God the Father,
Jesus Christ the Son,
and the Holy Spirit,
Amen.

י

BIBLIOGRAPHY

❖ Ackermann, Silke; Devoy, Louise. *'The Lord of the smoking mirror': Objectsassociated with John Dee in the British Museum; Studies in History and Philosophy of Science* Part A, Volume 43, Issue 3, September 2012.

❖ Asprem, Egil. *Arguing With Angels*. Albany, NY. State University of New York Press, 2012.

❖ Barrett, Francis. *The Magus or Celestial Intelligencer*. Lackington, Allen & Co, 1801.

❖ Casaubon, Meric, ed. *A True & Faithful Relation of What Passed for Many Years Between Dr. John Dee and Some Spirits*, 1659. Reprinted by Kessinger Publishing.

❖ Crowley, Aleister. *Magick in Theory and Practice*, contained in *Book Four*. Weiser Books, Second Edition, 1998.

❖ ______________. *The Vision and the Voice*. Weiser Books, 1999.

❖ Dee, John. *The Hieroglyphic Monad*. Boston. MA. Red Wheel/ Weiser Books, 2000.

❖ ________. *The Mathematical Preface to Elements of Geometry of Euclid of Megara*. London. Iohn Daye,1570.

❖ DeSalvo, John. *Decoding the Enochian Secrets*. Rochester, VT. Destiny Books, 2011.

❖ ____________. *The Lost Art of Enochian Magic*. Rochester, VT. Destiny Books, 2010.

✤ DuQuette, Lon Milo. *Enochian Vision Magick*. San Francisco, CA. Red Wheel/Weiser Books, 2008.

✤ French, Peter. *John Dee: The World of an Elizabethan Magus*. New York, NY. Routledge, 2006.

✤ Halliwell, James Orchard. ed. *The Private Diary of Dr. John Dee*. London. J.B. Nichols and Son, 1842.

✤ Hibner, Israel. *Mysterium Sigillorum, Herbarum and Lapidum*, London. W. Downing, 1698.

✤ James, Geoffrey. *The Enochian Evocation of Dr. John Dee*. San Francisco, CA. Red Wheel/Weiser Books, 2009.

✤ Küntz, Darcy, ed. *The Enochian Experiments of the Golden Dawn*. Holmes Publishing Group, Third Edition, 2007.

✤ Laycock, Donald C. *The Complete Enochian Dictionary*. San Francisco, CA. Red Wheel/Weiser Books, 2001.

✤ Leitch, Aaron. *The Angelical Language*: Volume I. Woodbury, MN. Llewellyn Publications, 2010.

✤ ___________. *The Angelical Language*: Volume II. Woodbury, MN. Llewellyn Publications, 2010.

✤ ___________. *The Essential Enochian Grimoire*. Woodbury, MN. Llewellyn Publications, 2014

✤ Levi, Eliphas. *The Magical Ritual of the Sanctum Regnum*,. Berwick, ME. Ibis Press, 2004.

✤ Mathers, S.L. MacGregor, trans. *The Book of the Sacred Magic of Abramelin the Mage*. Dover, 1975.

✤ ____________________, trans. *The Key of Solomon the King*. Weiser Books, 2006.

❈ McLean, Adam, ed. *A Treatise on Angel Magic*. York Beach, ME. Red Wheel/Weiser Books, 2006.

❈ Peterson, Joseph H., ed. *John Dee's Five Books of Mystery*. York Beach, ME. Red Wheel/Weiser Books, 2003.

❈ Regardie, Israel. *The Golden Dawn*. St. Paul, MN. Llewellyn Publications, Sixth Corrected Edition, 1989.

❈ ____________. *Ceremonial Magic*. Northamptonshire, UK. The Aquarian Press, 1980.

❈ Rowe, Benjamin. *Enochian Temples: Invoking the Cacodemons with the Temple*, published online, 1992.

❈ ____________. *The Book of the Seniors*, published online, 1992.

❈ Skinner, Stephen, ed. *Dr. John Dee's Spiritual Diaries*. Singapore. Golden Hoard Press, 2011.

❈ Szőnyi, György E. *John Dee's Occultism*. Albany, NY. State University of New York Press, 2004.

❈ Tyson, Donald. *Enochian Magic for Beginners*. Woodbury, MN. Llewellyn Publications, 2005.

❈ ____________, ed. *Three Books of Occult Philosophy*. St. Paul, MN. Llewellyn Publications, 2003.

❈ Whitby, Christopher. *John Dee's Actions With Spirits*. Oxfordshire. Routledge, 2013.

❈ Woolley, Benjamin. *The Queen's Conjurer*. New York, NY. Henry Holt and Company, 2001.

❈ Yates, Frances. *The Rosicrucian Enlightenment*. New York, NY. Routledge, 2007.

Index

I

J

K

L

M

O

P

Q

R

S

ABOUT THE AUTHOR

Frater Yechidah is a magician and author from Dublin, Ireland.

He has written extensively on occult topics, including articles for *Hidden Spirit*, *Hermetic Virtues*, and *The Gnostic*. He also blogs regularly about topics related to the Golden Dawn and Gnosticism.

He has been involved with a number of magical groups, including the Order of the Sons and Daughters of Light and the Hermetic Order of the Golden Dawn, and he is currently a member of the Ancient and Honourable Order of the Golden Dawn (www.ahogd.com).

י